Warner, Timothy L.,
Microsoft Azure /
[2020]
33305247901501
gi   08/19/20

Microsoft®
Azure®

D1571460

by Timothy Warner

for
dummies®
A Wiley Brand

Microsoft® Azure® For Dummies®

Published by: **John Wiley & Sons, Inc.**, 111 River Street, Hoboken, NJ 07030-5774, www.wiley.com

Copyright © 2020 by John Wiley & Sons, Inc., Hoboken, New Jersey

Published simultaneously in Canada

No part of this publication may be reproduced, stored in a retrieval system or transmitted in any form or by any means, electronic, mechanical, photocopying, recording, scanning or otherwise, except as permitted under Sections 107 or 108 of the 1976 United States Copyright Act, without the prior written permission of the Publisher. Requests to the Publisher for permission should be addressed to the Permissions Department, John Wiley & Sons, Inc., 111 River Street, Hoboken, NJ 07030, (201) 748-6011, fax (201) 748-6008, or online at http://www.wiley.com/go/permissions.

Trademarks: Wiley, For Dummies, the Dummies Man logo, Dummies.com, Making Everything Easier, and related trade dress are trademarks or registered trademarks of John Wiley & Sons, Inc. and may not be used without written permission. Microsoft and Azure are registered trademarks of Microsoft Corporation. All other trademarks are the property of their respective owners. John Wiley & Sons, Inc. is not associated with any product or vendor mentioned in this book.

LIMIT OF LIABILITY/DISCLAIMER OF WARRANTY: THE PUBLISHER AND THE AUTHOR MAKE NO REPRESENTATIONS OR WARRANTIES WITH RESPECT TO THE ACCURACY OR COMPLETENESS OF THE CONTENTS OF THIS WORK AND SPECIFICALLY DISCLAIM ALL WARRANTIES, INCLUDING WITHOUT LIMITATION WARRANTIES OF FITNESS FOR A PARTICULAR PURPOSE. NO WARRANTY MAY BE CREATED OR EXTENDED BY SALES OR PROMOTIONAL MATERIALS. THE ADVICE AND STRATEGIES CONTAINED HEREIN MAY NOT BE SUITABLE FOR EVERY SITUATION. THIS WORK IS SOLD WITH THE UNDERSTANDING THAT THE PUBLISHER IS NOT ENGAGED IN RENDERING LEGAL, ACCOUNTING, OR OTHER PROFESSIONAL SERVICES. IF PROFESSIONAL ASSISTANCE IS REQUIRED, THE SERVICES OF A COMPETENT PROFESSIONAL PERSON SHOULD BE SOUGHT. NEITHER THE PUBLISHER NOR THE AUTHOR SHALL BE LIABLE FOR DAMAGES ARISING HEREFROM. THE FACT THAT AN ORGANIZATION OR WEBSITE IS REFERRED TO IN THIS WORK AS A CITATION AND/OR A POTENTIAL SOURCE OF FURTHER INFORMATION DOES NOT MEAN THAT THE AUTHOR OR THE PUBLISHER ENDORSES THE INFORMATION THE ORGANIZATION OR WEBSITE MAY PROVIDE OR RECOMMENDATIONS IT MAY MAKE. FURTHER, READERS SHOULD BE AWARE THAT INTERNET WEBSITES LISTED IN THIS WORK MAY HAVE CHANGED OR DISAPPEARED BETWEEN WHEN THIS WORK WAS WRITTEN AND WHEN IT IS READ.

For general information on our other products and services, please contact our Customer Care Department within the U.S. at 877-762-2974, outside the U.S. at 317-572-3993, or fax 317-572-4002. For technical support, please visit https://hub.wiley.com/community/support/dummies.

Wiley publishes in a variety of print and electronic formats and by print-on-demand. Some material included with standard print versions of this book may not be included in e-books or in print-on-demand. If this book refers to media such as a CD or DVD that is not included in the version you purchased, you may download this material at http://booksupport.wiley.com. For more information about Wiley products, visit www.wiley.com.

Library of Congress Control Number: 2020931520

ISBN: 978-1-119-61214-8(pbk); 978-1-119-61218-6 (ebk); 978-1-119-61215-5 (ebk)

Manufactured in the United States of America

V10017599_021720

Contents at a Glance

Introduction 1

Part 1: Getting Started with Microsoft Azure 5
CHAPTER 1: Introducing Microsoft Azure 7
CHAPTER 2: Exploring Azure Resource Manager 27

Part 2: Deploying Compute Resources to Microsoft Azure 45
CHAPTER 3: Managing Storage in Azure 47
CHAPTER 4: Planning Your Virtual Network Topology 65
CHAPTER 5: Deploying and Configuring Azure Virtual Machines 87
CHAPTER 6: Shipping Docker Containers in Azure 115

Part 3: Deploying Platform Resources to Microsoft Azure 137
CHAPTER 7: Deploying and Configuring Azure App Service Apps 139
CHAPTER 8: Running Serverless Apps in Azure 167
CHAPTER 9: Managing Databases in Microsoft Azure 185

Part 4: Providing High Availability, Scalability, and Security for Your Azure Resources 209
CHAPTER 10: Backing Up and Restoring Your Azure Data 211
CHAPTER 11: Managing Identity and Access with Azure Active Directory 229
CHAPTER 12: Implementing Azure Governance 251

Part 5: Migrating to Microsoft Azure and Monitoring Your Infrastructure 267
CHAPTER 13: Extending Your On-Premises Environment to Azure 269
CHAPTER 14: Monitoring Your Azure Environment 301

Part 6: The Part of Tens 323
CHAPTER 15: Top Ten Azure News Resources 325
CHAPTER 16: Top Ten Azure Educational Resources 331

Index 339

Table of Contents

INTRODUCTION 1

About This Book... 1

Foolish Assumptions.. 2

Icons Used in This Book 3

Beyond the Book.. 4

Where to Go from Here 4

PART 1: GETTING STARTED WITH MICROSOFT AZURE 5

CHAPTER 1: **Introducing Microsoft Azure**........................ 7

What Is Cloud Computing?................................... 7

    NIST definition 9

    Cloud computing benefits 10

    Economies of scale 11

Understanding Cloud Computing Models 11

    Deployment models 12

    Service delivery models 14

Introducing Microsoft Azure Services........................ 17

    Azure history 17

    PaaS products 19

Starting Your First Azure Subscription 20

    Understanding subscription types 20

    Creating a free Azure account......................... 22

    Viewing subscription details 24

CHAPTER 2: **Exploring Azure Resource Manager** 27

Introducing Azure Resource Manager 27

    REST APIs 28

    Resource providers................................... 28

    JSON.. 30

    ARM management scopes 31

Getting Familiar with Azure Regions......................... 33

    Availability zones.................................... 33

    Geographies... 34

    Special regions...................................... 34

    Paired regions 35

    Feature availability 36

Introducing the Azure Management Tools 36
    Azure portal 36
    Azure PowerShell. 38
    Azure CLI/Azure Cloud Shell. 39
    Azure SDKs 41
    ARM REST API. 42

**PART 2: DEPLOYING COMPUTE RESOURCES
TO MICROSOFT AZURE** 45

CHAPTER 3: **Managing Storage in Azure** 47
Understanding Azure Storage Data Types. 47
    Unstructured data. 48
    Semistructured data 48
    Structured data 48
Working with a Storage Account. 49
    Creating a storage account 49
    Using the blob service. 54
    Understanding the file, table, and queue services. 59
Introducing Azure Disk Storage. 61

CHAPTER 4: **Planning Your Virtual Network Topology** 65
Understanding Virtual Network Components. .66
    Address space 66
    Subnets 66
Creating a Virtual Network. 68
    Deploying with the Azure portal 68
    Deploying with PowerShell. 71
Configuring Virtual Networks 73
    Deciding on a name resolution strategy 73
    Configuring network security groups. 74
    Understanding service endpoints. 78
Connecting Virtual Networks. 81
    Configuring VNet peering. 81
    Understanding service chaining 82

CHAPTER 5: **Deploying and Configuring Azure
Virtual Machines**. 87
Planning Your VM Deployment 88
    Understanding VMs. 88
    Starting your VM deployment from the Azure Marketplace. 89
    Starting your VM deployment from your
    on-premises environment 89

Recognizing Azure VM Components.............................91
    Compute...92
    Storage...93
    Network...93
Architectural Considerations.................................94
    High availability.................................94
    Scalability..95
Deploying Azure VMs from the Azure Marketplace...............96
    Deploying a Linux VM...............................96
    Deploying a Windows Server VM......................99
Configuring Your VMs...106
Starting, Stopping, and Resizing VMs.........................108
    Extending your VM's capabilities...................111

CHAPTER 6: **Shipping Docker Containers in Azure**..............115
Understanding Docker...116
    Using Docker containers............................117
    Setting up Docker on your workstation..............117
    Running containers in Azure........................120
Implementing Azure Container Instances.......................122
    Deploying an Azure container instance..............123
    Verifying and disposing of the container instance..124
Storing Images in Azure Container Registry...................126
    Deploying a container registry.....................126
    Pushing an image to a new container registry.......127
    Pulling the repository image via ACI...............128
Introducing Azure Kubernetes Service.........................131
    AKS architecture...................................131
    AKS administration notes...........................132
Using Containers with Azure App Service......................133

**PART 3: DEPLOYING PLATFORM RESOURCES
TO MICROSOFT AZURE**...137

CHAPTER 7: **Deploying and Configuring Azure
App Service Apps**...139
Introducing Azure App Service................................140
    Web apps...141
    API apps...141
    Mobile apps..141
    Logic apps...141
    Function apps......................................141
    App Service logical components.....................142

Deploying Your First Web App.................................144
   Deploying from the Azure portal...........................144
   Configuring Git...145
   Connecting to a web app from Visual Studio 147
   Deploying from Visual Studio 153
   Understanding deployment slots 155
Configuring a Web App..157
   Customizing app settings.................................158
   Adding a custom domain 158
   Binding a TLS/SSL certificate 160
   Configuring autoscaling..................................161
Monitoring a Web App 163
   Adding the Application Insights resource 164
   Enabling instrumentation in a web app....................165
   Viewing Application Insights telemetry data 165

CHAPTER 8: **Running Serverless Apps in Azure** 167
Defining Serverless 167
   Getting to know Azure Functions apps 168
   Getting to know Azure Logic Apps 168
   Understanding triggers, events, and actions................170
Working with Azure Functions.................................171
   Creating an Azure Function 171
   Configuring Function App settings 177
Building Workflows with Azure Logic Apps 179
   Creating an Azure Logic App 179
   Deploying the resource in the Azure portal.................180
   Defining the workflow....................................180
   Testing the trigger and action 183

CHAPTER 9: **Managing Databases in Microsoft Azure** 185
Revisiting the IaaS versus PaaS Question 185
   Controlling the environment..............................186
   Running any version of any database 186
   Using preinstalled VMs from Azure Marketplace.............186
Comparing Relational and Nonrelational Databases in Azure 187
   SQL Database...188
   SQL Database for MySQL Servers...........................189
   Azure Database for MariaDB Servers.......................189
   Azure Database for PostgreSQL Servers 189
Implementing SQL Database...................................190
   Understanding service tiers...............................190
   Deploying an SQL Database virtual server 191
   Deploying SQL Database 192

Configuring the database. 194

Inspecting the virtual server 198

Connecting to the database. 199

Implementing Azure Cosmos DB 200

Understanding Cosmos DB 201

Creating a Cosmos DB account. 202

Running and debugging a sample Cosmos DB application. 203

Interacting with Cosmos DB. 204

PART 4: PROVIDING HIGH AVAILABILITY, SCALABILITY, AND SECURITY FOR YOUR AZURE RESOURCES

. 209

CHAPTER 10: Backing Up and Restoring Your Azure Data

. 211

Protecting Your Storage Account's Blob Data. 212

Backing up and restoring individual storage blobs 212

Backing up storage blobs in bulk 216

Protecting Your Virtual Machines 217

Getting to know the Recovery Services vault. 217

Backing up VMs 219

Restoring VMs 221

Protecting Your App Services. 223

Backing up App Service apps. 223

Restoring App Service apps 224

Protecting Your Databases. 225

Backing up and restoring SQL Database .225

Backing up and restoring Cosmos DB 227

CHAPTER 11: Managing Identity and Access with Azure Active Directory

. 229

Understanding Active Directory 230

AD versus AD DS 231

Relationship between subscriptions and AD tenants 231

Creating Users and Groups 234

Adding a domain to your directory. 234

Understanding AD user and group types 235

Creating an AD group 237

Creating an Azure AD user. 238

Working with Azure AD user accounts. 238

Configuring Role-Based Access Control (RBAC) 242

Implementing built-in RBAC roles. 243

Adding an account to an Azure AD role 245

Touring Azure Advisor 247

CHAPTER 12: Implementing Azure Governance 251

    Implementing Taxonomic Tags 251

        Applying tags to resource groups and resources 252

        Reporting via tags 257

    Implementing Azure Policy 259

        Policy definition structure 259

        Policy life cycle 261

PART 5: MIGRATING TO MICROSOFT AZURE AND MONITORING YOUR INFRASTRUCTURE 267

CHAPTER 13: Extending Your On-Premises Environment to Azure 269

    Data Migration Options 269

        Blob copy 270

        Azure Data Box 271

        Azure Migrate: Database Assessment 272

    Server Migration Options................................... 277

        VHD upload 277

        Azure Migrate: Server Assessment 279

        Azure Migrate: Server Migration 281

    Hybrid Cloud Options..................................... 281

        S2S VPN.. 282

        ExpressRoute 286

    Introducing Azure Arc..................................... 288

        The Arc use case 288

        Arc family members 289

        Preparing your environment 289

        Adding a Windows Server system to Arc 290

        Adding a Linux system to Arc.............................. 294

        Managing local systems with Arc 295

CHAPTER 14: Monitoring Your Azure Environment 301

    Azure Monitor 302

        Enabling diagnostic logging 302

        Plotting resource metrics and raising alerts 310

    Azure Log Analytics....................................... 316

        Creating a Log Analytics workspace 316

        Connecting data sources to the workspace.................. 317

        Writing KQL queries 319

PART 6: THE PART OF TENS..323

CHAPTER 15: **Top Ten Azure News Resources**......................325

Azure Status...325
Azure Blog...326
Azure Updates...326
Azure.Source...327
Build5Nines Weekly...327
Azure Weekly (Endjin)...327
Azure Official YouTube Channel...............................328
Channel 9: Azure Friday...328
Azure Feedback...328
Tim's Twitter Feed...329

CHAPTER 16: **Top Ten Azure Educational Resources**............331

Azure Documentation...331
Azure Architecture Center...............................332
Azure REST API Browser...333
Microsoft @ edX...333
Microsoft Learn...334
Azure Certification...334
MeasureUp...335
Meetup...336
CloudSkills...337
Pluralsight...337

INDEX...339

Introduction

Microsoft Azure is a public cloud service in which you rent compute services from Microsoft that run in Microsoft's data centers. You pay only for the resources you use over the course of your billing period.

I wrote this book to give you a gentle yet thorough introduction to Microsoft Azure, showing you how it works and why you may want to use it to save your company money, time, effort, and sanity.

About This Book

You may wonder why you don't find a large number of Azure–related books in your local bookstores or at online retailers. The answer is quite simple: Azure changes often, so print publishers have a great deal of difficulty keeping up.

I've worked with Azure for several years and have regular contact with Azure team members at Microsoft, who find it to be just as time- and effort-intensive to stay current with the technologies as users do.

Thus, I wrote this book with the intention of helping you with the following:

» **Becoming comfortable with Microsoft Azure:** I give you this comfort by sticking to what Microsoft calls the "80 percent scenarios," or Azure deployments used by 80 percent of its customer base.

» **Gaining skill with programmatic deployment:** Along the way, I show you how to use Azure PowerShell, Azure Command-Line Interface (CLI), and Azure Resource Manager (ARM) templates to get your Azure work done. These Azure access methods change less frequently than the Azure portal graphical user interface (GUI).

>> **Becoming comfortable with tools and staying current:** You can expect the Azure portal to change such that what you see on your screen may not match what's in this book. That's to be expected! In the last section of the book, "The Part of Tens," I give you the skills to stay current on your own and not to feel blindsided when Azure looks different today from how it looked yesterday.

I include many web addresses, also called URLs, throughout this book. If Microsoft changes a page address, and the link I provide no longer works, don't fret! Simply run a Google search for the article title, and you'll find the updated page address nearly instantly.

Throughout this book, you'll find dozens of step-by-step procedures. I want you to keep the following points in mind as you work through them:

>> You need an Azure subscription to follow the steps. If you haven't already done so, you can create a free Azure account (https://azure.microsoft.com/free) that gives you 30 days to spend $200 USD on any Azure service. This quota should get you through this book's material so long as you delete your deployments when you finish using them.

>> I often provide sample values that work in my environment but may not work in yours. You should customize these procedures to suit your requirements.

>> If you require additional software to complete an exercise, I tell you at before the exercise. Software requirements are limited to free Microsoft software to minimize the financial impact that working through this book has on you.

I assume that you have an Internet connection; otherwise, you'd be unable to access Azure (unless you're using Azure Stack, but that's a subject for another book).

Finally, most of the Azure administration and development tools are available for Windows, macOS, and Linux. (I used a Windows 10 workstation.)

Foolish Assumptions

I wrote this book with several types of readers in mind. See whether you can place yourself roughly or exactly in any of the following descriptions:

>> You're an experienced IT professional who needs to know Azure for future initiatives at work.

>> You're an IT newcomer who wants to know Azure to futureproof your career.

>> You're proficient in other public cloud platforms, such as Amazon Web Services or Google Cloud Platform, and you want to see how Azure compares.

>> You're being forced to use Azure for your job.

>> You're tasked with convincing your boss and other decision-makers how valuable Azure could be to your business, and you want to make sure that you understand the basics.

>> You're already using Azure but want to fill in your knowledge or skills gaps.

Regardless of your present attitude and orientation toward Azure, I hope that by studying this book and applying its methods you can more knowledge about Azure and thereby excel in your profession.

Icons Used in This Book

If you've read a *For Dummies* book before, then you're probably familiar with the icons. If not, or if you want a formal description of each, then read on!

The Tip icon marks tips (duh!) and shortcuts that you can use to make working with Azure easier.

Remember icons mark especially important information. To siphon off the most important information in each chapter, skim the paragraphs that have these icons.

The Technical Stuff icon marks information of a highly technical nature that you can skip.

The Warning icon tells you to watch out! It marks important information that may save you headaches.

Beyond the Book

Beyond what's included between the covers of this book, I've created a Cheat Sheet that includes tips, tricks, and shortcuts for the Azure services you use over the course of the book. You can find the Cheat Sheet and other information related to this book (such as errata) by visiting https://www.dummies.com and typing *Azure For Dummies* in the Search box.

Where to Go from Here

Although I'd read this book in order starting with Chapter 1, you may not prefer to use that method. You can dip into any chapter with no formal dependency on those that come before it, so flip to the chapter that you want to begin with, and let's get to work!

1

Getting Started with Microsoft Azure

IN THIS PART . . .

Figuring out exactly what "cloud computing" means and how Microsoft Azure fits into the cloud computing picture

Differentiating the different cloud computing deployment and service delivery models

Understanding the basics of Azure Resource Manager

Gaining familiarity with the various Microsoft Azure administrative tools

Chapter **1**

Introducing Microsoft Azure

Welcome to cloud computing, and welcome to Microsoft Azure! I'm not sure what occurred in your professional or personal life to lead you to read this book, but I'm glad you're here with me. In this chapter, I cover ground-level terminology, beginning with precisely what buzzwords *the cloud* and *cloud computing* mean.

By the end of this chapter, you'll have your very own Azure subscription running at the free tier. Are you excited? I hope so!

What Is Cloud Computing?

My 9-year-old daughter Zoey knows what the cloud is. "It's where my iPad apps are stored," she says. "If I delete an app from my iPad, I can download it again from the cloud." I can't argue with that.

My 75-year-old mother told me that as far as she's aware, the cloud is "a part of the Internet where you can save your stuff." True enough.

Most people use cloud services whether they're aware of doing so or not. Think of your smartphone. Where do you think your photos, media, files, and settings are being backed up? What is behind your ability to retrieve your content wherever you are in the world, provided that you have an Internet connection?

Do you use a web-hosting company to host your personal website? Where is the physical server that houses your website?

These scenarios are examples of cloud computing, in which you simply rent resources on another organization's infrastructure.

The resources you rent consist of the following hardware and software components:

» **Compute:** *Compute* is raw computing power — the central processing unit (CPU) and random-access memory (RAM) that form the platform for applications and data.

» **Storage:** *Persistent storage* means you have a place on Microsoft's servers to store your files and other data. When you save a file to a cloud-hosted storage account, the file should remain in place forever, or at least until you move or delete it.

» **Network:** Azure provides a software-defined network infrastructure on which you can host your virtual machines and other Azure services. Because the cloud almost always involves an Internet connection, *online* and *cloud* are essentially synonymous. I say "almost always" because a business can create a private cloud that shares most attributes of a public cloud but is local to its private network environment. Microsoft also sells a private, portable version of Azure called Azure Stack.

» **Analytics:** You'll never get to touch the cloud provider's compute, storage, or network resources. The closest you'll get is viewing its telemetry data in your web browser or from a management app. Thus, Azure and other public cloud providers give you tools to see precisely how much of their services you consume each minute. Cloud analytics also gives you valuable troubleshooting and performance-tuning advice for your cloud infrastructure.

Businesses are interested in using the cloud because it allows them to offload a lot of what's scary, annoying, and/or expensive about maintaining an on-premises data center, such as the following:

» **Power:** It's potentially very expensive to provide electricity to all the equipment necessary to host your applications and services. And what happens if your on-campus data center experiences a utilities outage? When you move your data into the cloud, your provider takes on the risk of these issues.

>> **Capital expenditure:** When you run an on-premises data center, you either rent your physical servers or purchase them outright. As such, you're responsible for all hardware upgrades and repairs. All that hardware can be expensive too.

>> **Security and configuration overhead:** If you can't afford local systems administrators, or if your existing resources are stretched thin, it can be too easy to leave a vulnerability in place on an on-premises server that can be compromised by bad actors. By contrast, when you use a public cloud service like Azure, you rely upon Microsoft's human and machine learning–based threat intelligence to help keep your applications, services, and data safe.

Do you see the trend here? Cloud computing is popular because it's convenient for the end user and cheaper for the enterprise business. Before I go any further, however, I want to codify what I mean by *cloud computing.*

NIST definition

The National Institute of Standards and Technology (NIST, pronounced *nihst*), a research laboratory in the United States, developed the standard definition of cloud computing. According to NIST, the five essential characteristics of cloud computing are

>> **On-demand self-service:** A cloud customer can provision services at any time and is charged only for the resources that he or she consumes.

>> **Broad network access:** Cloud services are ordinarily offered globally, and the customer is encouraged to place services as geographically near its consumers as possible.

>> **Resource pooling:** Cloud services are *multitenant,* which means that different customers' environments are isolated. You should never, ever see another Azure customer's data, and vice versa.

>> **Rapid elasticity:** A cloud services customer can accommodate variable traffic patterns by configuring their services to scale accordingly. For instance, you can configure Azure to automatically duplicate your web servers to accommodate traffic spikes and then remove servers automatically when they are no longer needed.

>> **Measured service:** The cloud offers services on demand, which are metered; once again, customers pay only provisioned resources.

TECHNICAL STUFF

If you want to read the source material, check NIST Special Publication 800-145, *The NIST Definition of Cloud Computing,* which you can download from https://csrc.nist.gov/publications/detail/sp/800-145/final.

Cloud computing benefits

As I mention earlier in this chapter, cloud computing is attractive to both businesses and consumers because of its convenience, high availability, and potential cost savings. Specifically, Microsoft Azure or any other public cloud service uses a consumption-based spending model that's classified as an operational expenditure (OpEx).

Purchasing or leasing on-premises infrastructure is an up-front capital expenditure (CapEx). By contrast, the relatively predictable, recurring cost model of OpEx is appealing to cost-conscious organizations (and what organization isn't cost-conscious nowadays?).

The cloud's rapid scalability and elasticity are capabilities that only the largest companies in the world can afford to manage on their own. Microsoft Azure enables smaller companies and individuals to replicate a SQL database between geographical regions with a couple of mouse clicks. (See Figure 1-1.) Making high availability this accessible to customers is an enormous benefit of cloud computing.

FIGURE 1-1:
In Azure, you can make a database geographically available with only a couple of clicks.

OTHER CLOUD PROVIDERS

For completeness, I want you to know that although this book's focus is Microsoft Azure, other major public cloud providers also take advantage of economies of scale. These public cloud providers include, but aren't limited to, the following:

- Amazon Web Services (AWS)
- Google Cloud Platform (GCP)
- IBM Cloud
- Oracle Cloud
- Salesforce

Economies of scale

The term *economies of scale* means that a business that purchases its internal resources at a larger volume can pass along savings to its customers.

At this writing, Microsoft has its Azure product portfolio spread across 54 regions worldwide. Within each region are two or more physical data centers. Within each data center are untold numbers of server racks, blade servers, storage arrays, routers, switches, and so forth — an immense physical capacity. I think we can reasonably assume that Microsoft gets a discount from the original equipment manufacturers (OEMs) because it purchases in such huge volume. Microsoft's purchase discounts means that the company in turn extends the savings to its Azure customers. It's as simple as that.

Understanding Cloud Computing Models

The working definition of *cloud computing* is a subscription arrangement under which a person or business rents a cloud service provider's infrastructure and pays only for the services consumed. That definition is fine.

In this section, however, I want to sharpen your general understanding of cloud computing by explaining the deployment and service delivery models.

Deployment models

In Azure nomenclature, *deployment* refers to your provisioning resources in the Azure public cloud. You may be saying, "What's this? Why is Microsoft Azure called a public cloud? I thought you said that different Azure customers can never see each other's resources by default." Hang on; hang on. Let me explain.

Public cloud

Microsoft Azure is a public cloud because its global data center fabric is accessible by the general public. Microsoft takes Azure's multitenant nature very seriously; therefore, it adds layer after layer of physical and logical security to ensure that each customer's data is private. In fact, in many cases, even Microsoft doesn't have access to customers' data encryption keys!

Other major cloud service providers — including AWS, GCP, Oracle, and IBM (see the nearby sidebar "Other cloud providers") — are also considered to be public cloud platforms.

TECHNICAL STUFF

Microsoft has three additional, separate Azure clouds for exclusive governmental use. Thus, the Microsoft literature contains references to Azure Cloud, which refers to its public cloud, and to Azure Government Cloud, which refers to its sovereign, special-access clouds. No member of the general public can access an Azure Government Cloud without being associated with a government body that employs it.

Private cloud

As I mention earlier, very, very few businesses have enough financial, capital, and human resources to host their own cloud environments. Typically only the largest enterprise organizations can afford having their own private cloud infrastructure with redundant data centers, storage, networking, and compute, but they may have security prohibitions against storing data in Microsoft's (or any other cloud provider's) physical data centers.

Microsoft sells a portable version of the Azure cloud: Azure Stack, which consists of a server rack that a company leases or purchases from a Microsoft-affiliated hardware or service provider.

The idea is that you can bring the hallmarks of cloud computing — on-demand self-service, resource pooling, elasticity, and so forth — to your local environment without involving either the Internet or an external cloud provider unless you want to.

Your administrators and developers use the same Azure Resource Manager (ARM) application programming interface (API) to deploy resources locally to Azure Stack as they use to deploy to the Azure public cloud. This API makes it a snap to bring cloud-based services on premises, and vice versa. You'll learn about ARM in Chapter 2.

Hybrid cloud

When you combine the best of on-premises and cloud environments, you have a hybrid cloud.

In my professional experience, the hybrid cloud deployment model makes the most sense for most businesses. Why? A hybrid cloud allows the business to salvage (read: continue to use) the on-premises infrastructure that it's already paid for while leveraging the hyper scale of the Azure public cloud.

Take a look at Figure 1-2. In this topology, the on-premises network is extended to a virtual network running in Azure. You can do all sorts of nifty service management here, including

» Joining the Azure virtual machines (VMs) to your local Active Directory domain.

» Managing your on-premises servers by using Azure management tools.

» Providing nearly instant failover disaster recovery (DR) by using Azure as a DR site. Failover refers to having a replicated backup of your production servers available somewhere else so that you can shift from your failed primary environment to your backup environment within minutes. Failover is critical for businesses that cannot afford the downtime involved in restoring backups from a backup archive.

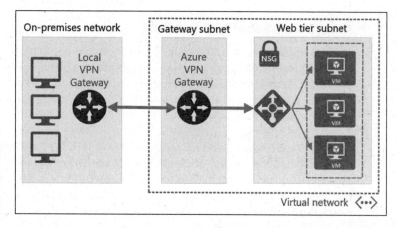

FIGURE 1-2:
A hybrid cloud in which the on-premises corporate network extends to Azure.

By the end of this book, you'll understand how to deploy the environment you see in Figure 1-2, but here's an overview of what's going on:

>> On the left side is a local business network that connects to the Internet via a virtual private network (VPN) gateway.

>> On the right (Azure) side is a three-VM deployment in a virtual network. A site-to-site VPN connects the local environment to the virtual network. Finally, an Azure load balancer spreads incoming traffic equally among the three identically configured web servers in the web tier subnet. As a result, the company's internal staff can access the Azure-based web application over a secure VPN tunnel and get a low-latency, reliable, always-on connection to boot.

REMEMBER

In this book, I refer to a local, physical network environment as an *on-premises environment*. In the wild, you'll see stray references to "on premise" — sadly, even in Microsoft's Azure documentation. Don't make this mistake. A *premise* is an idea; *premises* refers to a location.

In my experience, only small businesses are agile enough to do all their work in the Azure cloud. That said, you may find that after your organization gets its sea legs with Azure and begins to appreciate its availability, performance, scalability, and security possibilities, you'll be working to migrate more on-premises infrastructure into Azure, and you'll be targeting more of your line-of-business (LOB) applications to the cloud first.

Service delivery models

Organizations deploy applications in three primary ways: Software as a Service, Infrastructure as a Service, and Platform as a Service.

Software as a Service (SaaS)

An SaaS application is a finished, customer-facing application that runs in the cloud. Microsoft Office 365 is a perfect example. As shown in Figure 1-3, you can use Word Online to create, edit, and share documents with only a web browser; an Internet connection; and an Office 365 subscription, which you pay for each month on a subscription basis.

With SaaS applications, you have zero visibility into the back-end mechanics of the application. In the case of Word Online, you neither know nor care how often the back-end servers are backed up, where the Office 365 data centers are geographically located, and so forth. All you care about is whether you can get to your cloud-hosted documents and whether Word Online behaves as you expect.

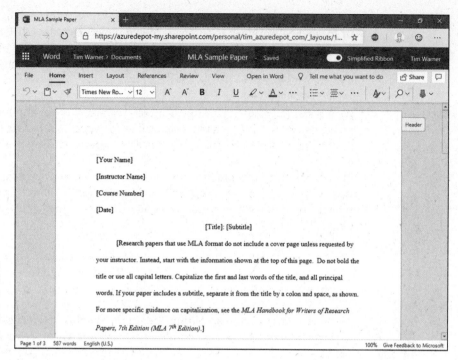

FIGURE 1-3:
Word Online, part
of the Microsoft
Office 365
product family, is
an example of an
SaaS application.

Platform as a Service (PaaS)

Much of my work as an Azure solution architect centers on explaining the benefits of PaaS over IaaS in certain scenarios.

Consider a business that runs a three-tier on-premises web application with VMs. The organization wants to move this application workload to Azure to take advantage of the benefits of cloud computing. Because the organization has always done business by using VMs, it assumes that the workload must by definition run in VMs in Azure.

Not so fast. Suppose that the workload consisted of a Microsoft-stack application. Maybe the business should consider using PaaS products such as Azure App Service and Azure SQL Database to leverage autoscale and pushbutton georeplication.

I discuss both Azure App Service and Azure SQL Database later in Part 3. For now, understand georeplication means placing synchronized copies of your service in other geographic regions for fault tolerance and placing those services closer to your users.

Or maybe the workload is an open-source project that uses PHP and MySQL. No problem. Azure App Service can handle that scenario. Microsoft also has a native hosted database platform for MySQL called (appropriately enough) Azure Database for MySQL.

With PaaS, Microsoft takes much more responsibility for the hosting environment. You're not 100 percent responsible for your VMs because PaaS products abstract all that plumbing and administrative overhead away from you.

The idea is that PaaS products free you to focus on your applications and, ultimately, on the people who use those applications. If PaaS has a trade-off, it's that relinquishing full-stack control is an adjustment for many old-salt systems and network administrators.

To sum up the major distinction between IaaS and PaaS, IaaS gives you full control of the environment, but you sacrifice scalability and agility. PaaS gives you full scalability and agility, but you sacrifice some control.

TIP

To be sure, the cloud computing literature contains references to other cloud deployment models, such as community cloud. You'll also see references to additional delivery models, such as Storage as a Service (STaaS) and Identity as a Service (IDaaS). This chapter focuses on the most commonly used cloud deployment and delivery models.

Infrastructure as a Service (IaaS)

I find that most businesses that migrate their applications and services to Azure use the IaaS model, if only because they've delivered their services via VMs in the past — the old "If it ain't broke, don't fix it" approach.

In large part, IaaS is where the customer hosts one or more VMs in a cloud. The customers remain responsible for the full life cycle of the VM, including

>> Configuration

>> Data protection

>> Performance tuning

>> Security

By hosting your VMs in Azure rather than in your on-premises environment, you save money because you don't have to provision the physical and logical resources locally. You also don't have to pay for the layers of geographic, physical, and logical redundancy included in Azure out of the box.

Thus, whereas SaaS is a service that's been fully abstracted in the cloud, and the customer simply uses the application, IaaS offers a split between Microsoft's responsibility (providing the hosting platform) and the customer's responsibility (maintaining the VMs over their life cycle).

WARNING

Cloud computing in general, and Microsoft Azure in particular, use what's called the *shared responsibility model.* In this model, Microsoft's responsibility is providing the tools you need to make your cloud deployments successful — Microsoft's data centers, the server, storage and networking hardware, and so on. Your responsibility is to use those tools to secure, optimize, and protect your deployments. Microsoft isn't going to configure, back up, and secure your VMs automatically; those tasks are your responsibility.

Introducing Microsoft Azure Services

The Microsoft Azure service catalog has hundreds of services. Listing all of them in this book would be a waste of ink and paper, because by the time you read this chapter, the service list will have expanded even more.

Microsoft maintains a services directory at `https://azure.microsoft.com/en-us/services`, but in this chapter, I give you a high-level tour of what Microsoft calls 80 percent services — the Azure products that 80 percent of the customer base uses.

Azure history

In October 2008, Microsoft announced Windows Azure at its Professional Developers Conference. Many people feel that this product was a direct answer to Amazon, which had already begun unveiling AWS to the general public.

The first Azure-hosted service was SQL Azure Relational Database, announced in March 2009. Then came support for PaaS websites and IaaS virtual machines in June 2012. Figure 1-4 shows what the Windows Azure portal looked like during that time.

Satya Nadella became Microsoft's chief operating officer in February 2014. Satya had a vision of Microsoft expanding its formerly proprietary borders, so Windows Azure became Microsoft Azure, and the Azure platform began to embrace open-source technologies and companies that Microsoft formerly considered to be hostile competitors.

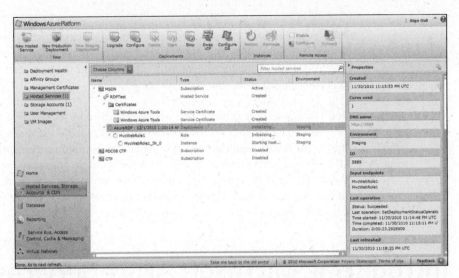

FIGURE 1-4:
The Windows
Azure portal,
circa 2012.

TIP

I can't overstate how important that simple name change was and is. Today, Microsoft Azure provides first-class support for Linux-based VMs and non-Microsoft web applications and services, which is a huge deal.

Finally, Microsoft introduced the RM deployment model at Microsoft Build 2014. The API behind Windows Azure was called Azure Service Management (ASM), and it suffered from several design and architectural pain points. ASM made it super-difficult to organize deployment resources, for example, and it was impossible to scope administrative access granularly.

The ARM API is modeled closely on the AWS API (you know the old saw "Imitation is the sincerest form of flattery"), with core architectural concepts such as resource groups and role-based access controls that were direct analogs of features in the AWS cloud.

To support old customers with old deployments, ARM still offers limited support for ASM deployments in the Azure portal (see Chapter 2). These resources are tagged with the suffix Classic. This book is committed to the ARM API, however, so I won't be addressing ASM IaaS products.

Azure Virtual Machines is Microsoft's Azure mainline IaaS product. Specifically, the Azure Marketplace in the Azure portal lists thousands of preconfigured VM images from Microsoft, endorsed Linux distributions, and third-party solution providers. You can see the gallery of VM images in Figure 1-5.

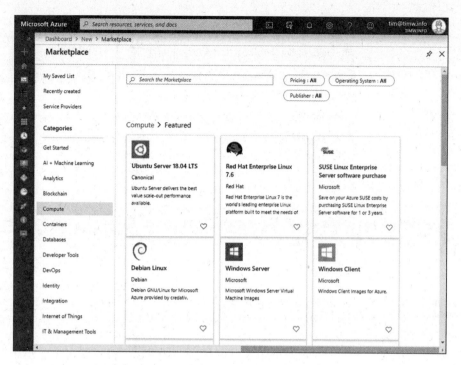

FIGURE 1-5:
The Azure
Marketplace
includes prebuilt
Windows and
Linux VM images.

You can migrate your on-premises physical and virtual machines to Azure, of course, as well as create custom VM images. I'll get to those topics in time; I promise.

PaaS products

The Azure product portfolio is filled with powerful, cost-saving PaaS offerings. Following are some of the more high-profile Azure PaaS products:

>> **App Service:** Web Apps, Mobile Apps, API Apps, Logic Apps, and Function Apps

>> **Databases:** Cosmos DB, Azure SQL Database, Azure Database for MySQL, and Azure Cache for Redis

>> **Containers:** Azure Container Instances, Azure Container Registry, and Azure Kubernetes Service

>> **DevOps:** Azure DevOps and Azure DevTest Labs

>> **Internet of Things (IoT):** Azure IoT Hub, Azure IoT Edge, Azure Sphere, and Azure Digital Twins

- » **Machine learning:** Azure Machine Learning Service, Azure Bot Service, Cognitive Services, and Azure Search

- » **Identity:** Azure Active Directory, Azure AD Business-to-Business, and Azure AD Business-to-Consumer

- » **Monitoring:** Application Insights, Azure Monitor, and Azure Log Analytics

- » **Migration:** Azure Site Recovery, Azure Cost Management, Azure Database Migration Service, and Azure Migrate

Starting Your First Azure Subscription

You can have a free, low-obligation trial of the Microsoft Azure platform with the Azure free account. *Low-obligation* means that you have to provide some personal details and a legitimate payment type. Microsoft uses your credit card information only for identity verification.

Many people have some trepidation about signing up for a public cloud service, even if it's promised to be free, for reasons such as these:

- » Does Microsoft begin to charge my credit card when the free trial period expires?

- » What if I accidentally leave an Azure service running? Will Microsoft ding my credit card for it?

I can address these and other perfectly reasonable concerns, starting by explaining how Azure subscriptions work.

Understanding subscription types

When you sign up for an Azure free account, you receive $200 (or the equivalent in your local currency) to spend on any Azure service over a 30-day period. At the end of the 30 days, Microsoft does not convert your account to pay as you go (PAYG), the typical paid subscription offer.

Instead, any running services you have are stopped, and to restart your services, you need to convert your trial account manually to a PAYG account or other subscription offer in the Azure portal.

That said, the Azure free account provides 12 months of free availability to several IaaS and PaaS services, including the following:

>> 750 hours of B1S General Purpose VMs running Windows Server or Linux

>> 5 GB locally redundant hot-tier blob storage

>> 10 web, mobile, or API apps with 1 GB storage

>> 5 GB Cosmos DB instance

>> 250 GB Azure SQL Database (S0 instance size)

>> 15 GB outbound data transfer from Azure

TECHNICAL STUFF

You can see a full list of Azure free tier services by looking up the Free services blade in the Azure portal or by visiting the Azure Free Account FAQ page at `https://azure.microsoft.com/en-us/free/free-account-faq`.

REMEMBER

"Blade" is the term Microsoft uses to describe any specific web page in the Azure portal. I use the word a lot in this book, and you'll see it all the time in the Azure documentation.

Additionally, several Azure services run on an always-free tier; you'll need to check `https://azure.microsoft.com/en-us` for specifics. Remember, however, that the free tier services aren't there for you to run production workloads. The tier exists to give you an opportunity to test Azure, to see whether it may fit your professional or personal needs.

Pay-As-You-Go (PAYG for short) is the most common standard subscription offer. Each month, you receive an invoice stating charges for the Azure resources you consume outside the Azure free-tier services.

The Enterprise Agreement (EA) is a special-purpose contract intended for larger businesses that are willing to commit to a three-year Azure subscription. Microsoft offers EA customers special discounts on Azure services and provides them a special management portal for analyzing spending, creating budgets, tracking use, and so forth.

Under EA, you pay your yearly fee up front and must use it or lose it. If you commit to $12,000 for the first year and spend only $9,000 by December 31, for example, you lose the remaining $3,000. At the end of each contract year, however, you can adjust your fee for the upcoming year to better match your use and expectations.

Several other Azure subscription offers grant recurring monthly credits, including these:

>> **Visual Studio:** Given to those who have a Visual Studio Online subscription

>> **Action Pack:** Given to Microsoft Partner Network members

>> **Azure for Students:** A free credit ($100) over 12 months for students with a verified academic email address

>> **Azure Pass:** Normally granted by Microsoft to Azure user groups and educational institutions, and intended for free distribution

Creating a free Azure account

To sign up for an Azure free account, you need an Internet connection and any modern web browser.

TIP

I suggest that you perform this procedure (and all procedures in this book) on a desktop or laptop computer rather than a tablet or smartphone. Microsoft makes the Azure portal as mobile-friendly as possible but given the amount of typing you'll be doing, I recommend using a larger computer.

Follow these steps to create your account:

1. **Browse to** `https://azure.microsoft.com/en-us` **and look for a free-account.**

Microsoft changes the Azure website regularly, so I hesitate to ask you to look in a particular spot for the link or a button. Somewhere on the page, you'll find the link or button to click.

2. **Sign in with your Microsoft account, or create a new one.**

The Azure free account is a Microsoft account, which powers all of the company's online services, including Xbox and Office 365. If you already have a Microsoft account, however, you may want to create a new one exclusively for Azure use. I suggest this because you probably want to keep your Azure business completely isolated from, say, your Xbox leisure.

3. **In the About You section, provide your contact details, and click Next.**

Microsoft needs this information to set up your Azure subscription. It also uses your telephone number, email address, and payment details to verify your identity.

4. **In the Identity Verification by Card section of the next page, provide valid credit card details.**

   Note that you can't use a prepaid credit card or gift card; the card has to be a legitimate credit or debit card with your name and billed to your address. Microsoft won't charge your account unless you upgrade to a paid subscription offer. That said, Microsoft may put a $1 verification hold on your credit card account; this hold is lifted within three to five business days.

   You can have only one Azure free account, and Microsoft performs the identity verification in part to prevent fraud.

5. **In the Agreement section, confirm that you agree to the subscription agreement, offer details, and privacy statement; then click Sign Up.**

6. **On the You're Ready to Start with Azure page that appears, click Go to the Portal.**

   You're done and ready to rock. That was easy, wasn't it?

You should now see the Azure portal, along with a Welcome to Microsoft Azure message, as shown in Figure 1-6.

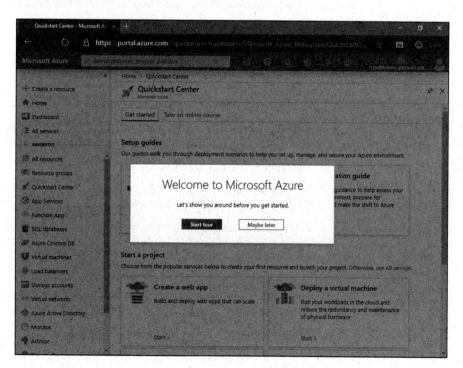

FIGURE 1-6:
Signing in to the Azure portal for the first time.

I formally introduce the Azure portal in Chapter 2. For now, bookmark this address (`https://portal.azure.com`), because you'll be using it a lot from now on.

Click Start Tour to take a spin around the Azure portal. In the background of Figure 1-6, you see the Quickstart Center; you can return to this blade at any time by typing **quickstart center** in the Search box on the top navigation bar. The Quickstart Center contains links to the documentation and to Microsoft Learn, Microsoft's free Azure education portal.

REMEMBER

The windows in the Azure portal are called *blades*.

Viewing subscription details

Follow these steps to view your Azure free-account subscription details:

1. **Type** subscriptions **in the Search box in the Azure portal.**

   The Subscriptions option should appear almost instantly. (I'm a huge fan of the global search feature in the Azure portal, and I hope you'll become one too.)

2. **In the Subscriptions blade, select your Free Trial subscription.**

   Before you click Free Trial, notice the information that the Subscriptions blade gives you: Your account role is Account Admin, and the status of the account is Active. So far, so good.

3. **Examine the various subscription management tools.**

   Figure 1-7 shows the following tools:

   - *A:* The Overview setting shows you the Essentials panel (shown on the right side of the figure), where you see details on your subscription status and metadata.

   - *B:* The Cost Management settings enable you to report on the Azure service you've consumed and/or are currently consuming.

   - *C:* The Payment Methods setting enables you to change the payment method associated with your subscription.

   - *D:* Upgrade Subscription enables you to convert your free trial to a PAYG subscription. If you convert before you spend the $200 or reach the 30 days, you keep your credit before the cost meter starts ticking.

   - *E:* The Manage button takes you to the Azure Account Center, where you can print past service invoices, set billing alerts, and change the account that owns the subscription.

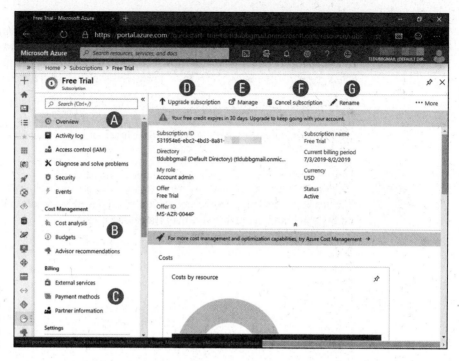

FIGURE 1-7:
Viewing your Free
Trial subscription
in the Azure
portal.

- *F:* The Cancel Subscription button enables you to . . . well, cancel your subscription. What else?

- *G:* The Rename button enables you to change the logical name of your subscription from Free Tier to something more meaningful to you and your organization.

If you decide to upgrade your subscription, Microsoft asks whether you want to buy a monthly support plan. As with the PAYG subscription, you can cancel a support plan at any time with no penalty. The three support tiers, each of which has a fixed monthly cost, are

>> **Developer plan:** Support for trial and nonproduction environments. You can interact with Azure support staff members from 9 a.m. to 5 p.m. in your time zone, with an initial response time of less than 8 business hours. As of this writing in November 2019, the monthly cost is $29.

>> **Standard plan:** Support for production environments. You receive 24/7 technical support and a response within 2 hours. As of this writing, the Standard plan costs $100 per month.

» **Professional Direct plan:** Support for businesses that rely heavily on Azure. You get 24/7 technical support and a response for critical issues within one hour. As of this writing, Microsoft charges $1,000 per month for this support plan.

» **Premier plan:** This support tier is aimed at businesses that want not only lightning-fast technical support but also architectural guidance from Microsoft Azure solutions experts. You need to contact Microsoft to get a Premier plan price quote.

REMEMBER

Unless you have an EA with Microsoft, you can cancel your Azure subscription at any time. Be aware, however, that you're required to delete all your resources before Microsoft will let you cancel the subscription.

Chapter **2**

Exploring Azure Resource Manager

I n this chapter, I give you a glimpse behind the proverbial curtain as I introduce you to the back-end services that comprise the Microsoft Azure public cloud.

At first blush, you may find the forthcoming discussions of REST APIs to be a bit (perhaps more than a bit) developerish and outside your professional comfort zone. Stay with me, please! I submit that any Azure professional, regardless of specialization, must have a solid understanding of Azure Resource Manager architecture; after all, it underlies every bit of Azure-based services.

Introducing Azure Resource Manager

Azure Resource Manager (most often abbreviated ARM and pronounced like the body part) is the deployment and management service underneath Microsoft Azure. Every action you take in Azure, regardless of the tool you use, calls the ARM REST APIs. The Azure portal is simply a web front end that abstracts ARM REST API requests and responses.

"What's a REST API, Tim?" you rightly ask. I answer that question next.

REST APIs

An application programming interface (API) is a software specification that allows interaction with other software applications. Twitter, for example, publishes its API specification to allow software developers to tap Twitter services for use in their own applications (fetching tweets, making posts, and so forth).

Representational state transfer (REST) is a software development methodology that defines how web-based APIs can communicate by using Hypertext Transfer Protocol (HTTP).

HTTP has five primary methods (also called *operations* or *verbs*) that a REST API call can undertake:

>> GET: Retrieve resource details

>> POST: Create a new resource

>> PUT: Update a resource (replace the existing resource)

>> PATCH: Incrementally update a resource (modify existing resource)

>> DELETE: Remove a resource

TECHNICAL STUFF

Four of the aforementioned HTTP methods deal with the four primary data operations in information technology: Create, Read, Update, and Delete. Because we in IT like puns and juvenile humor, we call these operations CRUD for short.

Hey, at this point don't get bogged down with the HTTP verbs. I describe them here only to give you fuller context.

Now I'll relate this REST API stuff to Microsoft Azure. ARM's REST API fundamentally defines Azure products and services, and specifies how you can use them within your subscriptions.

Every individual artifact you deploy in Azure represents a resource. Thus, virtual machines (VMs), web applications, databases, storage accounts, and key vaults are defined in the ARM REST API as discrete resource types.

Resource providers

In the ARM REST API definition, a *resource provider* is a service that delivers a specific Azure product. The Azure resource provider's namespace is arranged hierarchically.

To illustrate this namespace, consider the resource ID for one of my Azure storage accounts, named tlwstor270:

```
/subscriptions/2fbf906e-1101-4bc0-b64f-adc44e462fff/
    resourceGroups/twtech/providers/Microsoft.Storage/
    storageAccounts/tlwstor270
```

First of all, notice the forward slashes and the way the resource path resembles a Uniform Resource Identifier (URI). That's intentional because all REST APIs are web-based and use HTTP or HTTPS URIs exclusively. You can read the storage-account resource ID from left to right to traverse the ARM REST API namespace:

>> subscriptions: The node below slash (/), which is the top-level root of the ARM REST API hierarchy.

>> 2fb...: The subscription ID of the subscription that hosts my storage account.

>> resourceGroups: The resource group namespace. The resource group is the primary deployment unit in Azure.

>> twtech: The resource group that hosts my storage account.

>> providers: The resource provider level.

>> Microsoft.Storage: The resource provider that governs Azure storage services (of which the storage account is but one service).

>> storageAccounts: The resource group that hosts my storage account.

>> tlwstor270: A reference to the actual storage account.

TIP

If you've worked with REST APIs, you may want to use a third-party product such as Postman (https://www.getpostman.com) to interact with the ARM REST API. If you haven't, point your browser to https://resources.azure.com, sign in with your subscription owner account, and browse the ARM REST API and your Azure subscription resources graphically. Figure 2-1 shows the interface.

As I mention earlier, I have a storage account called tlwstor270 located in a resource group named twtech. Here's how to "walk the tree" by using Azure Resource Explorer:

1. **On the left navigation bar, expand Subscriptions and then expand your subscription.**

In Figure 2-1, I've expanded my subscription.

2. **Expand resourceGroups and then expand your target resource group.**

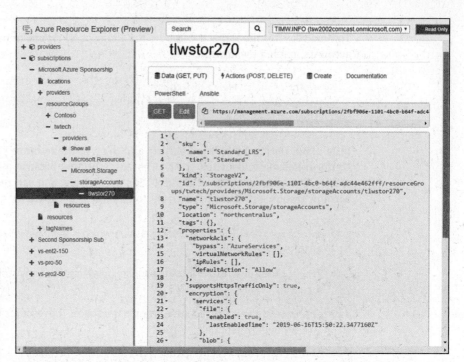

```
1 ⌄ {
2 ⌄     "sku": {
3             "name": "Standard_LRS",
4             "tier": "Standard"
5         },
6         "kind": "StorageV2",
7         "id": "/subscriptions/2fbf906e-1101-4bc0-b64f-adc44e462fff/resourceGro
    ups/twtech/providers/Microsoft.Storage/storageAccounts/tlwstor270",
8         "name": "tlwstor270",
9         "type": "Microsoft.Storage/storageAccounts",
10        "location": "northcentralus",
11        "tags": {},
12 ⌄     "properties": {
13 ⌄         "networkAcls": {
14                 "bypass": "AzureServices",
15                 "virtualNetworkRules": [],
16                 "ipRules": [],
17                 "defaultAction": "Allow"
18            },
19            "supportsHttpsTrafficOnly": true,
20 ⌄         "encryption": {
21 ⌄             "services": {
22 ⌄                 "file": {
23                         "enabled": true,
24                         "lastEnabledTime": "2019-06-16T15:50:22.3477160Z"
25                    },
26 ⌄                 "blob": {
```

FIGURE 2-1:
The Azure
Resource
Explorer allows
you to view the
ARM REST API
directly.

3. **Expand providers, expand Microsoft.Storage, and then select your storage account.**

4. **In the main screen, browse the JavaScript Object Notation (JSON) output that defines your storage account.**

   In Figure 2-1, the tlwstor270 storage account is the only resource in my twtech resource group, so it's easy to find the resource definition in the JSON output. Note the references to the HTTP verbs at the top of the screen: GET, PUT, POST, and DELETE.

WARNING

Although Azure Resource Explorer puts you in read-only mode by default, note the Read Only button at the top of the interface. If you have sufficient privilege, you could go beyond simple GET requests and perform PUTs, POSTs, and DELETEs on your Azure resources, so be careful!

JSON

RESTful APIs use JSON (ordinarily pronounced *jay-sahn*) data format to encode all request and response data, which is certainly true in ARM.

Douglas Crockford invented JSON in 2001 as a way to represent data in relatively compact, human-readable form. JSON documents are plain-text and can be opened in any text editor.

TIP

If you're an Azure professional, I recommend using Visual Studio Code as your text editor.

JSON elements consist of a comma-separated list of key/value pairs. Check out this JSON snippet from the Azure storage account I discussed previously. Pay attention to how much you can learn about this resource by viewing a small amount of code. Don't worry about understanding it yet — you're just getting started!

```
"sku": {
  "name": "Standard_LRS",
  "tier": "Standard"
},
"kind": "StorageV2",
"id": "/subscriptions/2fbf906e-1101/resourceGroups/twtech/
          providers/Microsoft.Storage/
          storageAccounts/tlwstor270",
"name": "tlwstor270",
"type": "Microsoft.Storage/storageAccounts",
"location": "northcentralus",
```

All deployments in Azure are recorded in JSON format. These ARM templates, as they're known, make it much easier to create reliable, repeatable Azure environments.

In the Azure portal in Figure 2-2, for example, you can see the trusty tlwstor270 storage account I created in my testing environment. I then select the Export template setting, and click Download to capture the storage account's ARM template definition. You can see this process in action in Figure 2-2.

I can't overstate how important it is to get comfortable with JSON in general and ARM templates in particular. The good news is that over the course of this book, you'll get lots of practical experience with both.

ARM management scopes

In a computer's file system, you have a defined hierarchy: volume, folder, sub-folders, and files. Permissions you set at a higher scope flow by inheritance to lower scopes. Giving Pat read-only access to your server's E drive, for example, results in Pat's inheriting that read-only access to all the E drive's folders, sub-folders, and files.

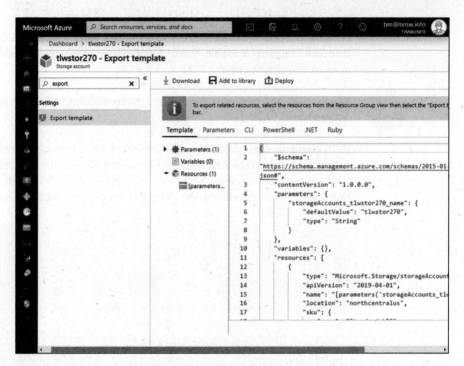

FIGURE 2-2:
You can locate and download the JSON source code behind every Azure resource.

Inheritance and multilayer scopes work much the same way in Azure. All your resource groups are contained within an Azure subscription, and you can roll one or more subscriptions up into a management group. These management scopes (see Figure 2-3) simplify granting role-based access control authorization assignments and governance policies to your resources and, ultimately, their users.

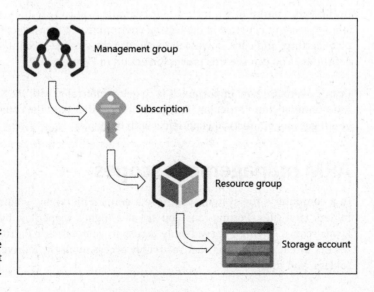

FIGURE 2-3:
Azure management scopes.

Let me give you an example of how an Azure administrator can combine these management scopes. Roll with me here for now; you'll understand these concepts intimately by the time you finish the book.

Suppose that an administrator needs to ensure that any VMs deployed by other Azure admins occur within only corporate authorized regions. But I'm going to complicate this scenario by saying that the organization's VMs are spread across 44 resource groups in 6 subscriptions. Whoa! Even with inheritance, the management overhead here would be significant.

But the situation isn't as bad as it may seem at first. The administrator creates a single management group that includes the six corporate subscriptions. Then she makes a single Azure policy that defines the resource deployment rule and associates the policy with the management group. The Azure Policy flows by inheritance through its enclosed subscriptions and resource groups to the existing and future VMs, which is powerful and efficient management.

Getting Familiar with Azure Regions

In public cloud computing, you store your resources in Microsoft's physical infrastructure. (Refer to Chapter 1.) This infrastructure consists of an enormous datacenter network spread around the world.

This world wide web (as it were) of Azure data centers means that you can place your cloud resources geographically close to your customers, thereby giving them low-latency, high-performance connections to your applications. At this writing, Microsoft has 54 regions spread across 140 countries. Each region consists of one or more discrete physical data centers with redundant, high-speed network interconnectivity.

Availability zones

When you host customer-facing services in Azure, high availability should be uppermost in your mind. What plans do you have if a failure occurs in your home region's data center?

Microsoft has been gradually rolling out availability zones throughout its region map. Essentially, an *availability zone* allows you to place replica VMs in different data centers in the same region. In other words, availability zones represent separate locations within a single Azure region.

Figure 2-4 illustrates this concept, with two identically configured web server VMs are placed in two availability zones in my home region. An Azure load balancer in front of the VMs makes both of them available under the same IP address or Domain Name System host name. With this setup, if one of my VMs goes offline (through my own error or a Microsoft data-center outage), my service remains online and functional.

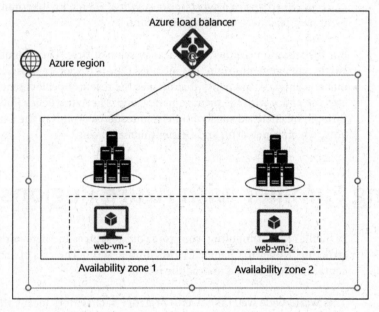

FIGURE 2-4:
Providing high availability for replica VMs by placing them in availability zones.

REMEMBER

In Azure nomenclature, *region* and *location* are interchangeable.

Geographies

Microsoft organizes its regions into geographies to support corporate compliance and data residency requirements.

Special regions

Azure is called a public cloud service because most of its regions and services are available for purchase by the general public. That said, Microsoft hosts special regions called government clouds or sovereign clouds for exclusive use by particular governmental bodies around the world (refer to Chapter 1).

**TECHNICAL
STUFF**

OPERATIONAL SECURITY

You may notice that I'm being intentionally vague in describing the network of data centers that make up Microsoft's global regions. This vagueness is by design, due to an information security principal known as *operational security*. Customers trust Microsoft to keep its regional data centers secure on physical and logical levels, so the company doesn't publish any more information on data-center internals than required to be worthy of trust.

In my career, I can count on two hands the number of Microsoft employees I've met who have visited an Azure data center. The practical guidance is that you should place your Azure resources in the regions that are physically closest to your customers. Furthermore, for high availability and to reach different audiences, you can redundantly host resources across multiple regions.

If you thirst for more information, check out Azure chief technical officer Mark Russinovich's video on operational security at https://azure.microsoft.com/en-us/resources/videos/build-2019-inside-azure-data center-architecture-with-mark-russinovich.

Azure Government regions are inaccessible (invisible) to nongovernment employees. At this writing, Microsoft maintains separate regions, availability zones, and data centers for the governments of the United States, China, and Germany.

Paired regions

Earlier in this chapter, I mention that you can place redundant copies of your Azure services in more than one region for failover redundancy. When you do so, you should first determine Microsoft's designated paired region to ensure minimal latency.

Microsoft builds additional high-speed network connectivity between paired regions, which assures customers that their multiregion deployments won't suffer undue latency.

Search https://docs.microsoft.com/azure for the article "Business continuity and disaster recovery (BCDR): Azure Paired Regions," which includes the master list of paired regions.

TIP

In my Azure consultancy, I recommend that customers test the latency between their location and Azure by visiting Azure Speed Test 2.0 at `https://azure speedtest.azurewebsites.net/`. You may find that the lowest-latency Azure region wasn't what you thought it was.

Feature availability

Azure product teams gradually roll out new features across the region map, so some products may not be available at the moment in your home region.

For this reason, it's important to keep an eye on the Products Available by Region page at `https://azure.microsoft.com/en-us/global-infrastructure/ services/`. The same guidance applies to Azure Government regions. Most of the time, I find that new features begin their life cycle in the Azure public cloud and only much later make their way to the sovereign clouds.

Introducing the Azure Management Tools

It's time to become familiar with the most common Azure management tools. All the step-by-step procedures I describe in this book assume that you're working on a Windows 10 workstation, but you can accomplish nearly every task in this book on a macOS or Linux system.

Azure portal

The Azure portal (`https://portal.azure.com`) is a responsive web application that forms the basic graphical administration platform in Azure. Figure 2-5 shows the Azure portal.

- » **Page header (A):** The top navigation bar is sometimes called *global navigation* because these controls are available everywhere in the Azure portal. Open the Favorites menu.

- » **Global search (B):** Search for any Azure resource. The search results include documentation links.

- » **Cloud Shell (C):** Open Azure Cloud Shell to perform command-line Azure work.

- » **Global subscription filter (D):** Display a subset of your Azure subscriptions to make your Azure portal view lists easier to browse.

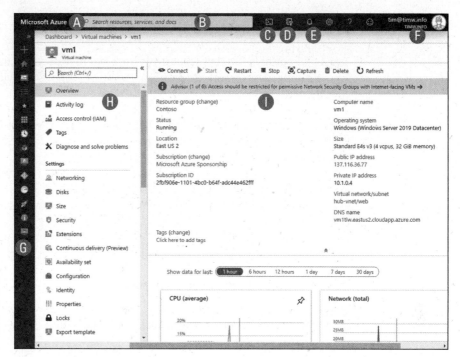

FIGURE 2-5:
The Azure portal is your administrative base of operations.

>> **Notifications (E):** Check the progress of current and past deployments.

>> **Your account (F):** Log out, switch directories, and edit your account profile.

>> **Favorites (G):** Load up your most frequently used Azure services.

>> **Resources pane (H):** Use the Search box to find the setting that you need to configure.

>> **Configuration blade (I):** *Blade* refers to the detail screens in which you do your Azure work. The horizontal scroll bar helps you move from side to side.

REMEMBER

Your Azure portal customization affects only your user account. Your colleague will have her own favorites list, subscription filters, custom dashboards, and so forth.

TIP

Responsive web applications rearrange themselves dynamically to accommodate different web browsers and screen sizes. Accessing the full portal on a smartphone usually isn't fun, however. Microsoft makes mobile versions of the Azure portal available for iOS and Android mobile devices. You can perform most administration tasks in this mobile app, including accessing Cloud Shell.

Azure PowerShell

The Azure portal is fun, but what if you're asked to deploy 10, 100, or 1,000 VMs? You certainly don't want to perform repetitive actions by clicking-clicking-clicking in the Azure portal.

For administrative automation, you Azure PowerShell. PowerShell is an automation language that you can use to perform any repetitive task in Windows Server, macOS, Linux, Azure, AWS . . . you get the picture.

If you haven't begun to skill up on PowerShell, today's the day; you need to have at least intermediate-level PowerShell skills to be fully productive in Azure.

Follow these steps to get the Az modules installed on your Windows 10 workstation:

1. **Open an elevated PowerShell console.**

   In Windows 10, open the Start menu, type PowerShell, right-click the icon, and choose Run as Administrator from the shortcut menu.

2. **Install the Az modules from the PowerShell Gallery.**

   Microsoft operates a curated PowerShell module repository called (appropriately enough) the PowerShell Gallery. Run the following command to download and install Azure PowerShell:

   ```
   Install-Module -Name -Az -Verbose -Force
   ```

   Technically, the -Verbose and -Force switch parameters are optional, but I suggest using -Verbose so that you can read detailed command output, and -Force to upgrade the modules if you already have them installed on your computer.

3. **Update your local help.**

   PowerShell doesn't ship with local help by default because the documentation changes so rapidly. Make sure that you have the most recent PowerShell command help at your disposal by using this command:

   ```
   Update-Help -Force -ErrorAction SilentlyContinue
   ```

   The -ErrorAction SilentlyContinue bit suppresses any errors or glitches that may occur during the help-file download. For a variety of reasons, you should expect to see an occasional error when running Update-Help. (Someone on the PowerShell team may have forgotten to create a help article for a command, for example.)

4. **Sign into your Azure subscription.**

Run the following command to generate a Sign In to Your Account dialog box. After you authenticate, you'll be brought back to the PowerShell console, all logged in and ready to rock.

```
Connect-AzAccount
```

5. **To close your PowerShell connection, close the console window.**

TIP

You'll need to use the aforementioned steps every time you want to manage Azure with PowerShell. However, you can automate Azure PowerShell sign-in by using a special Azure Active Directory account called a service principal. For details, see the Azure documentation article "Create an Azure Service Principal with Azure PowerShell" at https://docs.microsoft.com/en-us/powershell/azure/create-azure-service-principal-azureps?view=azps-3.2.0.

Azure CLI/Azure Cloud Shell

The Azure command-line interface (CLI) is . . . well, a cross-platform command-line interface for Azure. I've found that some Azure administrators and developers prefer the Azure CLI to Azure PowerShell because the CLI has an easier learning curve and can be lightning-fast, especially in interactive mode.

In this book, you work with the Azure CLI from within Azure Cloud Shell. Cloud Shell is a browser-based command-line environment that gives you access to PowerShell, Azure CLI, and a bunch of other administrative and development tools.

Follow these steps to start getting acquainted with Azure Cloud Shell and the Azure CLI:

1. **On the global navigation bar in the Azure portal, click Cloud Shell.**

The You Have No Storage Mounted dialog box opens.

2. **Select your Azure subscription, and click Create Storage.**

The first time you start Cloud Shell, you're required to specify a storage account. You use the storage account to store all your Cloud Shell resources (modules, scripts, and so forth).

Click Show Advanced Settings if you want to use an existing storage account or if you desire full control of the storage account's name and region.

You need to specify whether you want to start with Bash or PowerShell. I suggest you go with PowerShell.

3. On the Cloud Shell toolbar, ensure that PowerShell is the current environment.

You can do this by inspecting the first element on the Azure Cloud Shell toolbar. Note that you can switch between the Bash and PowerShell environments simply by making a choice from this menu.

You can start your Cloud Shell session from a PowerShell session or a bash shell session. These steps are in the PowerShell environment.

4. Run Get-CloudDrive to see your cloud drive information.

The command tells you everything you need to know about where your Cloud Shell files are. Your cloud drive points to a file share in the designated Azure storage account.

5. Type az interactive to start an interactive Azure CLI session.

6. Answer yes or no to the request to send telemetry information to Microsoft.

Be patient the first time you start the Azure CLI interactive environment. It normally takes a minute or longer to fully initialize.

7. Type the following command to view your available storage accounts:

```
az storage account list -o table
```

As you type, pay attention to the following behaviors in Azure CLI, which I think are extraordinarily helpful:

- Azure CLI provides autocomplete drop-down menus that help you complete commands. Take advantage of these menus. Press Tab to accept the highlighted option, or use the arrow keys to select an alternative.

- In the middle of the screen, Azure CLI provides inline documentation as you type.

- Azure CLI provides JSON output by default, but in this case, specify tabular format instead. Then run az configure to specify table or another default output format that better suits your comfort.

8. To exit Cloud Shell, close the pane.

TECHNICAL STUFF

Cloud Shell is so fast because Microsoft stages Docker containers in its global content delivery network. Azure uses your client IP address and geolocation to connect you to the Cloud Shell container nearest you, which offers the fastest connection.

TIP

Although I use Azure CLI from within Cloud Shell for this book, you can install Azure CLI on your Windows, macOS, or Linux workstation. Head to the Azure Downloads page at `https://azure.microsoft.com/en-us/downloads` to download the installer.

Azure SDKs

As discussed earlier in this chapter, a REST API is an HTTP-based interface that allows two software systems to communicate, and the Azure portal, PowerShell, and the Azure CLI are ways to *abstract* (hide the details of) the underlying ARM REST API.

For software developers, software development kits (SDKs) represent yet another API abstraction layer. As of this writing, actually, Azure SDKs are available for the following programming languages and frameworks:

» Android	» PHP
» Go	» Python
» iOS	» Ruby
» Java	» Swift
» .NET	» Windows
» Node.js	» Xamarin

An Azure SDK provides the project templates and code libraries you need to interact with Azure services. In this book, I use Visual Studio 2019 to work with Azure SDKs. As shown in Figure 2-6, all you have to do is enable the Azure development workload; Visual Studio takes care of the rest of the setup.

TIP

If you're new to Visual Studio, you may want to get more detailed instructions on modifying installed workloads. See the Microsoft documentation article "Modify Visual Studio" at `https://docs.microsoft.com/en-us/visualstudio/install/modify-visual-studio?view=vs-2019`.

Incidentally, if you're thinking, "Hey, I'm not a developer; I don't want to pay for Visual Studio!" hang on a second. Microsoft makes Visual Studio 2019 Community Edition free of charge for testing and development. Both Windows and macOS versions are available.

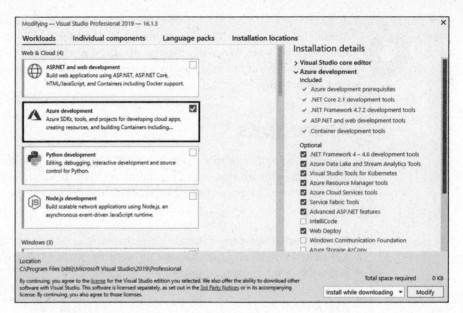

FIGURE 2-6:
Enable the Azure
development
workload in
Visual Studio
2019.

ARM REST API

You can get down to the "bare metal" of the ARM REST API if you want to. Figure 2-7 shows Azure Resource Explorer (`https://resources.azure.com`), a browser-based interface to the ARM REST API.

The annotations are as follows:

>> **A:** Choose the Azure AD directory to which you want to attach.

>> **B:** Set the environment to Read Only (the default) or Read/Write. Be careful when you work in Read/Write mode, because you're operating directly on your Azure resources.

>> **C:** Although Resource Explorer uses a well-known address, access is authenticated, and what you see in the interface reflects your user account's Azure AD and Azure resource permissions.

>> **D:** Browse your subscriptions and drill into your resources by using the ARM REST API resource provider namespace.

>> **E:** Perform ARM REST API operations by using the HTTPS verbs `GET`, `PUT`, `POST`, and `DELETE`.

>> **F:** View the resource definition in its native JSON format. If you put Resource Explorer in Read/Write mode, you can make changes directly.

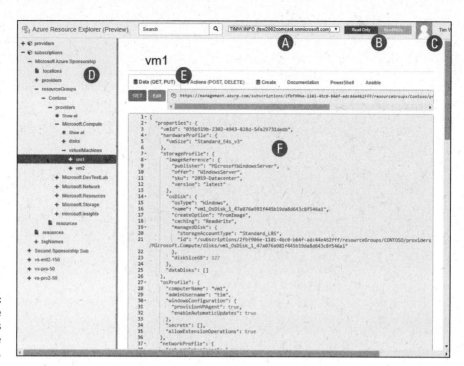

FIGURE 2-7:
Azure Resource
Explorer gives
you access to the
ARM APIs.

WARNING

As many people, including the folks in the open-source community, often say, "With great power comes great responsibility."

You may wonder when and why you'd ever need to interact with Azure at the basic REST API level. This type of interaction is more common than you think, however. Maybe you're be troubleshooting resource behavior and can't reach the control you need in the Azure portal or another abstraction layer. Or perhaps you're writing your own API and need to know how to structure ARM REST API calls for your own use.

2

Deploying Compute Resources to Microsoft Azure

IN THIS PART . . .

Managing Azure storage like a boss

Planning and implementing virtual networks in
Microsoft Azure

Deploying and configuring Windows Server and Linux
virtual machines (VMs)

Differentiating Docker containers from VMs and
learning how to wrangle them in the Azure public
cloud

Chapter **3**

Managing Storage in Azure

S torage is an example of a practically universal service in the Microsoft Azure cloud. Regardless of what kind of workload you're running — VMs, app service, functions, machine learning, or whatever — you're likely to require persistent object storage.

By the end of this chapter, you'll have a solid grasp of the Azure storage account: what it is, how it works, how to deploy it, and how to store and retrieve different data types.

Understanding Azure Storage Data Types

The Azure storage account represents a multipurpose container resource that provides highly available, persistent storage for three primary data types: unstructured, semistructured, and structured.

Unstructured data

Unstructured data is data that has no schema enforcing it. Think of *binary large objects* (blobs) as you would files, virtual hard disks, document files, and media files. All these objects are file-storage objects that can have any particular format and contents.

TECHNICAL STUFF

Although the term *blob* encompassed the word *large*, a blob object is a file of any size, whether it's a 1 KB text file or a 120 GB virtual hard disk file.

Semistructured data

Semistructured data doesn't have the column-row arrangement that relational data does, but it's not as freeform as pure binary unstructured data. The table service in the Azure storage account is semistructured in the form of key/value data pairs.

NoSQL databases are an example of semistructured data. As I discuss in Chapter 9, Cosmos DB is Azure's principal NoSQL database product.

Structured data

If you've worked with any relational database system, you understand *structured data* — data that's decomposed into one or more tables in which each column is bound by a particular data type.

So far, I've explained that an Azure storage account stores unstructured and semi-structured data. But what about structured data?

As it happens, the Azure storage account doesn't have a structured data storage option. Instead, you need to use one of Microsoft's relational data Platform as a Service (PaaS) products or run your database inside a virtual machine (VM).

Examples of structured databases in the Azure ecosystem include Azure SQL Database and Azure Database for MySQL Servers.

At this point, you understand that an Azure storage account blob service for unstructured data and table service for semistructured data. But you should be aware of two additional storage account services:

>> **Queue:** Supports asynchronous message delivery among application components. The service is fast and scalable, with low overhead.

>> **File:** Creates Server Message Block (SMB) and Network File System (NFS)-compatible file shares and accesses them from within or outside of Azure.

Working with a Storage Account

Now consider how to plan for Azure storage. The Azure general-purpose storage account includes several configuration options, so in the interest of cost-savings and security you want to make the right decisions.

Creating a storage account

Before you create your first storage account, you should understand some key facts. First, you need to determine what kind of storage account you need. Here are your choices:

>> **General-purpose v2:** Unless you have a compelling reason to choose otherwise, you should choose this type most often because it's the most fully featured option. It includes all four storage account services: blob, table, queue, and file.

>> **General-purpose v1:** This option exists mainly to support classic Azure deployments and has fewer features than v2.

>> **Blob storage:** This storage account supports only the blob service. At one time, you needed this type to specify access tiers, but now you don't need to choose this storage account type for new deployments.

Next, you have to address the question of performance tiers. Standard storage is less expensive and slower because it uses traditional mechanical hard drives on the Azure back end. Premium storage is more expensive and much faster because the Azure storage fabric uses solid-state drives that have no moving parts.

Whether you want to pay extra money for a faster storage account depends on what data you plan to store. If you plan to place database data and log files in a storage account, you probably need the robust, predictable performance of premium storage. For most other data, the standard performance tier should be fine.

Finally, you have to determine which storage-account replication option you need. Azure storage is highly available because Microsoft *replicates* (creates exact copies of) your storage account at least three times. Here are your options, from least to most expensive:

>> **Locally redundant storage (LRS):** Microsoft makes three copies of your storage account within a single data center in your home region.

>> **Zone-redundant storage (ZRS):** The three storage account copies are spread among different data centers in your home region.

>> **Georedundant storage (GRS):** Three storage account copies are spread across data centers in your home region, and another three copies are placed in a secondary region chosen by Microsoft. (Refer to Chapter 2 for more information about paired regions.)

>> **Read-access georedundant storage (RA-GRS):** This option is GRS, but you get read-only access to the contents of your secondary storage account.

The replication option you choose depends on your availability needs, compliance requirements, and so forth.

WARNING

Azure storage provides high availability, which means that your data is durable and not susceptible to loss or deletion. You still need to back up your storage account data, however. Microsoft doesn't do that for you. Just because Azure storage accounts are highly available doesn't mean that they're highly recoverable by default.

TECHNICAL STUFF

I decided not to discuss Azure resource pricing because that topic is beyond the scope of the book and because prices can change even more often than products do. For price information, visit https://azure.microsoft.com/en-us/pricing.

Table 3-1 summarizes the protection offered by each storage-account replication option.

TABLE 3-1   **Replication Protection**

Replication Option	Protects
LRS	Storage array within a single data center in your home region
ZRS	A single data center in your home region
GRS	Your home region

When you know what type of storage account you need, you can create a new storage account in the Azure portal. Go to https://portal.azure.com, log in with your subscription owner account, and then follow these steps:

1. **In the Azure portal, navigate to the Storage Accounts blade.**

You can do this in various ways, but I recommend typing **storage accounts** in the global Search box and selecting the appropriate link.

TIP

Don't select Storage Accounts (Classic), which concerns Azure Service Management. This book deals with Azure Resource Manager (ARM).

2. On the Storage Accounts blade, click Add.

3. On the Basics page, specify a subscription and a new or existing resource group.

4. Complete the form below Instance Details (see Figure 3-1) and click Next to continue.

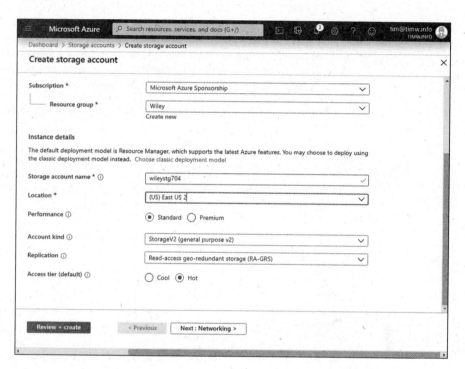

FIGURE 3-1:
Creating a general purpose storage account.

- *Storage Account Name:* This name needs to be globally unique and to contain only lowercase letters and numbers. The maximum length is 24 characters.

- *Location:* Place the storage account closest to the users who need its resources.

- *Performance:* Standard is lower-speed storage, whereas Premium is higher-speed (and more expensive) storage. Unless you have a need for more predictable input/output performance, choose Standard.

- *Account Kind:* You always want to select general-purpose v2.

- *Replication:* Unless you have a business need for higher availability, locally redundant storage (LRS) is a good starting choice. You can always change your mind later by visiting the storage account's Configuration blade.

- *Access Tier* (default): The Access Tier option may give you a price break depending on whether you access the storage account data frequently (Hot tier) or infrequently (Cold tier). I talk more about tiers later in this chapter.

5. **On the Networking page, click Next to continue.**

   The Network connectivity blade allows you to configure a service endpoint for the storage account, which integrates the storage account into an Azure virtual network. I talk about service endpoints in Chapter 4.

6. **Complete the form on the Advanced page (shown in Figure 3-2):**

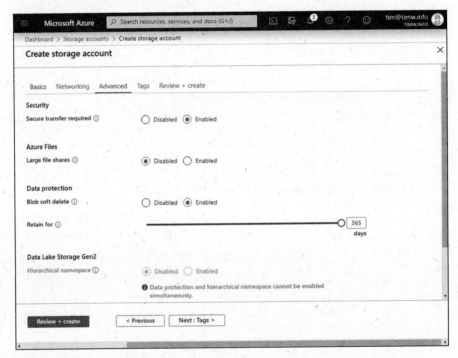

FIGURE 3-2:
Configuring advanced storage account options.

- *Secure Transfer Required:* Leave this option set to Enabled to ensure that you use encrypted HTTPS, not unencrypted HTTP, to access your storage account data.

- *Allow Access From:* Leave this option set to All Networks. Optionally, you can use service endpoints to integrate a storage account into a virtual network.

- *Blob Soft Delete:* Enable this option to create a sort of recycling bin for your deleted blob objects.

- *Hierarchical Namespace:* Leave this option set to Disabled. (I discuss Azure Data Lake Storage in Chapter 4.)

7. **On the Tags screen, click Next: Review + Create.**

Using taxonomic tags is a great way to categorize related Azure resources, but you don't need to worry about tags now.

8. **If validation passes, click Create to submit the deployment to ARM.**

If you receive a validation error, check the configuration-blade tabs; the one that contains the error should have a dot next to it.

REMEMBER

Don't freak out if the procedures I provide don't match what you see in the Azure portal. The reason is simple: Microsoft is continually tinkering with the portal, updating the user interface and adding or modifying services and settings. The important thing is to understand what you're configuring.

Figure 3-3 shows details on ARM deployment.

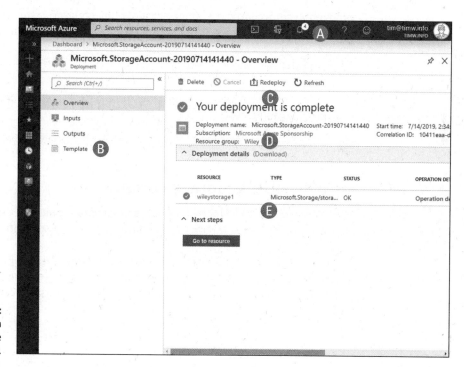

FIGURE 3-3:
Watching a
Microsoft Azure
deployment.

Following are some key features to note:

>> Open the Notification menu (A) to check the status of current and recent deployments.

>> Gain access to the deployment's underlying ARM template (B), which is useful for future automated deployments.

>> The Redeploy button (C) is useful if a deployment fails; you can fix the errors in the ARM template and pick up the deployment where it left off. This important ARM characteristic is called *idempotence*.

>> You can open the resource group associated with the deployment (D) and navigate to the Deployments setting to review this and other deployments, download template definitions, and so forth.

>> This list of granular deployment operations (E) is tremendously useful for troubleshooting failed deployments.

Using the blob service

Although general-purpose storage accounts have four discrete services intended for different data and object types, most of this chapter focuses on the blob service.

The reason for my choice is twofold:

>> This is a beginner's book, and the other three services are intended for a more advanced audience.

>> The blob service is the most frequently used Azure storage account service.

Installing Azure Storage Explorer

Azure Storage Explorer is a free, closed-source, cross-platform desktop application that enables you to interact with your Azure storage accounts.

Go to https://azure.microsoft.com/en-us/features/storage-explorer (or search for *Azure Storage Explorer* in your favorite search engine), download the program, and install it on your computer. Follow these steps to configure Storage Explorer:

1. **In the Connect to Azure Storage dialog box, select Add an Azure Account, set the Azure environment to Azure, and then click Next.**

   If the dialog box doesn't appear the first time you start Storage Explorer, click the Add Account button on the Storage Explorer sidebar. (The button's icon looks like an electrical plug.)

2. **Authenticate to Azure, using your administrative account.**

3. **In the Show Resources from These Subscriptions filter, ensure your target Azure subscription is selected, and click Apply.**

   I manage multiple subscriptions, so I like to focus only on the one(s) I'm working with.

Figure 3-4 shows Storage Explorer and the following features:

>> Click the Explorer button (A) to browse your storage account(s).

>> Click the Manage Accounts button (B) to filter the subscriptions that Storage Explorer shows in Explorer view.

>> Click the Add Account button (C) to sign in with more than one Azure AD account simultaneously.

>> Expand general-purpose storage accounts to see their services (D). The navigation works like a File Transfer Protocol client application.

>> View the properties of the current selection (E). By default, storage accounts use the following public endpoints for each service:

- Blob service: `https://<storage-acct-name>.blob.core.windows.net/`

- File service: `https://<storage-acct-name>.file.core.windows.net/`

- Queue service: `https://<storage-acct-name>.queue.core.windows.net/`

- Table service: `https://<storage-acct-name>.table.core.windows.net/`

>> Each service has its own toolbar (F). The blob service toolbar shown in Figure 3-4 is used for containers and file uploads/downloads, whereas the table service toolbar is used for data import/export and queries.

>> This pane (G) gives you granular interaction with your storage account.

>> The Activities pane (H) shows error, warning, and information messages from Storage Explorer.

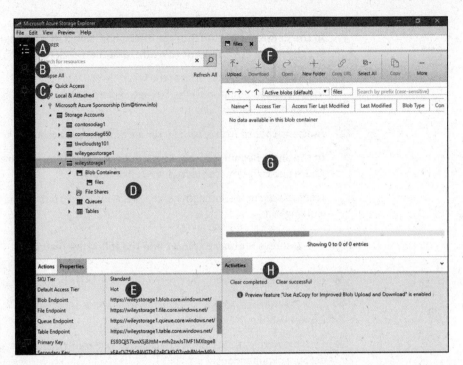

FIGURE 3-4:
Azure Storage
Explorer.

TIP

Storage Explorer is also available in the Azure portal. Browse to your storage account, and select the Storage Explorer setting.

Uploading blobs

Now it's time to create a blob container and upload some files to Azure. Follow these steps:

1. **Expand your storage account, right-click the Blob Container node, and choose Create Blob Container from the shortcut menu.**

   An intuitive name for the container is files. A container functions like a directory in a computer's file system.

2. **Select the files container, and click Upload on the Storage Account toolbar.**

   You could drag and drop files into the container, but I'm intentionally being more . . . er, intentional in my instruction.

3. **Add one or more files to your new container.**

   You can perform a file upload directly in the Azure portal. Navigate to the Containers blade, click into your new container, and then click Upload from the toolbar. You can then browse your computer for files and add them to Azure blob storage.

It's a good habit to right-click blobs in Storage Explorer to access handy administrative options from the shortcut menu, including downloading the object and changing its access tier. Figure 3-5 shows the shortcut menu you see when you right-click a blob.

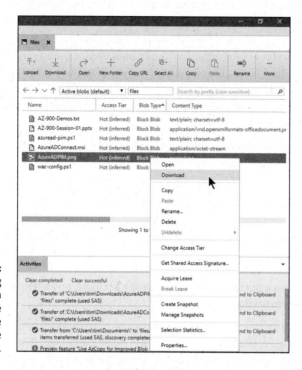

FIGURE 3-5:
Try right-clicking everything in Azure Storage Explorer to see what options are available.

TIP

Practice working with blob upload, download, and deletion by using keyboard shortcuts (which you can find at https://docs.microsoft.com/en-us/azure/vs-azure-tools-storage-explorer-accessibility#shortcut-keys) as well as Storage Explorer's menu and toolbar system. Make sure that you practice with test files and not production resources, however.

Changing blob access tiers

This section returns to the Azure portal so that you can modify a blob object's access tier. First, it's instructive to understand how Microsoft prices standard-tier storage accounts. You're charged for

>> **Storage volume:** Storage volume represents the amount of data in your blob service.

>> **REST API transactions:** Every time you interact with the blob service, that interaction translates into a read, write, update, or delete REST API call, and Microsoft charges you for each call.

>> **Data egress network traffic:** There's no charge for ingress (upload or inbound) traffic into the storage account, but you pay for egress (download or outbound) data transfer.

Depending on the pricing scheme, it may make sense for you to change the access tier for blobs that have different use scenarios. You have three tier options:

>> **Hot tier:** Optimized for frequently accessed data. You get a discount on transaction pricing.

>> **Cool tier:** Optimized for infrequently accessed data to be stored for at least 30 days. You get a discount on storage footprint.

>> **Archive tier:** Optimized for rarely accessed data (180 days or more). You get a discount on both storage footprint and transaction costs.

To modify the access tier for one of the blobs you uploaded into your files blob container, follow these steps:

1. **In the Azure portal, locate your storage account, and select the Containers setting.**

   You'll find some inconsistencies in the Azure portal and Azure documentation. The storage account Blobs service is also called Containers; if Microsoft changed the service name to Containers by the time you're reading this, you'll know why.

2. **Browse to the files container, select one of your blobs, and click Change Tier from the toolbar.**

   When you select a blob, Azure shows you all the blob's metadata.

3. **From the Access Tier drop-down menu, choose Archive, and then click Save to confirm your changes.**

   I show you the interface in Figure 3-6. The Azure portal should display a message informing you that marking the blob as Archive makes it inaccessible until you explicitly return it to the Hot or Cool tier.

Archived blobs are inaccessible unless you take them out of the Archive tier. This is a process Microsoft calls "rehydrating." To rehydrate an archived blob, repeat these steps, but choose Cool or Hot as the blob's new access tier.

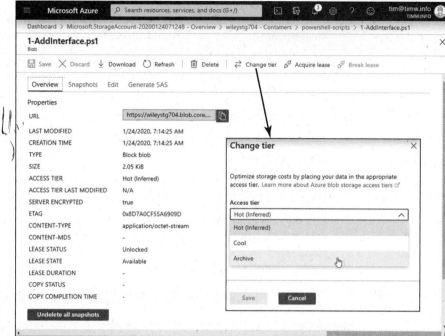

FIGURE 3-6:
Changing the access tier of a blob in an Azure storage account.

Understanding the file, table, and queue services

This section takes a brief look at the other three Azure storage account services.

File service

I consider the Azure Files service to be a sort of Swiss Army knife that has numerous use cases. For one thing, you store your Cloud Shell home folder environment in a file share. To get started with Cloud Shell, follow these steps:

1. **On the Azure portal top navigation bar, click Cloud Shell.**

2. **In the You Have No Storage Mounted dialog box, verify your Azure subscription and then click Show Advanced Settings.**

3. **Specify your cloud drive settings.**

   Feel free to reuse your existing storage account. Create a file share with an intuitive name such as cloud-drive. (*Note:* No spaces are allowed in file-share names.)

4. **Click Create Storage to continue.**

5. **When Cloud Shell loads, ensure that you're in the PowerShell environment.**

If you're not in the PowerShell environment, open the session menu and make the change. The session menu is the first button on the toolbar; it's a drop-down list that has two entries: PowerShell and Bash.

6. **Run the command `Get-CloudDrive`.**

This command shows the storage account and file share in which your Cloud Shell cloud drive exists.

7. **On the Cloud Shell toolbar, click the Upload/Download Files button, and choose Manage File Share from the drop-down list.**

Click the Upload button (see Figure 3-7) to upload script files, web pages, and other project artifacts and then access them from anywhere in the world via Cloud Shell.

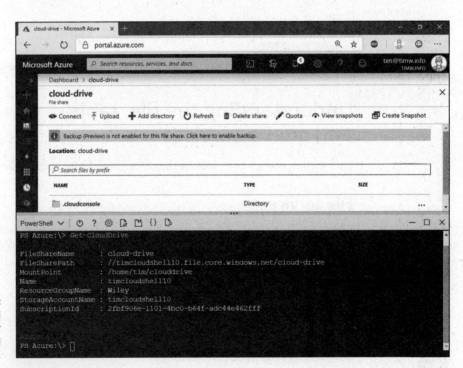

FIGURE 3-7:
Azure Cloud
Shell and your
personal cloud
share.

Table service

The Azure storage account table storage service is a NoSQL key-value store, which represents semistructured data. As I mention earlier in this chapter, many developers like programming against table storage because it's easy to work with, fast, scalable, and cost-effective.

Many Azure developers like the table service because it's a fast, scalable, low-cost method for storing application data either temporarily or permanently.

TECHNICAL STUFF

Azure table storage is aimed at high-capacity NoSQL storage within a single region. If you're looking for georeplication and worldwide scale, check the Azure Cosmos DB table API. For more information, visit https://docs.microsoft.com/en-us/azure/cosmos-db/table-introduction.

Queue service

If you're not a software developer, the concept of message queuing may seem foreign to you. The idea is that if you've separated your application into modular services (so-called *microservices* software architecture), you need a mechanism that enables these services to send and receive message data asynchronously.

Essentially, queue storage is a fast, scalable, yet relatively simple messaging platform. If developers need more advanced features (higher scale, guaranteed message delivery, transaction support, and so forth), refer them to the storage queue service's bigger sibling, Azure Service Bus.

Introducing Azure Disk Storage

Before Microsoft introduced Managed Disks, VM virtual hard disks (VHDs) were used in blob service for storage accounts. This arrangement wasn't ideal, for many reasons:

>> Mixing VHDs with other, random blobs made organization more difficult.

>> An administrator could easily delete VM disks by accident while cleaning out blob storage containers.

>> It's possible to grant the world anonymous access to blob containers. If the container stores VM VHDs, it creates a potentially catastrophic security problem.

>> Storage accounts have a fixed request rate of 20,000 input/output operations per second. If you put too many VHDs in a single storage account, your VM performance is crippled.

With Managed Disks, your VM operating system and data disks are stored and maintained by Microsoft. You're free to do whatever you want with your VHDs, but you don't have to deal with the headaches involved in storage account–based storage.

Before Managed Disks, VM disks were stored in general purpose storage accounts. This was a recipe for all sorts of potentially dangerous outcomes. For example, I once had a colleague allow anonymous public access to a storage account blob container that contained not only static website assets but Azure VM disks!

To illustrate how to work with Managed Disks, follow these steps to use Azure Cloud Shell and Azure CLI to create a resource group and VM. Don't worry about the VM details here; I deep-dive into VM care and feeding in this book in Chapter 5.

1. **In the Azure portal, open Cloud Shell.**

   For this exercise, it doesn't matter whether you're in the Bash or PowerShell environment.

2. **Use the Azure command-line interface (CLI) to create a new resource group.**

   You don't have to use the same name and region that I do. Be creative. Don't worry about cost, because you're setting up this environment only for practice. When you finish using it, you can delete it. Here's the code:

   ```
   az group create --name SimpleVM --location eastus
   ```

   Don't be surprised to see the Azure CLI output in JSON (JavaScript Object Notation), which is the default output format.

   Run az configure to change your Azure CLI defaults, including specifying table as your default output format.

   TIP

3. **Run az vm create to create a Windows Server 2016 VM quickly.**

   Normally, I don't recommend this method, because Azure CLI doesn't provide any administrative flexibility. For purposes of this step, however, it's fine.

   In the following code, myPassword is a placeholder; use your own strong password instead. Also, type the following command on one line, and ignore my backslashes. The backslashes are visual indications that the command has been broken into multiple lines to make it easier to read:

   ```
   az vm create \
   --resource-group SimpleVM \
   --name WindowsVM \
   --image win2016data center \
   --admin-username azureuser \
   --admin-password myPassword
   ```

4. **When deployment is complete, navigate to the Disks blade.**

   A fast way is to type **disks** in the Azure portal's global Search box.

5. Select your disk in the list, and inspect its properties.

Figure 3-8 shows some of the cool things you can do with VM disks on the Disks blade in the Azure portal:

- Set the account type (A). Somewhat surprisingly, the quick-create operation here chose the more expensive but higher-performing Premium SSD option.

- Download the VHD to your computer (B).

- View, deploy, or download the underlying ARM template (C).

- Make a backup copy of the disk (D).

WARNING

For most VM disk activities, the associated VM has to be stopped and deallocated. Keep this requirement in mind if you need to perform VHD configuration on a production VM.

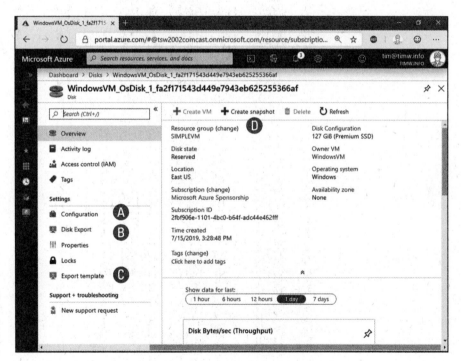

FIGURE 3-8:
Use Managed Disk storage for your VMs in Azure.

Chapter **4**

Planning Your Virtual Network Topology

P eople at Microsoft told me a couple of years ago that networking was the number-one support request in Azure. This makes sense to me for at least a couple of reasons:

» Ethernet and TCP/IP internetworking is a complicated subject that's deep enough to build an entire career on.

» Software-defined networking in the Azure cloud is vastly different from on-premises hardware networking.

» The costs and consequences of making a mistake with Azure networking are high.

In this chapter, I lay the groundwork for Azure networking. I talk about the virtual network, which forms the boundary in which you place your virtual machine (VM) and potentially other Azure services.

Understanding Virtual Network Components

The *virtual network* (VNet) is a strong isolation and communications boundary in Azure. A common beginner's mistake is placing VMs on separate VNets and expecting communication between them to be possible by default — because, say, the VNets are in the same Azure region and subscription.

Not true! Although VMs within a single VNet can communicate just fine by default (barring firewall deny rules, naturally), no direct communication is possible between VNets without additional administrative intervention.

For now, I'll start the VNet discussion by explaining the various components of such a network.

Address space

The *address space* is the top-level private IPv4 (Internet Protocol version 4) address range that you define for your VNet. Microsoft's best-practice guidance here is to ensure you have no IP address overlap among your VNets or your on-premises networks.

All network communications within a VNet take place only in Azure; thus, your address space must come from the private, nonroutable IPv4 address ranges defined in Request for Comments (RFC) 1918:

» 10.0.0.0–10.255.255.255 (/8 prefix)

» 172.16.0.0–172.31.255.255 (/12 prefix)

» 192.168.0.0– 92.168.255.255 (/16 prefix)

TECHNICAL STUFF

To learn more about the private IP address ranges, read the RFC 1918 source document at https://tools.ietf.org/html/rfc1918.

Subnets

Your VNet address space is worthless unless and until you define one or more subnets. What's cool about subnets is that Azure system routing takes care of directing traffic among the subnets of a single VNet. No router is required.

TECHNICAL STUFF

IPv6

I'd like to chat with you for a moment about Internet Protocol version 6, called IPv6 for short. The public IPv4 address space has long since been exhausted, and the world has been slowly embracing IPv6. Most businesses that use IPv6 do so in what's called a *dual-stack* configuration, using both IPv4 and IPv6.

The long story short is that Azure virtual networks support IPv6, but as of this writing, the feature is in public preview. Because public-preview features have no service-level agreement or support guarantee, you shouldn't use IPv6 in VNets in production at this time. By contrast, IPv6 for the Azure public load balancer is in general availability status; therefore, you're encouraged to use this feature in production.

The most common architectural pattern places each application tier in its own subnet — perhaps one subnet for the web front-end tier, one for the business logic tier, and one for the data tier. This way, you can sculpt your traffic rules more easily because the VMs on each subnet have the same network traffic requirements.

Azure always reserves five IP addresses from each subnet for its own use. Suppose that you create a subnet that uses the address 192.168.10.0/24. Here's what happens:

» 192.168.10.0 is reserved because it's the subnet's network ID.

» 192.168.10.1 through 192.168.10.3 are reserved for Azure's private use.

» 192.168.10.4 is the first usable IP address in the subnet and is distributed by Azure's Dynamic Host Configuration Protocol.

» 192.168.10.255 is reserved for protocol conformance.

WARNING

Azure is a metered service, and every service has a predefined capacity limit. In a single subscription in a single region, you can define up to 1,000 VNets and 3,000 subnets per virtual network. Those capacities seem to be absurdly high at first blush. The day will come when you'll run into one of these service limits, however, and I don't want you to be surprised. For more details, visit the Azure docs article "Azure subscription and service limits, quotas, and constraints" at https://docs.microsoft.com/en-us/azure/azure-subscription-service-limits.

Creating a Virtual Network

Figure 4-1 shows the environment deployed in this chapter.

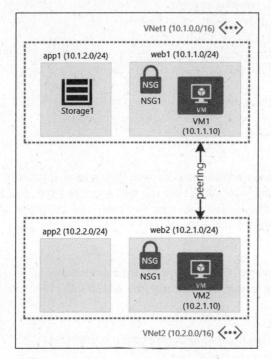

FIGURE 4-1:
The Azure virtual network infrastructure used in this chapter.

The topology has the following notable features:

» The VNet is divided into two subnets to reflect common application tiers.

» Each VNet is protected by a single network security group (NSG).

» A service endpoint links a storage account to a VNet.

» VNet peering logically connects VNet1 and VNet2.

Deploying with the Azure portal

When you're signed into the Azure portal with your administrative account, follow these steps to deploy your first Azure virtual network:

1. **Either create a new resource group or add to an existing resource group.**

2. **Use the global Search bar in the Azure portal to browse to the Virtual Networks blade.**

3. **Click Add.**

4. **Fill out the Create Virtual Network Configuration blade, and click Create to submit the deployment.**

   For practice, use the following values:

   - *Name:* VNet1

   - *Address Space:* 10.2.0.0/16

   - *Subscription:* [your subscription]

   - *Resource Group:* Wiley

   - *Location:* Whichever Azure region is closest to you. (These examples use East US 2.)

   - *Subnet Name:* web1 (Azure always names the default subnet "default"; you're changing its name to make it more descriptive.)

   - *Subnet Address Range:* 10.2.1.0/24

   - *DDoS Protection:* Basic

   - *Service Endpoints:* Disabled

   - *Firewall:* Disabled

You can see my completed configuration blade in Figure 4-2.

After Azure deploys the new VNet, you need to revisit its configuration settings to define the second subnet. Follow these steps to accomplish that goal:

1. **Navigate to the VNet1 Configuration blade.**

2. **In the VNet's Settings list, select Subnets; then click the Subnet button.**

3. **Fill out the form on the Add Subnet blade, and then click Create to complete the configuration.**

   Use the following values:

   - *Name:* app1

   - *Address Range:* 10.1.2.0/24

   - *Network Security Group:* None

   - *Route Table:* None

   - *Service Endpoints Services*: 0 selected

   - *Delegate Subnet to a Service:* None

FIGURE 4-2:
The completed
virtual network
configuration.

Software-defined networking can become abstract and difficult to envision. In the VNet1 Settings list, click Diagram, as shown in Figure 4-3. Azure creates a vector diagram that depicts your virtual network; clicking an element in the graphic takes you to that resource's settings.

I find these diagrams invaluable for figuring out how my VNets are laid out. What's even cooler is that you can

>> As I mentioned earlier, click any of the diagram shapes in the Azure portal to go to their configuration blades.

>> Click Download Topology to download a scalable vector graphics (SVG) format image for use in your architectural documentation.

TIP

If you don't own a Microsoft Visio license, consider getting one. Visio makes creating Azure diagrams simple. I highly recommend that anyone with work that involves Azure invest in Visio so they can make visualizing cloud-based resources easier.

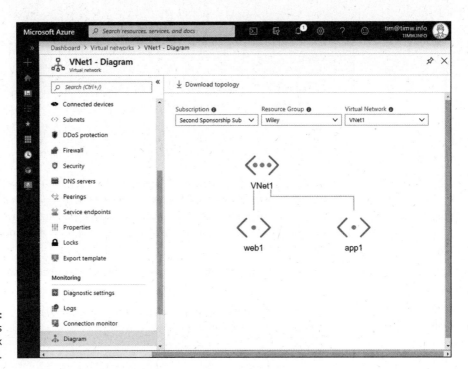

FIGURE 4-3:
Azure generates nifty network diagrams for you.

Specifically, import the VNet topology image into Visio, right-click it, and choose Group⇨Ungroup from Visio's shortcut menu. Now you have access to all the shapes. You should also download the Azure Visio stencils at `https://www.microsoft.com/en-us/download/details.aspx?id=41937`.

Deploying with PowerShell

You can deploy the second VNet by using Cloud Shell and PowerShell. Because limited space is available on this page, I've broken the code in the following steps across multiple lines, but you should type the code as single lines. I've used a backtick (`) as a line-continuation character to make the PowerShell code easier to understand, but you shouldn't add it in Cloud Shell. Follow these steps to deploy the VNet:

1. **In the Azure portal, click Cloud Shell to open a Cloud Shell session.**

If the session opens in Bash, use the Cloud Shell's drop-down menu to switch to PowerShell.

If you have multiple subscriptions, you may need to run Set-AzContext to ensure you're focused on the right one. If you have only one subscription, then you can proceed directly.

2. Enter the following code to run `New-AzVirtualNetwork` and define the VNet:

```
New-AzVirtualNetwork `
   -ResourceGroupName Wiley `
   -Location EastUS2 `
   -Name VNet2 `
   -AddressPrefix 10.3.0.0/16
```

Note the backtick (`) characters in my code. This is not the single quotation mark, but instead the key above the Tab key on the keyboard. In PowerShell, you use the backtick to continue a code line to the next line. I do it here only to keep the code readable on the page; you may omit them if you don't mind having the code lines run long in Cloud Shell.

3. Run `Add-AzVirtualNetworkSubnetConfig` to define the web2 and app2 subnets.

Variables in PowerShell start with a dollar sign. Here's the code:

```
$subnetConfig1 = Add-AzVirtualNetworkSubnetConfig `
   -Name web2 `
   -AddressPrefix 10.3.1.0/24 `
   -VirtualNetwork 'VNet2'

$subnetConfig2 = Add-AzVirtualNetworkSubnetConfig `
   -Name app2 `
   -AddressPrefix 10.3.2.0/24 `
   -VirtualNetwork 'VNet2'
```

4. Use the PowerShell pipeline and the `Set-AzVirtualNetwork` command to commit the configuration.

The PowerShell pipeline allows you to feed the output from one command to a subsequent command. Here's the code:

```
$subnetConfig1 | Set-AzVirtualNetwork
$subnetConfig2 | Set-AzVirtualNetwork
```

TIP

One reason why performing Azure deployments programmatically is considered more efficient than doing it in the Azure portal is that you can specify all aspects of the deployment. In the preceding example, both subnets are defined simultaneously. The Azure portal form allows you to specify only your first subnet.

Configuring Virtual Networks

Thus far, this chapter has laid the foundation for future VM and Azure service internetworking. Before you populate your VNet, you need to make some tweaks to ensure that it's behaving the way you want it to.

Deciding on a name resolution strategy

Azure-provided name resolution, enabled by default in your VNets, ensures that your VMs can communicate via short host name as well as by IP address. The problem some businesses have, however, is they want their cloud VMs to use a custom DNS domain name (company.com, for example).

If you need VMs in different VNets to resolve one another's host names, or if you want to use a custom fully qualified domain name for your cloud VMs, then you need to configure custom name resolution. For instance, you can do either of the following:

>> Deploy a private Azure Domain Name System (DNS) zone and link the zone to both subnets.

>> Deploy DNS server VMs in each VNet and configure them to forward name resolution queries to each other.

In your VNets, browse to the DNS servers setting. You should see the default (Azure-provided) setting. If you need to override DNS, select Custom and then supply one or more custom DNS server IPv4 addresses. These addresses might point to

>> On-premises DNS servers (if you're running in a hybrid cloud)

>> A DNS server VM(s) running in the local VNet

>> An Azure-provided virtual IP address (168.63.129.16)

TIP

168.63.129.16 is a good IP address to know, because you may want your VMs to fall back to an Azure-provided DNS if a recursive name lookup fails with the pre-scribed list of custom DNS servers.

WARNING

Never attempt to configure TCP/IP properties from within a VM in Azure. If you do so, you'll immediately lose a network connection to your VM. Remember you're dealing with cloud-based software-defined networking here, not your local physical or virtual servers. You need to perform all your VM networking configuration in Azure Resource Manager (ARM), whether you use the Azure portal, PowerShell, or the Azure command-line interface (CLI).

Configuring network security groups

NSGs are traffic filters that you can associate with VM virtual network interface cards and/or VNet subnets. I recommend that you associate NSGs with subnets to reduce future troubleshooting effort and to apply the same inbound and outbound traffic rules to multiple VMs simultaneously.

An NSG consists of one or more access rules that have the following properties:

>> **Priority:** Lower-priority values are evaluated first. As you add rules, make sure to leave space between them to allow room for future growth.

>> **Name:** I suggest that you name your NSG rules as descriptively as possible (such as HTTP-in-Allow).

>> **Port:** This property is the Transmission Control Protocol (TCP) or User Datagram Protocol (UDP) port assignment.

>> **Protocol:** This property is TCP, UDP, or both.

>> **Source:** This property is where the traffic stream originates.

>> **Destination:** This property is where the traffic stream is going.

>> **Action:** This property is Allow or Deny.

An NSG runs each traffic stream through its inbound or outbound rules list, depending on the direction of traffic. The first rule that applies becomes the effective rule. Unless you have a catch-all rule to deny all unclassified traffic, you open up the possibility of connection types you don't want, and that could compromise your VM's security.

Tables 4-1 and 4-2 summarizes the default inbound and outbound rules for NSGs.

TABLE 4-1

Default Inbound Security Rules

Rule	Description
AllowVnetInBound	Allows inbound traffic originating in this VNet and any peered VNets
AllowAzureLoadBalancerInBound	Allows health-probe traffic inbound from any Azure load balancer IP address
DenyAllInBound	Catch-all rule ensuring that any inbound traffic not caught by a previous rule is denied

TABLE 4-2

Default Outbound Security Rules

Rule	Description
AllowVnetOutBound	Allows outbound traffic from this VNet and to any peered VNets
AllowInternetBound	Allows VMs to reach the public Internet from within the VNet
DenyAllInBound	Catch-all rule ensuring that any outbound traffic not caught by a previous rule is denied

TIP

Although Microsoft created the default inbound and outbound NSG security rules for your convenience, you're not obligated to use them. I feel that they're too permissive, so I create the DenyAllInbound and DenyAllOutBound rules manually and don't use the other default rules.

The VNet shown in Figure 4-1 earlier in this chapter includes NSG1 for filtering traffic and contains the default inbound and outbound rules.

TIP

Because you have the same access requirements in VNet2, you associate NSG1 with both subnets.

To create the NSG and allow inbound HTTP traffic (TCP port 80), follow these steps:

1. **Use the Azure portal's global search to find the Network Security Groups blade; then click Add on the toolbar.**

   REMEMBER

   Don't select the Network Security Groups (Classic) option. The focus of this book is ARM.

2. **Complete the form on the Create Network Security Group blade and then click Create.**

   Use these properties:

   - *Name:* NSG1

   - *Subscription:* [your subscription]

   - *Resource Group:* Wiley

   - *Location:* East US 2 (use your home region; these examples use mine)

3. **After deployment, select your NSG and browse to the Inbound Security Rules setting in the Settings list.**

   Note that there are separate settings for inbound and outbound security rules. The Default Rules button toggles their state. Leave both settings enabled for this exercise.

4. **Click Add.**

5. **Complete the form on the Add Inbound Security Rule blade and then click Create.**

By default, Azure places you in Advanced view, which is where you want to be. (If you like, click Basic to see the simplified view.)

Use these configuration properties for NSG1:

- *Source:* Service Tag, Internet.

  Your source can be a comma-separated list of IP addresses or address ranges, a service tag, or an application security group. For now, understand that this rule applies to inbound traffic originating from the public Internet.

- *Source Port Ranges:* Any (denoted by the asterisk)

- *Destination:* VirtualNetwork (service tags to the rescue)

- *Destination Port Ranges*: 80

- *Protocol:* TCP

- *Action:* Allow

- *Priority:* 100

- *Name:* HTTP-In-Allow

- *Description:* (add if you want to)

6. **Create a new outbound (I repeat: outbound) security rule for NSG1.**

This rule allows traffic from the web1 subnet to the storage account that you'll place on the app1 subnet.

Use these properties:

- *Source:* Virtual Network

- *Source Port Ranges:* Any

- *Destination:* Service tag, Storage

- *Destination Port Ranges:* Any

- *Protocol:* Any

- *Action:* Allow

- *Priority:* 100

- *Name:* Storage-Out-Allow

- *Description:* (fill in if you want to)

Figure 4–4 shows my completed NSG1 configuration on the MSG1 Overview page.

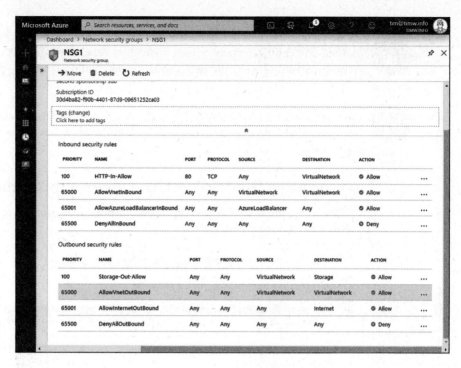

Dashboard > Network security groups > NSG1

NSG1
Network security group

→ Move 🗑 Delete ↻ Refresh

Second sponsorship Sub

Subscription ID
30d4ba82-f90b-4401-87d9-09651252ca03

Tags (change)
Click here to add tags

Inbound security rules

PRIORITY	NAME	PORT	PROTOCOL	SOURCE	DESTINATION	ACTION	
100	HTTP-In-Allow	80	TCP	Any	VirtualNetwork	⊘ Allow	...
65000	AllowVnetInBound	Any	Any	VirtualNetwork	VirtualNetwork	⊘ Allow	...
65001	AllowAzureLoadBalancerInBound	Any	Any	AzureLoadBalancer	Any	⊘ Allow	...
65500	DenyAllInBound	Any	Any	Any	Any	⊘ Deny	...

Outbound security rules

PRIORITY	NAME	PORT	PROTOCOL	SOURCE	DESTINATION	ACTION	
100	Storage-Out-Allow	Any	Any	VirtualNetwork	Storage	⊘ Allow	...
65000	AllowVnetOutBound	Any	Any	VirtualNetwork	VirtualNetwork	⊘ Allow	...
65001	AllowInternetOutBound	Any	Any	Any	Internet	⊘ Allow	...
65500	DenyAllOutBound	Any	Any	Any	Any	⊘ Deny	...

FIGURE 4-4:
NSG1
configuration.

Adding service tags and application security groups

Service tags are labels that aggregate pools of IP address prefixes and make crafting accurate NSG rules much easier. Some common service tags are

>> **VirtualNetwork:** All virtual network address spaces, for both local and peered VNets

>> **Internet:** All public IP addresses, both Azure-owned and public

>> **AzureLoadBalancer:** The virtual IP addresses of your deployed Azure load balancers

>> **AzureCloud:** Azure public IP address space

>> **Storage:** IP address range for the Azure Storage service

Application security groups (ASGs) are in effect user-created service tags. With them, you can group resources in an administrator-defined way to ease NSG rule assignment. You might create an ASG called web-servers that applies to the web-server VMs in your deployment, for example.

REMEMBER

Sadly, using the default inbound and outbound rules is an all-or-nothing proposition: You can't selectively delete individual default inbound or outbound rules. Thus, instead of using the default rules, you should plan to re-create what you need.

TECHNICAL STUFF

For more information on ASGs, read the Azure docs article "Security Groups" at https://docs.microsoft.com/en-us/azure/virtual-network/security-overview.

Associating the NSG with the appropriate subnets

Follow these steps to link your new NSG with the web1 subnet on VNet1 and the web2 subnet on the VNet2 subnet:

1. **On the NSG1 Configuration blade, select Subnets.**

2. **On the Subnets blade, click Associate.**

3. **On the Associate subnets blade, choose the appropriate virtual network and subnet.**

   You need to complete this procedure twice: once for VNet1/web1 and once for VNet2/web2.

Understanding service endpoints

Service endpoints secure certain Azure services by limiting their connectivity to a virtual network. You might have a storage account that contains sensitive data that should be accessed only by VMs located on a particular VNet. In this case, creating a service endpoint for the service account on the appropriate virtual network accomplishes your goal.

Other Azure products that can be bound to VNets via service endpoints include SQL Database, Cosmos DB, Key Vault, and App Service.

This section walks you through the configuration. To create a Microsoft.Storage service endpoint on the Vnet1 app1 subnet, follow these steps:

1. **In the Azure portal, browse to VNet1, and select the Service Endpoints setting.**

2. **On the toolbar, click Add.**

3. **On the Add Service Endpoints blade, select Microsoft.Storage as the service and app1 as the subnet; then click Add to complete the configuration.**

You're not finished with your work, however: You need to associate a storage account with the app1 subnet. You see, defining the service endpoint on the VNet opens up the possibility of integrating a storage account into the network. You next need to go to the storage account to complete the configuration.

In this case, you ignore service endpoint policies because, as of this writing, it's a public preview feature with no service-level agreement (SLA) associated with it. Service endpoint policies allow you to more granularly filter VNet traffic to Azure services.

4. **Open Storage Explorer, and ensure that you can connect to a storage account.**

   If you created a storage account in Chapter 3, you can use that storage account. You should be able to access the files' blob container and the blobs inside.

5. **Back in the Azure portal, browse to the VNet1 resource, and select the Service Endpoints setting.**

6. **From the Microsoft.Storage context menu (that is, the ellipses at the end of the row; I show you this in Figure 4-5), and choose Configure Virtual Networks in a storage account.**

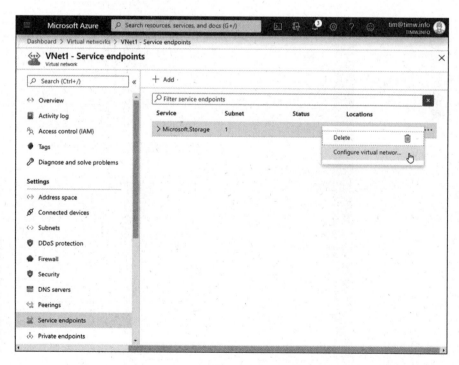

FIGURE 4-5: In the Azure portal, most resources have a context menu from which you can select configuration options.

7. On the Storage Accounts blade, select your storage account and the Firewalls and Virtual Networks setting.

8. In the Allow Access From section, select Selected Networks.

9. In the Virtual Networks section, choose Add Existing Virtual Network.

10. Browse to the VNet1 virtual network and app1 subnet, and click Add.

11. Click Save to complete the configuration.

The storage account's Firewalls and Virtual Networks blade contains some additional options once you've enabled service endpoints:

- *Add Your Client IP Address:* If you don't select this option, you won't be able to access the storage account from your current workstation.

- *Allow Trusted Microsoft Services to Access This Storage Account:* Enable this option to ensure other Azure services (such as Key Vault, Azure AD, and so on) can reach the storage account and vice versa.

12. Close and reopen Storage Explorer.

13. Test connectivity to your storage account.

You should see the error message shown in Figure 4-6.

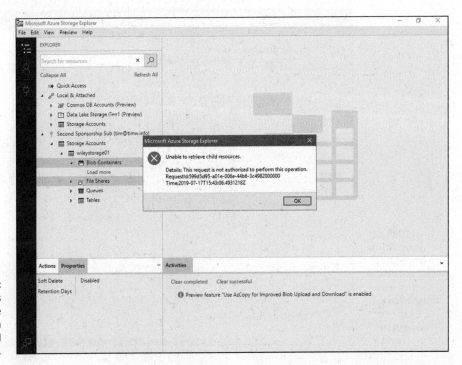

FIGURE 4-6:
Service endpoints secure Azure resources to a particular virtual network.

Connecting Virtual Networks

Here are two ways to logically link two VNets to support topologies that require it:

» Production/development VNets that support inter-VNet communication

» Hub-spoke VNet architectures in which the hub VNet has a link to the on-premises environment

Azure provides us two options for linking VNets, which I describe next.

Configuring VNet peering

VNet peering is one way to seamlessly connect two Azure virtual networks. Until late 2018, virtual network gateways and a VNet-to-VNet virtual private network (VPN) were needed to connect VNets located in different regions. Nowadays, VNets in different regions and even in different Azure subscriptions can be peered.

Network traffic across a VNet peering is private, occurring over the Azure network backbone and using private IP addresses. No VPN expense or overhead is required to do peering, although you can deploy a VNet-to-VNet VPN if your security needs dictate. You can configure both sides of a peering from the perspective of only one VNet, however.

Follow these steps to configure a VNet peering between your VNet1 and VNet2 virtual networks:

1. **In the Azure portal, browse to VNet1, select the Peerings setting, and click Add.**

2. **Fill out the form on the Add Peering blade and then click OK.**

   Use these configuration properties:

   - *Name of the Peering from VNet1 to Remote Virtual Network:* vnet1-to-vnet2-peering

   - *Virtual Network Deployment Model:* Resource manager

   - *Subscription:* [your subscription]

   - *Virtual Network:* VNet2

   - *Name of the Peering from Remote Virtual network to VNet1:* vnet2-to-vnet1-peering

(Not too long ago, you had to configure the peering in both VNets; it's nice to have the convenience to define both sides in one configuration blade now.)

- *Allow Virtual Network Access (Both Directions):* Enabled

- *Configure Forwarded Traffic Settings (Both Directions):* Disabled

- *Allow Gateway Transit:* Not selected

3. **Click OK to submit the configuration to ARM.**

Eventually, the VNet1 and VNet2 Peerings blades should show the peering status as Connected. You now have a routing path between the two VNets that involves only Azure — no public Internet (or VPN connection) involved.

Understanding service chaining

When you select a peering in the Azure portal, you can customize the peering relationship to accomplish routing goals. For example, you may have a spoke VNet that must reach your on-premises environment by transiting through a hub VNet.

It's important for you to know that VNet peerings are not transitive. Figure 4-7 shows a common hub-spoke VNet topology.

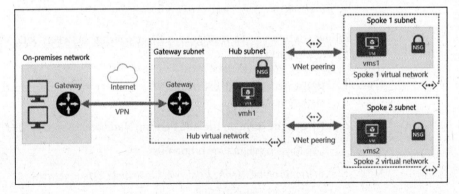

FIGURE 4-7:
A hub-and-spoke
virtual network
topology.

In the figure, the Hub virtual network serves as a transit point between Azure and the business's local network environment. (I address VPNs and the hybrid cloud in Chapter 13.)

Figure 4-5 also shows two peerings to Spoke 1 and Spoke 2. The no-transitivity property means that vms1 in Spoke 1 can't communicate directly with vms2 in

Spoke 2 through the Hub by default. To fix this problem, you could do one of the following:

>> Create a third peering between Spoke 1 and Spoke 2.

>> Configure a network virtual appliance and route traffic explicitly.

Do you see what I'm talking about here? Many businesses require more than one virtual network in Azure, and oftentimes you need to configure connectivity between them. For instance, a business might use peering to link development and production VNets.

Another use case is placing a network virtual appliance such as an enterprise firewall in the Hub network and "sharing" that device for traffic in other, linked VNets. Strictly speaking, this is what Microsoft means by the term "service chaining."

A route table is necessary in Azure when you need to control how traffic flows within and between VNets. The route table defines one or more "next hop" destination IP addresses; if you've worked with static IP routing in your local environment, then the Azure route table should be easy for you to pick up.

Follow these steps to create a sample route table, assuming that the NVA listens for traffic on the private IP address 10.1.1.100:

1. **Use global search in the Azure portal to find the Route Tables blade.**

2. **On the Route Tables blade, click Add.**

3. **Complete the form on the Create Route Table blade and then click Create.**

   Here are the properties to use:

   - *Name:* nva-next-hop

   - *Subscription, Resource Group, Location:* Use the values you've been using thus far

   - *Virtual Network Gateway Route Propagation:* Disabled

4. **Select the nva-next-hop route table, navigate to the Routes blade, and click Add.**

TECHNICAL
STUFF

CONFIGURING PEERING

Before continuing, I need to address how to allow the Hub virtual network to forward traffic from either spoke to the other or through the VPN tunnel to an on-premises network.

For the Spoke 1 and Spoke 2 peerings, enable the Use Remote Gateways option to instruct Azure to allow traffic from the spokes through the VPN gateway in Hub. Note that you configure the setting on the spoke rather than on the Hub sides of the peerings.

In the Hub VNet's peering properties, enable the Allow Gateway Transit option. This option instructs Azure to allow peered VNets to use this VNet's VPN gateway. Also enable the Allow Forwarded Traffic option for both Spoke 1 and Spoke 2 so that the spokes can communicate through the Hub VNet in theory.

"In theory, Tim?" you ask. "What the heck does that mean?" Well, to support full VNet transitive communication, you have to use *service chaining*, in which you deploy a network virtual appliance to your Hub VNet and implement user-defined routes.

The figure shows an NVA virtual machine configured as a router that can forward IP traffic from other VNets. You associate a user-defined route (also known as an Azure route table) with each Spoke VNet to provide a next-hop routing address of 10.1.1.100: the network virtual appliance. In so doing, you override Azure system routes with your own custom routes.

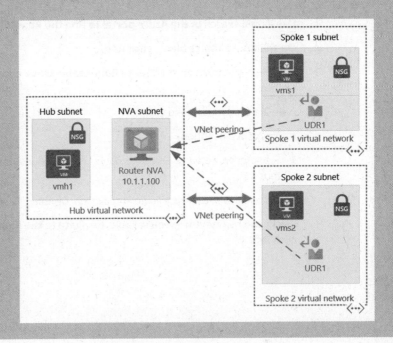

WHAT IS AN NVA?

A *network virtual appliance* (NVA) is an ordinary VM that runs in Azure but has a fundamentally different purpose from that of most VMs. Normally, an NVA has more than one virtual network interface card attached to multiple subnets within a VNet; is configured for IP forwarding; and runs a third-party enterprise network traffic management application.

Leading providers of enterprise load balancers, firewalls, proxy servers, and other devices publish preconfigured NVAs to the Azure Marketplace, for example. These VMs normally run a thin, specialized Linux version and are configured via a web interface. To browse the NVAs in the Azure Marketplace, visit `https://azure.microsoft.com/en-us/solutions/network-appliances`.

5. **Fill in the form on the Add Route blade and then click OK to submit your configuration.**

Specify the following properties:

- *Route Name:* nva-default-route

- *Address Prefix:* 0.0.0.0/0.

  This special IP address range, known as a *default route,* applies to every traffic bit outbound from the subnet(s) with which this route table is associated.

- *Next Hop Type:* Virtual Appliance.

  The other options are Virtual Network, Internet, and Virtual Network Gateway. Remember when you learned about service tags and network security groups? That's what these identifiers are as well.

- *Next Hop Address:* 10.1.1.100

A note from ARM reminds you to enable IP forwarding on the NVA. You configure this forwarding as a property of the NVA's network interface card settings.

6. **Associate the route table with the appropriate subnet(s).**

To do this, open the Subnets blade in the route table's Settings list, and select Associate. As shown in the figure in "Configuring peering" earlier in this chapter, you need to associate your new route table with the Spoke 1 and Spoke 2 subnets to force their outbound traffic through the NVA located in the Hub VNet.

The hub-and-spoke VNet design pattern and service chaining are not uncommon scenarios. I see these topologies all the time in my work as an Azure solution architect. User-defined route tables allow you to move from Azure-provided routing, which works well enough, to custom routing, in which you granularly shape how traffic flows within VNets, between VNets, and between a transit VNet and your on-premises networks.

REMEMBER

Don't forget about your NSGs and their inbound and outbound rules. When you create more complex VNet topologies, such as service chaining and peering, you'll most likely need to tweak existing NSG rules and/or create new ones to accommodate the new traffic flows.

Chapter **5**

Deploying and Configuring Azure Virtual Machines

I n my experience as an Azure solutions architect, I find that most of my clients naturally think of virtual machines (VMs) in two situations:

» When they're migrating their existing workloads to Azure
» When they're deploying new workloads directly to the cloud

One of my joys as a cloud consultant is showing customers that they don't have to use Azure VMs. Azure includes many wonderful Platform as a Service (PaaS) options, such as Azure App Service and Azure SQL Database, that can provide geo-scaling and fast agility.

If you need full stack control of your environment, Azure fully supports VMs. In this chapter, I explain the various Azure VM options and how to deploy and configure Windows Server and Linux VMs in Azure.

Planning Your VM Deployment

You may recall the carpenter's aphorism "Measure twice, cut once," which stresses the importance of planning before you jump into a project. With Azure VM deployment, you need to think carefully to make the right decisions the first time; otherwise, you risk having to delete and re-create your VM.

Before you plan your deployment, however, you need to understand how VMs operate in Azure.

Understanding VMs

A VM is a software representation of a computer. Each Azure region consists of multiple data centers; each data center consists of thousands of hardware blade servers. VMs run within this massive compute fabric.

Each VM is allocated virtual hardware resources from its parent hardware host:

>> Compute (CPU [central processing unit] and RAM [random-access memory])

>> Storage

>> Network

TECHNICAL STUFF

Microsoft's data center servers run a specialized Windows Server Core version, and your VMs reside on Microsoft Hyper-V hosts. By contrast, Amazon Web Services (AWS) runs its Elastic Compute Cloud VM instances under the open-source Xen hypervisor.

As of this writing, the Microsoft Azure VMs service supports the following 64-bit versions:

>> Windows 7

>> Windows 8.1

>> Windows 10

>> Windows Server 2008 R2

>> Windows Server 2012 R2

>> Windows Server 2016

>> Windows Server 2019

TIP Microsoft supports Windows Client VM images in Azure only for development purposes. The idea is that developers can deploy Windows Client VMs to use as test agents against cloud-based line-of-business applications.

Azure also supports the following endorsed 64-bit Linux distributions:

- » CentOS
- » CoreOS
- » Debian
- » OpenSUSE
- » Oracle Linux
- » Red Hat Enterprise Linux
- » SUSE Enterprise Linux
- » Ubuntu

Starting your VM deployment from the Azure Marketplace

Perhaps the fastest way to deploy a VM in Azure is to do so from the Azure Marketplace. Azure Marketplace is an online bazaar consisting of thousands of Microsoft and non-Microsoft VM images, including all the naked operating system (OS) images described earlier in this chapter. Figure 5-1 shows the Azure Marketplace.

You get to the Azure Marketplace from the Azure portal by entering **marketplace** in the global Search box.

Starting your VM deployment from your on-premises environment

In Chapter 13, I explain how to use Azure Migrate to migrate your on-premises physical and virtual servers to Azure. That said, you can always upload your generalized OS images to Azure. To do this, you need a fast Internet connection or a private connection to the Azure cloud; that's all.

FIGURE 5-1:
Azure
Marketplace is a
one-stop shop for
several VM types.

WARNING

The instructions I provide here are illustrative, not comprehensive. Consult the Azure documentation for full, step-by-step guidance on preparing your on-premises Linux and Windows Server VMs for upload to Azure.

Here's the general workflow:

1. **Prepare your VM disks for upload to Azure.**

If your on-premises VMs aren't Hyper-V, you need to use appropriate tools to convert them. Although Azure supports Hyper-V Generation 2 virtual hard disks (VHDs), the disks need to be in .vhd format (not .vhdx) to work in Azure.

To convert a .vhdx virtual disk to a fixed-size .vhd, you can run the Convert-VHD PowerShell cmdlet on your local Hyper-V host like so:

```
Convert-VHD –Path d:\dev\vm1-gen2.vhdx –DestinationPath d:\dev\vm1-gen1.
    vhd –VHDType Fixed
```

TIP

By the way, PowerShell commands are commonly called "cmdlets," pronounced *command-lets*.

Note also that your OS VHD must be generalized. Generalization removes all unique information from the VM disk image, including security identifiers, static IP address, host name, and so on. In Windows Server, you can use the built-in Sysprep utility.

2. **Upload your generalized OS image to the blob service of an Azure storage account.**

Refer to Chapter 3 for more information about using storage accounts and the Azure Storage Explorer tool.

3. **Add the uploaded VHD to the Azure Managed Storage service with Azure PowerShell, as follows.**

(a) *Define some variables to make your code tidier:*

```
$vmName = "vm1"
$rgName = "myResourceGroup"
$location = "EastUS"
$imageName = "myImage"
$osVhdUri = "https://mystorageaccount.blob.core.windows.
    net/vhds/vm1-gen1.vhd"
```

(b) *Create what Microsoft calls a* managed image:

```
$imageConfig = New-AzImageConfig -Location $location
$imageConfig = Set-AzImageOsDisk -Image $imageConfig
    -OsType Windows -OsState Generalized -BlobUri $osVhdUri
$image = New-AzImage -ImageName $imageName
    -ResourceGroupName $rgName -Image $imageConfig
```

4. **Use the managed image for your VM deployments.**

Recognizing Azure VM Components

At a higher level of abstraction, an Azure virtual machine is a cloud resource that consists of the following three subsystems:

» Compute

» Storage

» Network

Before I explain how to deploy and configure a VM, I'll go over how Azure VMs implement these subsystems.

Compute

You're charged for each minute that your Azure VMs are allocated and running. *Allocated* means that Microsoft reserves hardware compute power — primarily CPU and RAM resources — for your VM.

The available VM instance sizes are divided into families. Table 5-1 lists the Windows Server VM sizes and the intended workload for each size, which will help you get a feel for the difference among the VM size families. You can find the associated Linux VM sizes in the Azure documentation (https://docs.microsoft.com/en-us/azure/virtual-machines/linux/sizes).

TABLE 5-1   ## Windows Server VM Sizes in Azure

Family	Sizes	Intended Workload
General-purpose	B, Dsv3, Dv3, Dasv3, Dav3, DSv2, Dv2, Av2, DC	Testing and development
Compute-optimized	Fsv2	Web servers
Memory-optimized	Esv3, Ev3, Easv3, Eav3, Mv2, M, DSv2, Dv2	Database servers
Storage-optimized	Lsv2	Big data workloads
GPU	NC, NCv2, NCv3, ND, NDv2, NV, NVv3	Heavy graphic rendering jobs
High-performance compute	HB, HC, H	High performance computing

TIP

If you're not bound to a particular Azure region for compliance purposes, consider shopping around before deploying your VMs, because running VMs in different regions creates significantly different costs. Price differences are due to electricity costs, physical plant costs, and the like, which vary based on the regions in which Azure data centers reside.

Over time, you'll come to recognize which family a particular VM size comes from by inspecting its ID tag. D-series VMs, for example, are general-purpose and therefore are used most often by Azure customers. Note that these sizes are versioned; you can expect a v3 image to have features that v2 images don't, for example.

TIP

Don't worry if you deploy a VM at a size that turns out to be insufficient for your needs from a cost or performance perspective. You can resize VMs dynamically to align better with your situation.

Storage

Azure uses a feature called Managed Disks to store your OS and data VHDs. What's cool about Managed Disks is that you don't have to manage the underlying storage account infrastructure, which once was the case.

The big question about your VM disk storage relates to performance. Here are your options:

>> **Standard HDD storage:** Lower-speed and lowest-price mechanical disk storage. Offers 2,000 maximum input/output operations per second (IOPS).

>> **Standard SSD storage:** Balance between affordability and speed; underlying disks are solid-state. Offers 6,000 maximum IOPS.

>> **Premium SSD storage:** High-speed but higher-price solid-state disk storage. Offers 20,000 maximum IOPS.

>> **Ultra disk storage:** Super-high speed, highest-price solid-state disk storage. Offers 160,000 maximum IOPS.

Which storage tier is right for your VM workload depends on your need for speed and high availability. For example, a testing/development VM normally requires Standard HDD storage. On the other hand, a production database server VM may need the speed and predictable performance provided by Premium SSD storage.

Network

The main idea I want to drive home here is that your VM's networking configuration is independent of the VM resource itself. Understand that a VM's networking stack consists of the following components:

>> VM resource

>> Virtual network interface resource

>> (optional) Public IP address resource

>> (optional) Network security group resource

You configure TCP/IP protocol properties on the virtual network interface card (vNIC) rather than on the VM. This capability is cool for many reasons, not the least of which is that you can detach a vNIC from one VM and attach it to another. Portability!

Architectural Considerations

The process of deploying a VM in Azure has quite a few moving parts, and it's worth your while to take the most important of these parts — high availability and scalability — into account before you log into the Azure portal.

High availability

You don't want to have a single point of failure in your VM deployment. If your workload has a front-end web tier, you probably want at least two identically configured VM instances so that your service remains online if one node goes offline (expectedly or unexpectedly).

Microsoft offers a 99.99 percent high availability service-level agreement (SLA) when you place two or more matching VM nodes in separate availability zones. The SLA is 99.95 percent when you place two or more identical VM instances in an availability set. Finally, the SLA is 99.9 percent if you have a single VM instance using premium storage.

REMEMBER

You're responsible for configuring matching VM nodes. Azure doesn't automatically spawn additional identical VM nodes, as it does with, say, Azure App Service. To make replica VMs, all sorts of possibilities exist: You could do so manually in the Azure portal or use Azure Resource Manager templates to automate the process.

Take a look at Figure 5-2 to get a handle on the difference between availability sets and availability zones.

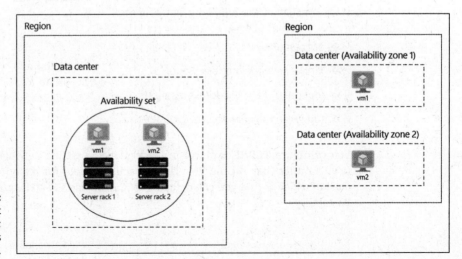

FIGURE 5-2:
Availability set on the left; availability zones on the right.

An *availability set* is a container object that you can populate with VM instances in the same region. Availability sets protect your VM tier against failures within a single data center in your home region. Your VMs are placed on separate hardware hosts on separate racks; thus, if Microsoft has a power or switch failure on a rack, or if it needs to take your hardware host offline, your service remains available because you have at least one member hosted elsewhere.

By contrast, *availability zones* protect against entire data center failures within your home region. You place your VMs in separate data centers in the region. You don't have to worry about latency, because Microsoft has redundant power, cooling, and network links among regional data center clusters.

WARNING

If you forget to place a VM in an availability zone or availability set during deployment, you need to redeploy to make this change. Yes, it's a pain, so make sure you do this task right the first time.

"Why wouldn't you always choose availability zones, then?" you may ask. The answer is simple: Microsoft hasn't enabled availability zones for all public regions yet, so that option may not be available in your region. In time, I'm sure that availability zones will be offered in all regions.

Thus, Microsoft's guidance is that if your Azure region supports availability zones, then you should use them. Otherwise, use availability sets to provide high availability for your Azure VMs.

Scalability

Scalability refers to your ability to resize your VM. It also means that you can scale your VM by deploying additional instances. A PaaS service such as Azure App Service can handle automatic scaling for you; this feature is a powerful differentiator between PaaS and IaaS.

For now, the closest thing Azure VMs have to horizontal autoscaling is Virtual Machine Scale Sets (VMSS). With VMSS, you can create a cluster of VMs and instruct Azure to autoscale based on your specs for CPU load, time schedule, and so on.

VMSS has some complications, however:

- » It's expensive, because you pay for each VM in your cluster.
- » It requires you to have networking knowledge, because you need an Azure load balancer.
- » You have to configure and synchronize your workload manually.

Whether you decide to use scale sets or create identical VM replicas on your own depends on how comfortable you are with conducting VM deployments and configuring VMs. Scale sets are intended to abstract away much of the underlying infrastructure complexity.

Deploying Azure VMs from the Azure Marketplace

I have a feeling that you've been waiting for this part of the chapter, in which I explain how to work with the Azure technology directly. Thanks for your patience.

Deploying a Linux VM

I'll start with Linux because I never cease to get a kick out of the fact that Microsoft supports Linux natively in Azure. I've been a Microsoft specialist since 1997, and it was inconceivable up until a handful of years ago that we'd be able to run non-Windows VMs by using Microsoft technologies.

In this section, I explain how to deploy a simple Linux web server in a new virtual network, using an Ubuntu Linux 18.04 Long-Term Support (LTS) VM image from the Azure Marketplace.

Deploying from the Azure portal

Follow these steps to deploy a Linux VM in the Azure portal:

1. **Choose Favorites ⇨ Create a Resource, and choose Ubuntu Server 18.04 LTS.**

   TIP

   Alternatively, you can browse to the Virtual Machines blade and click Add to deploy a new resource.

   If Ubuntu doesn't show up in the Azure Marketplace list, type its name to find it in the VM template gallery.

2. **On the Create a Virtual Machine blade, complete the Basics tab.**

   Figure 5-3 shows the Create a Virtual Machine blade. Oh, boy, it's tough not to feel overwhelmed when you see all the tabs: Basics, Disks, Networking, Management, Advanced, Tags, and Review + Create.

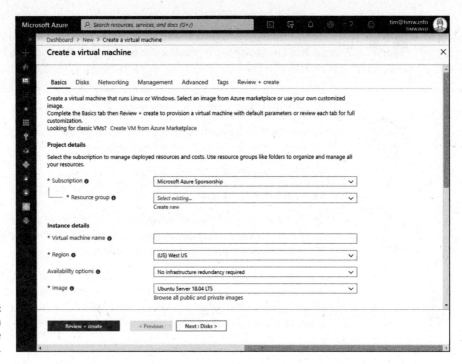

FIGURE 5-3:
The Create a
Virtual Machine
blade.

From now on, when I give you suggested choices on these deployment blades, I'll leave out fields you already know about, such as Subscription, Resource Group, and Region. Use the following information to complete the other fields:

- *Virtual Machine Name:* The name needs to be unique only within your resource group. Pay attention to the validation helpers that pop up when you place your cursor in a field.

- *Availability Options:* If you don't see both Availability Zone and Availability Set in the drop-down menu, choose a different region. (East US 2 is a good choice.) Because this is a practice deployment, you can choose No Infrastructure Redundancy Required.

- *Image:* You specified the Ubuntu image in step 1, but if you're curious about other options, open the drop-down menu to see the most popular VM images. You can also click Browse All Public and Private Images to view all templates in the Azure Marketplace.

- *Size:* For now, accept the Microsoft-recommended default VM size.

- *Authentication Type:* Linux VMs are different from Windows because you can use Secure Shell (SSH) key-based authentication or password-based authentication. For this exercise, choose password.

REMEMBER

You should choose a creative default administrator account name. ARM won't let you use commonly guessed administrator account names such as root or admin.

- *Public Inbound Ports:* For testing purposes, associate a public IP address with this VM, and connect to the instance via SSH.

You'll tighten network security group security later to prevent unauthorized access attempts by Internet-based bad actors.

TIP

- *Select Inbound Ports:* Choose SSH.

3. **Complete the Disks tab.**

This tab is where you make an initial choice about the VM's OS and data disks. Choose Standard HDD to save money. (Refer to "Storage" earlier in this chapter for more information about the various options.)

The number of data disks you can create depends on your chosen VM instance size. You can always add data disks later, so for now, proceed to the next blade. Note that the default number of data disks Azure provides the new VM is zero; it's up to you as administrator to decide whether you want to use them.

4. **Complete the Networking tab.**

You have some crucially important decisions to make in terms of where you want to place your VM and how you want to configure its connectivity. Here are the configuration options:

- *Virtual Network:* The template deploys a new virtual network by default. That's what you want here, so leave this setting alone.

If you place your VM on the wrong virtual network, you'll need to redeploy it to move it, which is a pain, so try to make the right choice the first time around.

WARNING

- *Subnet:* Leave this setting at its default.

- *Public IP:* Leave this setting at its default. You do in fact want a public IP address, at least initially.

- *NIC Network Security Group:* Select Basic.

- *Public Inbound Ports:* Allow Selected Ports.

- *Select Inbound Ports:* Select SSH.

- *Accelerated Networking:* Not all VM templates support this option. For VM templates that support this feature, accelerated networking gives the VMs a network speed boost by allowing the VM to use the Azure networking backbone more directly.

- *Load Balancing:* Select No.

5. **Complete the Management tab.**

   Ensure that Boot Diagnostics is enabled and all other options are off. Boot Diagnostics is required to use the VM serial console, so it's always a good idea to enable it sooner rather than later.

6. **Review the Advanced and Tags tabs.**

   You don't need any of these options right now, but they're worth examining. Extensions allow you to inject agent software and/or management scripts into the VM. You can handle configuration after deployment, however.

   Taxonomic tags are a way to track resources across subscriptions for accounting purposes.

7. **Submit the deployment, and monitor progress.**

   Click the Review + Create tab; then click Create after ARM informs you that your selections passed validation. If an error occurs, ARM places a red dot next to the configuration blade(s) where it detects invalid settings.

Connecting to the VM

Use Azure Cloud Shell to make an SSH connection to your VM. Follow these steps:

1. **In Azure portal, browse to the Overview blade of your newly created VM, and note the public IP address.**

   You can see my VM's configuration in Figure 5-4.

2. **Open Cloud Shell, and connect to your Linux VM by specifying your default administrator account name and the VM's public IP address.**

   To connect to my Linux VM at 13.68.104.88 using my `tim` admin account, I type

   ```
   ssh tim@13.68.104.88
   ```

   Type **yes** to accept the VM's public key and then type your password to enter the SSH session. At this point, you're working directly on the Linux VM.

TIP

You can get help for any Linux command by typing **man <command-name>**. Scroll through the Help document with your arrow keys, and press Q to quit.

Deploying a Windows Server VM

In this section, I explain how to create a Windows Server VM by using Visual Studio 2019 Community Edition and an ARM template.

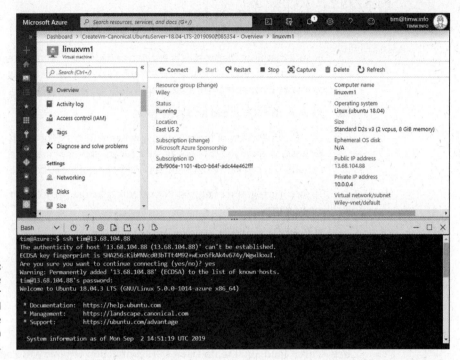

FIGURE 5-4:
Most admins use SSH (with or without Cloud Shell) to manage Linux VMs in Azure.

Visual Studio 2019 Community Edition (`https://visualstudio.microsoft.com/vs/community`) is a free Visual Studio version that you can use for testing, development, and open-source projects.

TIP

Although I use Windows as the workstation OS in this book, Microsoft does make a Visual Studio version for macOS. Visit `https://visualstudio.microsoft.com/vs/mac` for details.

This procedure is especially important for you to understand for two reasons:

» ARM templates form a basis for administrative automation, development, and operations.

» You'll use ARM templates to complete tasks that I cover later in the book.

Setting up your development environment

Follow these high-level steps to get your Visual Studio environment set up:

1. **Download Visual Studio 2019 Community Edition, and run the installer.**

You need administrative permissions on your Windows 10 workstation to install the software.

2. Choose the Azure workload.

This step is the most important one. Visual Studio is an integrated development environment that supports multiple development languages and frameworks. For the purpose of deploying a Windows Server VM, you need to install the Microsoft Azure software development kits and tools.

Figure 5-5 illustrates the user interface. You can leave the Azure workload components set at their defaults.

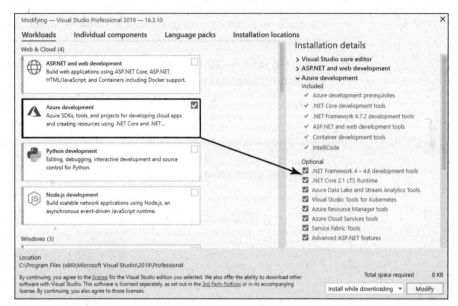

FIGURE 5-5:
Installing the
Azure SDKs
in Visual
Studio 2019.

3. After installation, open Visual Studio, and log in to your Azure administrator account.

When you start Visual Studio 2019, you'll see a Get Started page. Click Continue Without Code; then open the Cloud Explorer extension by choosing View ⇨ Cloud Explorer. Authenticate to Azure Active Directory, and select the Azure subscription(s) you want to work with.

Deploying the VM

Assuming that you have Visual Studio open and you're logged into your Azure subscription, you're ready to rock. In this section, you're deploying a Windows Server VM from the Azure Quickstart Templates gallery, which you can find at `https://azure.microsoft.com/en-us/resources/templates`. I'm using a template definition that includes Managed Disks. Follow these steps:

1. **In Visual Studio, choose File ⇨ New ⇨ Project.**

   The Create a New Project dialog box opens.

2. **Search the Visual Studio template gallery for Azure Resource Group, select it, and click Next.**

3. **Name and save your project.**

   Choose a meaningful project name such as Simple Windows VM, choose your favorite directory location, and click Create.

4. **Select the 101-vm-with-standardssd-disk template in the Azure Quickstart Templates gallery and click OK.**

   Figure 5-6 shows the interface.

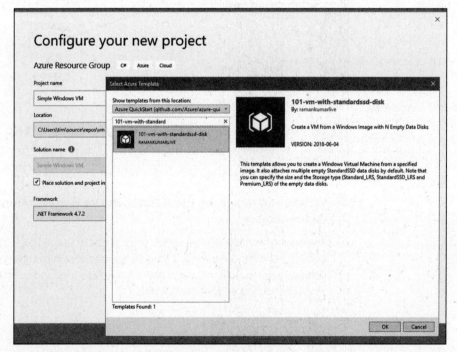

FIGURE 5-6:
Creating a resource group deployment project in Visual Studio 2019.

5. **Double-click your azuredeploy.json template file.**

   This action loads the JavaScript Object Notation (JSON) file into your code editor. Pay particular attention to the JSON Outline pane, shown in Figure 5-7.

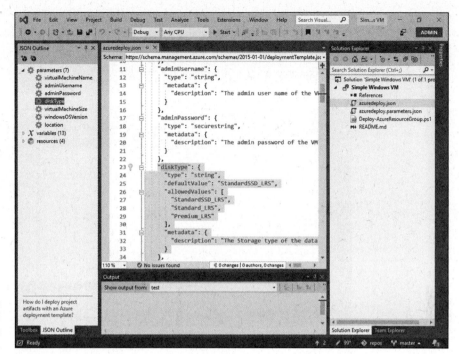

FIGURE 5-7:
The ARM
template in the
code editor.

6. **Browse the ARM template's contents.**

The three elements shown in JSON Outline view are

- *parameters:* You supply these values to the template at deployment time. Note the `allowedValues` element on lines 26–30; the template author prepopulated the VM disk types to make validation and deployment simpler.

- *variables:* These values represent fixed or dynamic data that is referenced internally within the template.

- *resources:* In this deployment, you create four resource types: virtual machine, virtual NIC, virtual network, and public IP address.

7. **In Solution Explorer, right-click the project and choose Validate from the shortcut menu.**

The Validate to Resource Group dialog box opens.

8. **Fill in the fields of the dialog box and then click Edit Parameters to supply parameter values.**

You can see my environment in Figure 5-8.

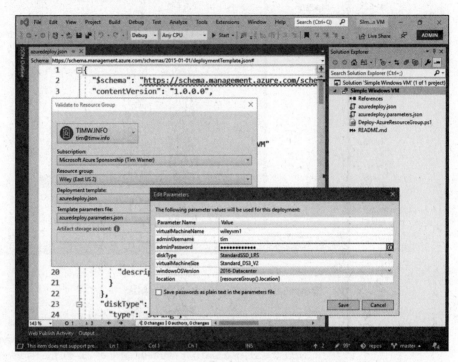

FIGURE 5-8:
Validating our
ARM template.

REMEMBER

Visual Studio allows you to validate your template before deploying it to Azure. The resource group is the fundamental deployment unit in Azure. Therefore, your deployments must specify a new or existing resource group.

9. **Click Validate, and watch the Output window for status messages.**

Make sure to look behind your Visual Studio application; Azure spawns a PowerShell console session to prompt you to confirm the admin password.

The feedback you're looking for in the Output window is

```
Template is valid.
```

If the template fails validation, Visual Studio is pretty good about telling you the template code line(s) on which it found an issue. You can debug and retry validation as many times you need to until the template passes.

TECHNICAL
STUFF

IDEM WHAT?

Azure Resource Manager templates use a declarative syntax that is described as idempotent. In ARM, *idempotency* allows you to run the same deployment multiple times without fear of deleting existing resources.

First, declarative code describes how you want the end state to look. The template code leaves the how of the deployment to the ARM platform. Declarative code is fundamentally different from imperative code such as C#, in which the programmer must instruct the .NET framework precisely what to do and when (and how) to do it.

By default, ARM deployments run in incremental mode, in which ARM operates under this assumption: "Make sure that the resource group contains all the template resources, but don't remove any existing resources that don't exist in the template definition."

You can also run deployments in Complete mode. In this mode, ARM operates under this assumption: "The only resources that this resource group should contain are those defined in the template." Any nonreferenced existing resources are deleted in this case.

TIP

10. **Deploy the VM by right-clicking the project in Solution Explorer and choosing Deploy from the shortcut menu.**

The shortcut menu contains a reference to your validation configuration.

11. **Monitor progress, and verify that the VM exists in the Azure portal.**

You'll know that the deployment completed successfully when you see the following status line in the Output window:

```
Successfully deployed template 'azuredeploy.json' to resource group
    'your-resource-group'.
```

Connecting to the VM

You normally use Remote Desktop Protocol to manage Windows Servers remotely on-premises, and Azure is no different. Browse to your new VM's Overview blade, and click Connect. The Remote Desktop Connection dialog box opens (see Figure 5-9). You can download the .rdp connection file and open it from here.

As shown in Figure 5-9, the steps to make an RDP connection are

1. Click Connect from the Overview blade toolbar.

2. Download the RDP connection file to your local computer.

3. Open the connection using your preferred RDP client software.

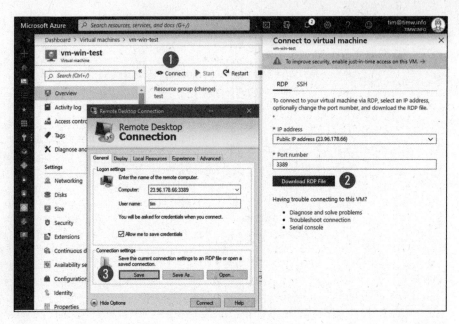

FIGURE 5-9:
Remote Desktop
Connection works
the same way
with Azure VMs
as it does
on-premises VMs.

TIP

Microsoft makes a native Remote Desktop Protocol client for macOS; it's available in the Mac App Store.

Configuring Your VMs

Configuration management in the Azure cloud is essentially the same as it is on-premises. You want to get your configuration right as early in the VM's life cycle as possible.

First, I explain how to tweak networking, a VM's crucially important and potentially vulnerable subsystem.

WARNING

Don't attempt to configure your Azure VM's networking settings from within the VM. If you do, you'll lock yourself out of the VM. Instead, you need to perform all your TCP/IP configuration in ARM.

It isn't the VM resource but its vNIC that contains the machine's IP configuration. Follow these steps to configure TCP/IP for a Windows Server VM:

1. **Open the Windows Server VM's settings blade, and select Networking.**

The Networking blade gives you at-a-glance TCP/IP configuration, with direct hyperlinks to associated network resources:

- vNIC

- Virtual network

- Public IP address

- Network security group

I show you this interface in Figure 5-10. If you deployed the Windows Server VM from the Simple Windows VM template you used in the previous exercise, you'll be unpleasantly surprised to see you don't have a NSG protecting the VM. You can fix that situation.

2. **In the Azure Search box, browse to the Network Security Groups blade, and click Add.**

WARNING

Make sure to place any additional NSGs in the same Azure region as your NSG. Otherwise, neither your VMs nor your VNet will be able to use them.

If you've been reading this book sequentially (and I dearly hope you have), you already know how to create NSGs.

3. **Add a single inbound rule to allow inbound Remote Desktop Protocol traffic.**

You learn how to create network security groups in Chapter 4.

4. **Browse to your VM's Networking blade, and select its vNIC.**

You want to associate your new NSG with the VM's vNIC to protect it against Internet-based access.

5. **From the Network Interface settings menu, choose Network Security Group, click Edit, select your new NSG, and click OK.**

Now we're talking! With this simple step, you've dramatically reduced the attack surface of this new VM.

6. **In the Network Interface settings, select the IP Configurations setting and then click ipconfig1.**

A vNIC always has a single IP configuration called (unimaginatively enough) ipconfig1. You specify your private and public IP addresses in the IP configuration.

Figure 5-10 walks you through the click path of finding where IP addresses are stored in Azure:

a. In the network interface's settings list, click IP Configurations.

b. Click ipconfig1, the default IP configuration.

c. Adjust the public and private IP addresses as needed.

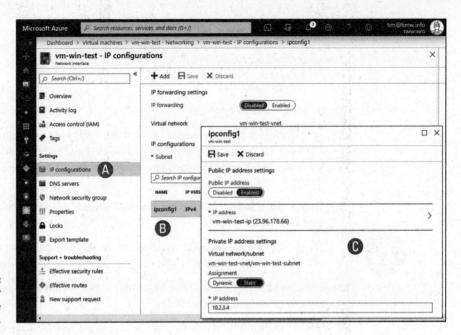

FIGURE 5-10:
Azure VM TCP/IP
settings in the
Azure portal.

TIP

Here are some points to ponder concerning your Azure VM's IP addresses:

- Remember that giving a VM a public IP address may not be required or even a good idea. Plenty of other options exist for Internet-based access to your VMs, such as Azure Firewall, a manually configured jump box, a load balancer, or a virtual private network.

- Your private IP address comes from its subnet on its given virtual network. You can assign a static private IP address here instead of relying on Azure dynamic address distribution.

7. **Revisit the VM's Networking blade and verify your changes.**

   You should see the NSG inbound port rules at least. Good deal!

Starting, Stopping, and Resizing VMs

REMEMBER

Before I teach you how to start and stop VMs, I want to remind you that Microsoft charges you for each minute the VM is running or stopped but in an allocated state. A rule I stated earlier applies here too: Perform as much Azure-related VM management as possible from outside the VM.

If you shut down the VM by using the Azure portal, PowerShell, or the Azure command-line interface, depending on what parameters you add, you shut down and deallocate the VM, which stops billing.

Just know that deallocating a VM releases any dynamic resources it has been assigned, such as public/private IP addresses and temporary storage.

Starting and stopping a VM

You may have noticed the Start, Restart, and Stop buttons on the VM's Overview blade in the Azure portal. You can use those buttons to control your VM's allocation state (and, therefore, billing), but I'm going to teach you how to stop and start a VM by using PowerShell. Figure 5-11 shows the interface.

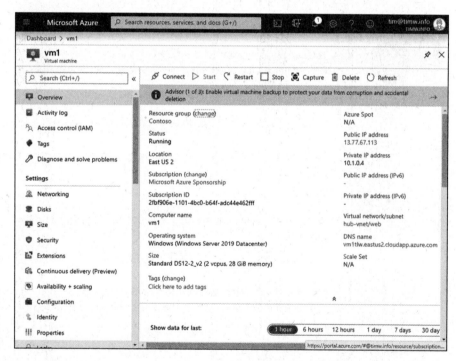

FIGURE 5-11: Use the toolbar to start, stop, or restart a VM in the Azure portal.

When you use Cloud Shell, Azure automatically authenticates your user account to Azure Active Directory. By contrast, you need to authenticate manually before you can use Azure PowerShell on your local computer.

Follow these steps to use PowerShell on your Windows 10 workstation to stop and then start a given VM:

1. **Open an administrative PowerShell console, and log into Azure.**

To do so, run Connect-AzAccount, and authenticate to Azure.

TIP

If you have more than one subscription, and Azure associates your session with the incorrect one, use the following command to make the switch:

```
Set-AzContext -SubscriptionName 'MySubscription'
```

2. **List the VMs in a resource group.**

You may not remember your VM's name, but if you remember the resource group name, try this:

```
Get-AzVM -ResourceGroupName 'Wiley'
```

TIP

You can enclose string (character) data in either single or double quotes in PowerShell. PowerShell was designed not to be fussy about such things.

3. **Stop the target VM with this command:**

```
Stop-AzVM -Name 'vm-win-test' -ResourceGroupName 'Wiley' -Force
```

Make sure to include the -Force switch parameter to ensure that you both stop and deallocate the VM.

4. **Start the VM.**

Whoa — whiplash! But this step is a good learning opportunity. Check out this technique:

```
Get-AzVM -Name 'vm-win-test' -ResourceGroupName 'Wiley' | Start-AzVM
```

The pipe (|) character passes the results of the first segment (getting a reference to the target VM) to the second segment. This technique is called *pipelining*.

Resizing a VM

As I mention earlier, the ability to resize your VM dynamically is a huge paradigm shift from maintaining on-premises hardware.

WARNING

VM resizes in Azure have one drawback: They restart your VM. Be sure to perform this operation only during a predefined maintenance window.

To resize a VM, follow these steps:

1. **In your VM settings, select Size.**

   The Size blade contains a table of all VM sizes that are available in your region. Not all VM sizes are available in every region.

2. **Edit the filters to filter available VM sizes.**

   You can filter the VM size by using any combination of the following properties:

   - *Size:* Choices are Small, Medium, and Large.

   - *Generation:* Choices are Current, Previous, and Older.

   - *Family:* Choices are General Purpose, GPU, High Performance Compute, Compute Optimized, Memory Optimized, and Storage Optimized.

   - *Premium Disk:* Choices are Supported and Not Supported.

   - *vCPUs:* Choices range from 1 to 64 vCPU cores.

   - *RAM:* Choices range from 2 to 432 GB.

3. **Select your desired VM size, and click Resize.**

   Your VM restarts with the new virtual hardware resources. Isn't that a world easier than requesting, ordering, and installing hardware in your on-premises data center?

Extending your VM's capabilities

As you enter this chapter's home stretch, I want to show you how to configure basic diagnostics logging for Windows Server and Linux VMs in Azure.

Enabling diagnostic logging

Microsoft offers three increasingly granular monitoring options for Linux and Windows Server VMs:

>> **Host-level metrics:** Basic CPU, disk, and network utilization data pulled by the Azure platform that requires no agent software

>> **Guest-level monitoring:** More detailed monitoring; requires the Azure Diagnostics agent

>> **Azure Monitor Log Analytics:** Most robust monitoring; requires the Log Analytics agent and an associated Azure Monitor Log Analytics workspace

In this chapter, I work with guest-level monitoring. To access it, open the Diagnostic Settings blade, and select Enable Guest-Level Monitoring.

Guest-level monitoring picks up the following data from your Windows Server VMs:

>> **Selected performance monitor counters:** CPU, memory, disk, and network.

>> **Event log messages:** Application, Security, and System.

>> **CPU kernel crash dump data:** This data can be helpful to Microsoft support representatives to diagnose problems with your VM.

Guest-level monitoring includes the following metrics and logs from your Linux VMs:

>> CPU, memory, network, file system, and disk metrics

>> Syslog log data for authentication, task scheduling, CPU, and other facilities

TECHNICAL STUFF

In Azure monitoring nomenclature, a *metric* is a time series of measured values that are stored for later analysis.

Viewing diagnostics data in Azure Monitor

Suppose that you need to plot CPU utilization data for the Linux and Windows Server VMs you've created to generate baseline data for your manager.

Follow these steps to create a monitoring chart in Azure Monitor:

1. **In the Azure portal, open Monitor, and navigate to the Metrics blade.**

I show you Azure Monitor in Figure 5-12.

2. **In the Chart Title field, give the new chart a descriptive name.**

For this exercise, I called mine Windows Server vs. Linux CPU Comparison.

3. **Configure the initial metric row to plot CPU data for one of your VMs.**

Here are the properties I specified for my Windows Server VM:

- *Resource:* vm-win-test

- *Metric Namespace:* Virtual Machine Host

- *Metric:* Percentage CPU

- *Aggregation:* Avg

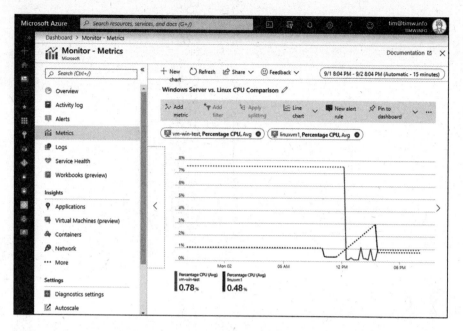

FIGURE 5-12:
Azure Monitor is a central point for infrastructure and application monitoring.

4. **Click Add Metric, and configure the metric row to plot CPU for your other VM.**

Being able to plot metrics from multiple Azure resources can be enormously helpful in your monitoring.

5. **Experiment with the other metrics controls in Azure Monitor.**

Check out these controls:

- *New Chart:* You can create a chart showing something such as Azure storage account read transactions.

- *Line Chart:* Try changing the plot type to observe how the view changes your data's visibility.

- *New Alert Rule:* You can generate alerts, notifications, and remediation actions based on defined metric thresholds (such as triggering an alert when your Linux VM exceeds your predefined CPU utilization threshold).

- *Pin to Dashboard:* You can use the Azure dashboard as a business intelligence dashboard.

IN THIS CHAPTER

» **Understanding Docker and containers**

» **Reviewing Azure support for Docker container**

» **Implementing Azure Container Instances and Azure Container Registry**

» **Touring Azure Kubernetes Service**

» **Deploying a Docker container in an Azure App Service web application**

Chapter **6**

Shipping Docker Containers in Azure

D ocker containers are taking over the world!

Okay, maybe I need to tone down the hyperbole. Many businesses are realizing the financial benefits of using Docker containers in their development and production environments. In a nutshell, Docker containers make it a lot faster and easier for developers to build software products.

Microsoft supports Docker containers in its cloud in myriad ways. You may not be a Docker expert by the time you finish this chapter, but I'm entirely confident that you'll grasp the use of containers and the possibilities of using Docker in Azure.

Understanding Docker

If you've read Chapter 5, you probably have a pretty good idea of what virtual machines (VMs) are and how they work. To me, Docker containers represent a more agile degree of virtualization. Containers allow developers or administrators to package an application and all its dependencies into a single, modular unit that can be deployed quickly.

REMEMBER

A Docker container is a virtualized application, not an entire VM. You might create and run Docker containers running different databases and database versions against which to test your application. These containers contain (see what I did there?) only the database engine binaries and their dependencies — nothing more.

Whereas each VM may weigh hundreds of gigabytes and need to be updated, backed up, monitored, and maintained, containers can range from less than 100 MB to a few gigabytes.

Like VMs, containers share hardware resources with their container host server. Unlike VMs, containers are defined fundamentally in plain-text Dockerfiles, which contain the instructions for building a container.

The idea is to put all the assets that will comprise your container in a single directory and create a Dockerfile that orchestrates the container's composition. Then you compile the Dockerfile into a binary image, which serves as your deployment unit. Finally, you create as many containers as you need by deploying instances of your image template. Figure 6-1 illustrates the Docker deployment process.

TIP

Docker is an enormous topic that could fill a separate book. If you want to know more about creating container images, check out the Docker documentation at https://docs.docker.com.

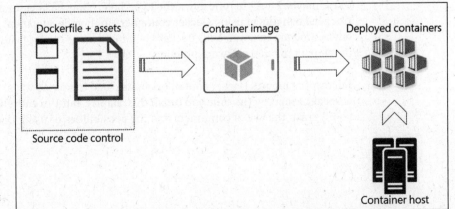

FIGURE 6-1:
The Docker container deployment process.

TECHNICAL
STUFF

Application virtualization existed in Linux long before Docker. Docker is a business that simply standardized and extended these preexisting technologies. Microsoft and Docker partnered primarily to bring Docker containers to Windows Server, and this chapter deals almost exclusively with Windows Server containers.

Using Docker containers

Developers love Docker containers because containers are agile. As I mention earlier, Dockerfiles are plain-text documents, which means that development teams can store them in source-code control and track their changes over time.

Suppose that Jane Developer needs to test her business's line-of-business application against three MySQL database versions. Starting three separate VMs is ordinarily a slow, labor-intensive process. This pain becomes greater when she needs to spin up and work with multiple instances of each VM-based MySQL installation. If the VM's guest operating system needs an update or if MySQL requires an update, the process is even slower.

By contrast, Jane can use the Docker command-line interface or a hosted container platform to start up any number of MySQL containers running different software versions. When she finishes testing, she disposes of the containers with a single command. If MySQL needs an update, she or a teammate can simply edit the Dockerfile and recompile an image.

Portability is another huge advantage of containers. Microsoft Azure is a Hyper-V ecosystem. What if you need to migrate your VMs to, say, Google Cloud Platform, where they use another hypervisor?

I've spent way too much time reconfiguring virtual machines so they fit into different cloud providers' ecosystems. With Docker, you have a universal format that works across any cloud that supports Docker.

As long as you have the Docker daemon (server service) component available, you can run your containers almost anywhere with no modification.

Setting up Docker on your workstation

The Docker run-time environment is relatively lightweight and portable. In this section, I show you how to install Docker Desktop on your Windows 10 workstation.

REMEMBER

For purposes of this book, I assume that you're working on a Windows 10–based computer. Docker Desktop and its associated tools are also available for macOS and Linux, however. Docker does a good job of standardizing the user interface, so you should find the following steps work for you if you are on macOS or Linux.

Installing Docker Desktop

Follow these steps to set up Docker on your Windows 10 system:

1. **Register for a free user account at Docker Hub.**

   Docker Hub (https://hub.docker.com) is the main public repository for Docker containers.

2. **Download and install Docker Desktop from** https://www.docker.com/products/docker-desktop.

   The website encourages you to work through an interactive tutorial; do so at your leisure.

3. **Accept the default settings during installation.**

   The exception to this rule occurs when the installer asks whether you want to use Windows containers instead of Linux containers. Select Windows containers. You won't see this option on macOS or Linux computers.

4. **Restart your computer.**

   The installer requires you to log out and restart to install the Hyper-V and Containers Windows 10 features.

5. **Verify that the Docker service is running.**

   Docker Desktop appears as an icon in the Windows notification area (see Figure 6-2).

   Right-click the Docker icon, and you'll see all sorts of options on the shortcut menu (including to Switch to Windows Containers if you forgot to enable that feature during installation). Figure 6-2 shows Switch to Linux Containers, which Docker displays if you're currently configured for Windows containers.

REMEMBER

The Docker service needs to run with elevated permissions. If you find that Docker Desktop doesn't put its icon in your notification area, run the app from the Desktop or Start-menu shortcut as an administrator.

Running the hello-world container

Docker's hello-world reference image can give you a feel for how to use Docker from the client's perspective. Follow these steps:

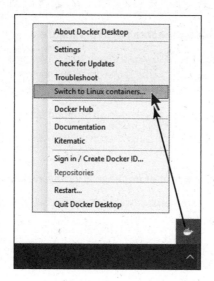

FIGURE 6-2:
Docker Desktop
is easily
accessible from
the Windows
notification area.

1. **Open an elevated PowerShell or Command Prompt console.**

To do so, find the PowerShell or Command Prompt icon on your Start menu or taskbar, right-click it, and choose Run as Administrator from the shortcut menu.

2. **Check your Docker version by running** `docker - version`**.**

This step is a sanity check to make sure that the Docker command-line interface and server components are functional.

3. **Check for any locally available container images by running** `docker images`**.**

You should see only the Repository, Tag, Image ID, Created, and Size properties with no images. (You correct that situation in Step 4.) You can also use `Docker info` to see more condensed metadata.

4. **Pull and run the hello-world image from Docker Hub.**

Issue the command `docker run hello-world` and watch what Docker does:

(a) *Docker checks whether the image exists on your local system. It doesn't.*

(b) *Docker issues a pull command to retrieve the latest version of the hello-world image from Docker Hub.*

(c) *Docker runs the container. hello-world displays* `Hello from Docker!`*, confirming that the image ran correctly.*

5. Run `docker ps -a` **to view the container's running state.**

Docker is telling you it ran the hello-world image as a container and that it exited as soon as the image ran. In the real world, you may want Docker containers to run longer. You can also attach to and detach from containers.

6. Run `docker container prune` **to remove all stopped containers.**

In this case, you have only one container. Rerun `docker ps -a` to verify that the container is gone.

7. Verify that the hello-world container image is locally available.

Use the `docker images` command; you should see the hello-world image listed.

Cool! With this whirlwind tour of Docker, you've seen that the ordinary user's workflow with containers is

1. Pull container images as needed from a central repository.

2. Run new containers based on those images.

3. Dispose of containers when they're no longer needed.

TECHNICAL STUFF

When you install Docker Desktop on your Windows 10 system, you're installing both the Docker daemon and the Docker CLI (client). If you right-click the Docker icon in your notification area, you can open Kitematic (a graphical Docker front end) from the shortcut menu. Kitematic can be helpful to Docker beginners who aren't yet comfortable running Docker commands from the command line.

Running containers in Azure

"All this Docker Desktop stuff is well and good, Tim," you may be saying, "but when will I get to Azure?" You're there now.

THE WINDOWS HELLO-WORLD CONTAINER

TECHNICAL STUFF

If you're wondering exactly what the Windows hello-world container does, let me enlighten you. This container derives from a Windows Nano Server image. (Nano is a super-stripped-down Windows Server version.) The container starts a `cmd.exe` console process, which in turn displays the contents of a file called `hello.txt`. These file contents represent the output you see in your Docker CLI session, after which the container terminates automatically.

In the Azure ecosystem, the following resources support Docker containers natively:

>> VM-based container hosts

>> Azure Container Instances

>> Azure Container Registry

>> Azure Kubernetes Service

>> Azure App Service Web App for Containers

I'll discuss each option briefly before you get your hands dirty with the technologies.

VM-based container hosts

Here, I'm speaking of starting a Linux or Windows Server VM in an Azure virtual network, installing the Docker daemon and launching Docker containers from there. Although this strategy works, it makes little sense to me under most circumstances, given the Platform as a Service (PaaS) resources that are already available and ready for your consumption.

Azure Container Instances

Azure Container Instances (ACI) is for Azure professionals who need to run Docker containers quickly without worrying about the overhead of installing and maintaining the Docker daemon and client. ACI is excellent for one-off container work, in which centralized management and orchestration are unnecessary.

Azure Container Registry

By now, you know about Docker Hub, the public image repository hosted by Docker. Microsoft publishes the bulk of its publicly accessible container images to Docker Hub. On the other hand, Azure Container Registry (ACR) is designed for businesses whose teams need a private, central image registry from which they can work with their own internal Docker images.

Azure Kubernetes Service (AKS)

Azure Kubernetes (pronounced *koo-burr-NET-eez*) Service, or AKS, is a container orchestration platform for Docker containers that was developed by Google. It allows you to create a compute cluster that provides powerful centralized management for your container workloads.

AKS is popular because many businesses use Dockers to host multitiered applications consisting of multiple containers that need to be managed as a group. It also provides high availability, scheduled application upgrades, and massively parallel scaling.

In a nutshell, AKS is Azure's hosted Kubernetes cluster service. You still get to work with the native Kubernetes client tools such as the web UI and the kubectl command-line client, but you can take advantage of seamless integration with other Azure services and features.

Azure App Service Web App for Containers

Azure App Service is a hosted web application service in Azure that can integrate with Docker container-based apps. App Service, which I discuss in Chapter 7, allows you to easily

>> Integrate your application in a build/release pipeline

>> Autoscale your application to meet usage spikes

>> Let Microsoft take care of patching, backing up, and maintaining the underlying host environment

Therefore, Web App for Containers combines the agility of containers with the powerful App Service PaaS platform.

Implementing Azure Container Instances

It's time to log in to the Azure portal and drill into each of these Docker-related Azure resources. This section covers the following tasks:

>> Defining a new container instance with Microsoft's publicly available Internet Information Services (IIS) web server container from Docker Hub

>> Associating a public IP address resource with the container so that you can reach it from your workstation

>> Testing connectivity with your browser

>> Removing the container

To complete any of these jobs, you need to log in to the Azure portal with your administrative account.

Deploying an Azure container instance

Follow these steps to deploy an IIS-based Windows Server container with a public IP address:

1. **Navigate to the Container Instances blade, and click Add.**

   To get to the Container instances blade, type **azure container** in the global Search box.

2. **Fill out the Basics tab, which appears by default and is shown in Figure 6-3. Click Next to continue.**

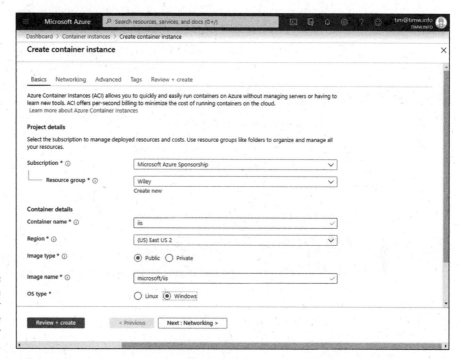

FIGURE 6-3: Deploying a Docker container using the Azure Container Instance service.

You need to complete the following items:

- *Subscription & Resource Group:* Choose the option that meets your requirements.

- *Container Name and Region:* The name needs to be unique within your resource group. Select the Azure region closest to you.

- *Image Type:* Public is the appropriate option when you're pulling the IIS image from the Docker Hub, as in this example. You'd choose Private to authenticate to a private image repository.

- *Image Name:* Type the name of the image — in this case, **microsoft/iis**, which is an extremely popular container image.

- *OS Type:* Select the OS you're using.

- *Size:* Accept the default setting. Your container will run on a host VM under the hood, even though you'll never interact with the host directly.

3. **Fill out the Networking tab.**

   Complete these items:

   - *Include Public IP Address:* Select Yes. You need a public IP address to connect to the container from over the public Internet.

   - *Ports:* Because you're deploying a web server container, you need to access TCP port 80 (HTTP) on the container.

   - *DNS Name Label:* This field is optional, but it's a good idea to supply a name label that you'll recognize in case your public IP address changes for some reason. Note that this host name needs to be globally unique, so you may need to apply some creativity in coming up with a name.

4. **Submit the deployment.**

   To do so, click Review + Create and then click Create.

5. **Monitor deployment progress.**

Verifying and disposing of the container instance

Follow these steps to get familiar with the ACI Azure portal experience and verify connectivity to your new IIS container:

1. **On the Container Instances blade, select a container instance.**

   You can select the IIS container you created in the previous procedure. Selecting the container instance takes you to its Overview blade.

2. **On the Essentials pane of the Overview blade, verify the Status and IP Address fields.**

   The container status should be Running. Make a note of the public IP address, because you'll need it in Step 3.

3. **Copy the container's IP address, paste it into the Address field of a new web-browser tab, and press Enter.**

   If all goes well, you should see the blue Windows Server IIS test page. If so, you've launched an Internet-accessible container.

4. **Back in the Azure portal, click the Containers setting.**

5. **On the Containers blade, click Connect.**

   You're making a terminal connection to this container.

6. **In the Choose Start Up Command window, type /bin/bash and then click Connect.**

   When you reach a command prompt, you can use command-line tools to perform tasks such as copying files to the container and downloading configuration files. Figure 6-4 shows the running container superimposed over the ACI instance metadata in the Azure portal.

TIP

   It's convenient to attach to your container through the Azure portal. Be aware, though, that other methods exist, some through the Docker command-line interface on your workstation or Azure PowerShell.

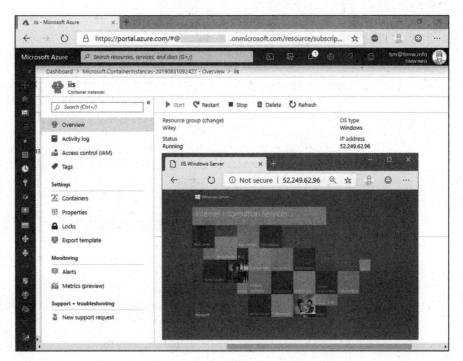

FIGURE 6-4:
Running the IIS web server as a container with the ACI service.

7. **Browse to the container instance's Overview page, click Delete, and confirm your choice.**

   The Overview toolbar has Stop, Restart, and Delete controls. Although Docker containers are ordinarily considered to be ephemeral and disposal, you may want to stop and restart the same container in the future. In this case, you no longer need the container, so you can delete it from your subscription.

CHAPTER 6 **Shipping Docker Containers in Azure** 125

CHECKING YOUR UNDERSTANDING

As your guide through Azure, I find it absolutely crucial that you understand why you're taking these steps and why you should care. If you're a web developer, you'll want to test your site code against a running web server. In the demo in this section, you used an existing IIS container image at Docker Hub.

What I want you to think of next is what happens if your team wants to use its own customized Docker images rather than the public Docker Hub.

Great question! You can do that with the ACR, which is the next stop on this Docker-in-Azure trolley ride.

Storing Images in Azure Container Registry

I want to be respectful of your network bandwidth, so in this section, you'll push the (relatively) small hello-world container you pulled from Docker Hub in an earlier section to your new container registry.

Azure Container Registry (ACR) is a cloud-hosted repository for Docker images. ACR provides a centralized storage/management location for your team's images; these images are accessible only to Azure users to whom you give proper permissions.

Deploying a container registry

Before you push a container to ACR, you need to deploy the registry. Follow these steps:

1. **In the Azure portal, browse to the Container Registries blade, and click Add. The Create Container Registry form appears.**

2. **Complete the Create Container Registry form.**

   Following are the settings you need to address:

   - *Registry Name:* You can choose any name for your registry as long as it's globally unique. Azure will not let you proceed if you happen to choose a name that's already in use.

   - *Subscription, Resource Group, and Location:* Choose your subscription and desired resource group and Azure region.

- *Admin User:* Enable this option. Doing so will make authenticating to your registry easier.

- *SKU:* Choose Basic. SKU is short for *stock-keeping unit,* and Basic is the lowest-cost ACR pricing tier. The Standard and Premium SKUs offer higher performance and scale.

3. **Click Create to submit the deployment.**

   In most cases, Azure completes the deployment in less than one minute.

4. **When deployment is complete, open your new registry in the Azure portal and note the content of the Login Server field.**

   You'll need this DNS name in the next section, where you push a container image to the registry. The registry takes the name *<your-registry-name>.* azurecr.io.

Pushing an image to a new container registry

To show you how to push an image to a container registry, I'm using the hello-world image you worked with in "Setting up Docker on your workstation" earlier in this chapter. To push an image to a container registry, follow these steps:

1. **Obtain your admin credentials from your registry's Access Keys settings blade.**

   I show you this blade in Figure 6-5. Specifically, you'll need to note the Username field, which should be your registry name, and one of the two passwords. It doesn't matter which password you copy; you need one to complete Step 2.

2. **Open a command prompt session and log in to your container registry using the** docker login **command.**

   Supply the registry short name (twwiley, in my case) as the user name and the previously copied password as the password. Here's the command:

   ```
   docker login twwiley.azurecr.io
   ```

   If all goes well, you see a Login succeeded status message.

3. **Define a tag for the hello-world image.**

   A tag looks like <owner-name>/<image-name>, but in this case, the owner is the registry. Here's the command I use for my twwiley registry:

   ```
   docker tag hello-world twwiley.azurecr.io/hello-world
   ```

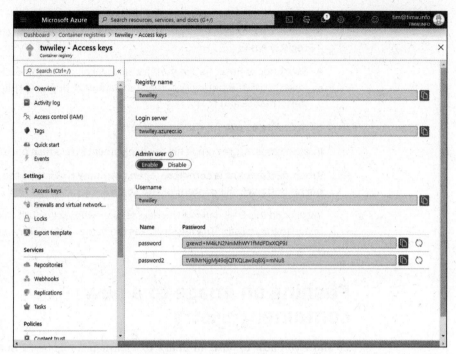

FIGURE 6-5:
Retrieving admin
credentials from
our Azure
Container
Registry.

4. **Push the hello-world image to your registry.**

To do this, use this command:

```
docker push twwiley.azurecr.io/hello-world
```

The amount of time that this process takes depends upon your upstream
network bandwidth to Azure.

5. **Verify that the hello-world image appears in your container registry.**

To do so, navigate to the registry's Repositories blade. You'll find that the Azure
portal doesn't give you too many options for what you can do with this
container image. The implication is you'll interact with the image by using the
Docker CLI, an automation tool, or a tool chain.

Pulling the repository image via ACI

Once you've placed a Docker image into a registry, you can use the docker pull
command to download the image and spawn containers on your local system
based on the image.

TECHNICAL STUFF

HOW THIS STUFF WORKS IN THE REAL WORLD

Consider how a development team might stitch together solutions by using ACIs and ACRs. The dev team, working in conjunction with the ops team (DevOps), might place all assets and associated Dockerfiles in a central source-code repository.

Automatically, on a schedule, or manually, the team can push new and/or updated Docker container image builds to their registry. Then, when a developer needs to start a new container, he or she can do so from ACI, either automatically, on schedule, or as needed. For now, you should know that Azure DevOps is a platform from which you can orchestrate the entire container life cycle in an almost completely automated process.

In this section, you'll run the registry-housed hello-world container image from the ACI service. To do so, follow these steps:

1. **Navigate to the Container Instances blade, and add a new container instance.**

2. **Specify the image type, image name, and OS type.**

   Here's the info:

   - *Image Type:* Choose Private when you're pulling the image from a private, Azure-based container registry; otherwise, choose Public.

   - *Image Name:* For my registry, I use twwiley.azurecr.io/hello-world. Substitute your own registry name.

   - *Image Registry:* Add your login server, user name, and password.

   - *OS Type:* Select the OS you're using.

3. **Submit the deployment by clicking Review + Create and then clicking Create.**

   You don't need to worry about networking, tagging, and the like.

4. **If the deployment fails, read the operation details.**

   ARM may validate yet still fail the deployment. If this happens, as in the case of any failed deployment, read all the operational details that Azure offers.

Figure 6-6 shows a failed ACI deployment. The banner explains the problem in plain English. In this case, Linux was specified as the container type instead of Windows. You can also click Operation Details to get more detailed feedback from ARM.

A failed deployment is no big deal, though. You can rerun deployment templates as many times as you need to until you get it right. Just click the Redeploy button shown in Figure 6-6. By default, deployments don't delete existing resources. Instead, the template picks up where it left off, so to speak, until your deployment matches the underlying template definition.

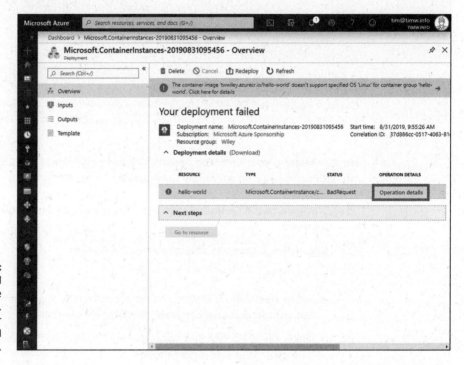

FIGURE 6-6:
Don't be fearful when an Azure deployment fails. Read the error messages, and learn from them.

TECHNICAL STUFF

Another place to research deployment details (successful or failed) is the Resource Groups blade in the Azure portal. Open a resource group, and navigate to the Deployments blade. Every deployment in Azure is recorded for your reference and/ or troubleshooting pleasure.

Everything I've explained about container support in Azure is well and good, but frankly, ACI suffers a fatal flaw: It has no orchestration. The chances are good that your developers will need to deploy multiple containers simultaneously and manage them as a group. Your business may also require your containers to be capable of horizontal scaling to adapt to user load and to be highly available. In other words, the ACI service is fine for relatively simple container deployments, but you'll need a container orchestration platform for anything beyond the most basic of container use cases in business.

To accomplish these requirements and more, you need a container orchestration platform, such as AKS.

Introducing Azure Kubernetes Service

AKS began life as Azure Container Service (ACS), which supported multiple container orchestration platforms, including Kubernetes, Swarm, and DC/OS. The downsides of ACS were its complexity and the fact that most customers wanted first-class support for Kubernetes only. Therefore, although you may see an occasional reference to ACS in the Azure portal or elsewhere, I want you to ignore them and focus exclusively on AKS.

I don't have the space to walk through how to deploy and manage an AKS cluster. Instead, I'll describe the AKS architecture, explain some of its benefits, and give you a bird's-eye perspective on using AKS in Azure.

REMEMBER

Developers don't necessarily start containers because they're fun to use; developers start containers because they're practical. Containers host application components such as web servers or a database servers and then form application solutions. Therefore, I want you to relate the words *container* and *application* from now on.

AKS architecture

Figure 6-7 shows the basic elements of AKS:

>> **Master node:** Microsoft abstracts the control plane (called the *master node* in Kubernetes nomenclature), so you can focus on your worker nodes and pods. This hosted Platform as a Service (PaaS) platform is one reason why many businesses love AKS. The master node is responsible for scheduling all the communications between Kubernetes and your underlying cluster.

>> **Worker node:** In AKS, the worker nodes are the VMs that make up your cluster. The cluster gives you lots of parallel computing, the ability to move pods between nodes easily, to perform rolling updates of nodes without taking down the entire cluster, and so on. One option is using ACI to serve as worker nodes.

 Figure 6-7 also shows ACR, from which AKS can pull stored images. Isn't all this Azure integration compelling?

>> **Pod:** The pod is the smallest deployable unit in the AKS ecosystem. A pod may contain one Docker container, or it might contain a bunch of containers that you need to stay together, communicate with one another, and behave as a cohesive unit.

Are you with me so far?

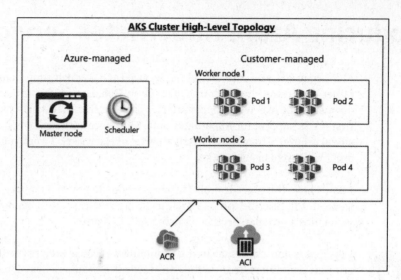

FIGURE 6-7:
AKS high-level architecture.

AKS administration notes

Before I move on, I'll review how developers and administrators interact with AKS. From a control-plane perspective, you have AZR, with which you can protect your AKS cluster with role-based access control, upgrade your Kubernetes version, scale out the cluster, add or remove worker nodes, and so on.

From the application-plane perspective, Microsoft wanted to ensure that customers don't have to learn a new tool set to work with containers in AKS.

kubectl command-line tool

Most Kubernetes professionals use the kubectl (generally pronounced *KOOB-see-tee-el*, *KOOB-control*, or *KOOB-cuttle*) to interact with their Kubernetes cluster and its pods programmatically. If you have Azure CLI installed on your workstation, you can install kubectl easily by issuing the following command:

```
az aks install-cli
```

In fact, Azure CLI seems to borrow quite a bit from kubectl syntax in terms of the app context command workflow. To list your running pods (containers) with kubectl, for example, run

```
$ kubectl get pods

                               READY    STATUS     RESTARTS    AGE
  azure-database-3406967446-nmpcf    1/1      Running    0           25m
  azure-web-3309479140-3dfh0         1/1      Running    0           13m
```

Kubernetes Web UI

The Kubernetes Web UI is a graphical dashboard that gives administrators and developers a robust control surface. Figure 6-8 shows the interface.

FIGURE 6-8:
The Kubernetes
Web UI
Dashboard.

Once again, you should use Azure CLI to connect to the dashboard; doing so isn't possible from the Azure portal. Here's the relevant command:

```
az aks browse --resource-group myResourceGroup --name myAKSCluster
```

TECHNICAL STUFF

The `az aks browse` command creates a proxy between your workstation and the AKS cluster running in Azure; it provides the connection URL in its output. The typical connection URL is http://127.0.0.1:8001.

Using Containers with Azure App Service

I'll close this chapter by showing you how to combine containers with Azure App Service. (Chapter 7 takes a deep dive into Azure App Service.)

Azure Web App for Containers allows you to plug your existing container-based apps into an Azure App Service app. For businesses that aren't using an orchestration/scaling platform like AKS, this feature is a great way to autoscale an app without additional investment and complexity.

"But you can't host non-.NET apps in App Service, right?" you ask. That's incorrect, I'm happy to report. Your containers can use any supported run-time environment, including the following:

>> .NET Core

>> Node.js

>> PHP

>> Java

>> Python

>> Ruby

This procedure uses the Cloud Shell in the Azure portal. To create a new Azure App Service web app that uses a Linux container pulled from the Docker Hub as its code base, follow these steps:

1. **In the Azure portal, start Cloud Shell, and select the Bash environment.**

   It doesn't matter which shell you choose, because Azure CLI is available in both.

TIP

   Although you're creating this App Service web app by using Azure CLI, you could have used the Azure portal, PowerShell, a software development kit (SDK), or the Azure REST API. Because Microsoft makes so many updates to the Azure portal, you may be better off focusing primarily on Azure CLI or PowerShell to have a more stable and familiar deployment environment.

2. **Use Azure CLI to create a new resource group.**

   Use your own resource group name and location. This is what I used:

   ```
   az group create --name containerApp --location "East US 2"
   ```

3. **Create an app service plan to power the web app.**

   The app service plan defines the underlying compute layer (VM) that hosts your web application. Here, you create a Linux-powered service plan by using the B1 VM instance size:

   ```
   az appservice plan create --name myAppServicePlan
           --resource-group containerApp --sku B1
       --is-linux
   ```

4. Define the web app.

I named my app go-container-704 to make the name globally unique and pulled the microsoft/azure-appservices-go-quickstart container image from Docker Hub. You can examine the container by visiting `https://hub.docker.com/r/microsoft/azure-appservices-go-quickstart/`.

```
az webapp create --resource-group containerApp
          --plan myAppServicePlan --name go-container-704
          --deployment-container-image-name microsoft/
    azure-appservices-go-quickstart
```

TIP

You can examine the container by visiting `https://hub.docker.com/r/microsoft/azure-appservices-go-quickstart`.

5. Browse to the app.

The format of the URL for projects is http:// http://<*app_name*>.azurewebsites.net/hello. Use that address (substituting your own app name).

6. Verify that you see the simple `Hello, world!` message shown in Figure 6-9.

Your new container-backed app appears on the App Services blade in the Azure portal.

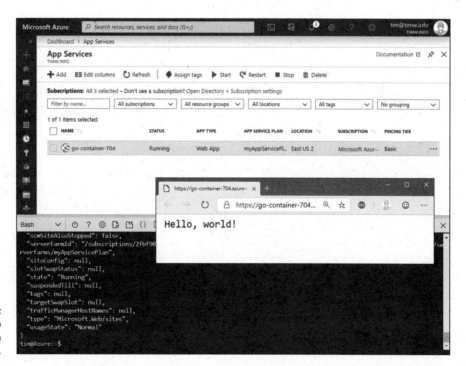

FIGURE 6-9: A new Azure web app powered by a Docker container.

**TECHNICAL
STUFF**

CLOUD SHELL IS A CONTAINER

It's timely and relevant for me to inform you now that when you open Cloud Shell in the Azure portal or directly via https://shell.azure.com, you're actually attaching to a Docker container start for you from the closest geographical location. The bash container is a virtualized bash shell session, and the PowerShell container is a virtualized PowerShell core (pwsh) session. Your persistent user data is shared across both container types and is located in a file share in your designated storage account.

7. **Clean up the environment.**

   Because you stored this test web app in its own resource group, cleaning up is a breeze. Run one final Azure CLI command, and confirm your choice:

   ```
   az group delete --name containerApp
   ```

3

Deploying Platform Resources to Microsoft Azure

IN THIS PART . . .

Deploying and configuring App Service apps

Comprehending "serverless computing" in Azure by working with Azure WebJobs, Functions, and Logic Apps

Characterizing relational and nonrelational database options in Azure

Gaining hands-on familiarity with Azure SQL Database and Cosmos DB

Chapter **7**

Deploying and Configuring Azure App Service Apps

O ne of my many joys in working as a Microsoft Azure solutions consultant is watching my customers' faces when they discover the power and agility of Azure Platform as a Service (PaaS) resources; Azure App Service is chief among them.

Azure App Service frees you up to focus on your line-of-business applications instead of managing VM infrastructure. App Service provides hyperscale and seamlessly integrates with other Azure products like storage accounts and Azure SQL Database databases.

By the end of this chapter, you'll understand App Service's place in the Azure product portfolio. You'll also be comfortable creating and configuring App Service web apps. Particular programming languages are beyond the scope of this book, of course, so I focus on the hows and whys of App Service and leave the code base to you and your team.

Introducing Azure App Service

In a nutshell, App Service is a Hypertext Transfer Protocol (HTTP)-based web application hosting service. Think of GoDaddy, but with much more power. The idea is that if you're willing to surrender full control app's underlying infrastructure (which is what Azure Virtual Machines is for) you'll receive in exchange

>> Global replication and geoavailability

>> Dynamic autoscaling

>> Native integration into continuous integration/continuous deployment pipelines

Yes, App Service uses virtual machines (VMs) under the hood, but you never have to worry about maintaining them; Microsoft does that for you. Instead, you focus nearly exclusively on your source code and your application.

DEVELOPMENT FRAMEWORKS AND COMPUTE ENVIRONMENTS

I can't devote space in this book to programming, but you should know that App Service supports several development frameworks, including the following:

- .NET Framework
- .NET Core
- Java
- Ruby
- Node.js
- Python
- PHP

You can use any of the following as your underlying compute environment in App Service:

- Windows Server VM
- Linux VM
- Docker container

This chapter focuses almost exclusively on web apps, but in Chapter 8 you meet other App Service family members.

Web apps

The static or dynamic *web application* is the most commonly used option in App Service. Your hosted web apps can be linked to cloud- or on-premises databases, API web services, and content delivery networks.

API apps

An *application programming interface* (API) is a mechanism that offers programmatic (noninteractive) access to your application by using HTTP requests and responses — a programming paradigm known as Representational State Transfer (REST). Nowadays, Microsoft supports API apps from App Service and the API Management service.

Mobile apps

A *mobile app* provides the back end to an iOS or Android application. Azure mobile apps provide features most smartphone consumers have grown to expect as part of the mobile apps they use, such as social media sign-in, push notifications, and offline data synchronization.

Logic apps

A *logic app* provides a way for developers to build business workflows without having to know all the underlying APIs in different services. You might create a logic app that triggers whenever someone mentions your company's name on Twitter, for example. Then this app may perform several actions, such as posting a notification message in your sales department's Slack channel or creating a record in your customer relationship management database.

Function apps

A *function app* allows developers to run specific code at specific times without worrying about the underlying infrastructure. That's why function apps are called *serverless* applications, or *Code as a Service (CaaS)* solutions. One of my consulting clients has a function app that sends a confirmation email message to a prospective customer whenever that user creates a new account on his website.

Function apps support the C#, F#, and Java programming languages.

REMEMBER

Both logic apps and function apps operate on the basis of a trigger. This trigger could be a manual execution command, a time schedule, or a discrete operation that occurs inside or outside Azure.

App Service logical components

Figure 7-1 shows the components that make up App Service. An App Service web app is powered by an associated App Service plan. This plan is an abstraction layer; you control how much virtual compute you need to power your application or applications, and you dynamically scale vertically to suit your performance requirements and budgetary needs.

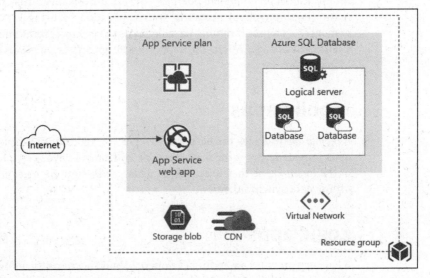

FIGURE 7-1:
App Service required and optional components.

In Figure 7-1, the App Service plan is the only required component. You can extend the app's capabilities by integrating it with any of the following:

>> **Storage account:** An App Service plan has persistent storage, but many developers like to use a flexible storage account for additional space.

>> **Virtual network:** You can link an App Service app to a virtual network — perhaps to connect your web app to a database running on a VM.

>> **Databases:** Most web apps nowadays use relational, nonrelational, and/or in-memory databases to store temporary or persistent data.

>> **Content delivery network:** You can place static website assets in a storage account and let Azure distribute the assets globally. This way, your users get a much faster experience because their browsers pull your site content from a low-latency, geographically close source.

App Service plans are organized in three increasingly powerful (and expensive) tiers:

>> **Dev/Test:** F- and B-series VMs with minimal compute and no extra features. This compute level is the least expensive but offers few features and shouldn't be used for production apps.

>> **Production:** S- and P-series VMs with a good balance of compute power and features. This tier should be your App Service starting point.

>> **Isolated:** Called the App Service Environment and very expensive; Microsoft allocates hardware so that your web app is screened from the public Internet.

You can move within or between tiers as necessary. This capability is one of the greatest attributes of public cloud services. Figure 7-2 shows an App Service plan.

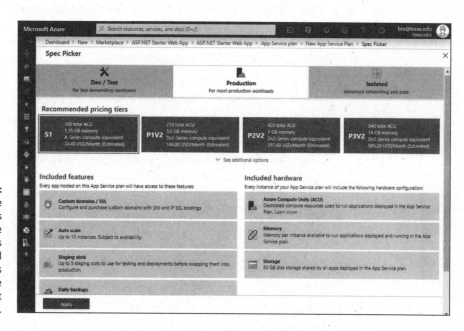

FIGURE 7-2: An App Service plan provides raw compute power as well as potentially useful website features such as autoscale and deployment slots.

TECHNICAL STUFF

Azure uses the Azure Compute Unit as a standardized method to classify compute power. You see it referenced in Azure VMs, App Service, and any other Azure resource that uses VMs. Having a standardized performance metric is crucial, because Microsoft uses several types of hardware in its data centers.

WARNING

Just because you can associate more than one web app into a single App Service plan doesn't mean that you should. Sure, you can save money (the App Service plan incurs run-time costs based on instance size), but the more apps you pack into a single plan, the greater the burden on the underlying VM.

Deploying Your First Web App

In this section, you get down to business by deploying two simple web applications, the first from the Azure portal via Azure Marketplace and the second from Visual Studio via a built-in project template. You need to have both Visual Studio 2019 and the Azure workload installed.

TIP

You can download and use Visual Studio 2019 Community Edition for free; grab the software at https://visualstudio.microsoft.com/vs.

Deploying from the Azure portal

Follow these steps to deploy your first web app from the Azure portal:

1. **In the Azure portal menu, select Create a Resource; then search for** ASP.NET Empty Web App. **Next, click Create.**

For this exercise, choose the ASP.NET Empty Web App template. This web app contains example code to give you something to look at and interact with.

2. **Complete the ASP.NET Empty Web App creation form as follows (see Figure 7-3):**

- *App Name:* Your app name needs to be globally unique, because Microsoft places it in the azurewebsites.net DNS domain. But you can and should bind your own corporate DNS domain to your site as soon as possible after you create the web app.

- *App Service Plan/Location:* Create a new App Service plan in your home location. Choose S1 Standard, which is the smallest VM instance size that unlocks production-level features.

- *Application Insights:* Select the Disable option. (I discuss web app monitoring later in this chapter in the "Monitoring a Web App" section.)

3. **Click Create to submit the deployment.**

4. **Open the web app.**

To do this, browse to the new web app's Overview blade, and select the contents of the URL property. The web app should display boilerplate content provided by Microsoft.

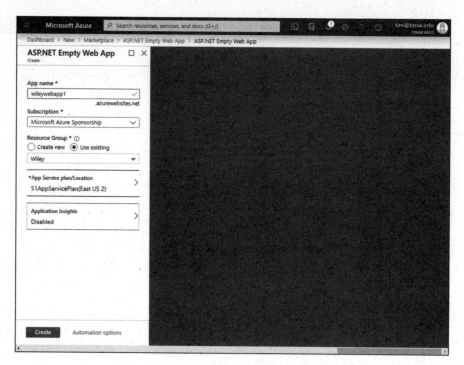

FIGURE 7-3:
Creating an Azure App Service web app.

Configuring Git

TECHNICAL STUFF

Git is a free, open-source, cross-platform version-control system invented by Linux originator Linus Torvalds. It's a distributed system in which each developer has a full copy of the repository; optionally, developers push their changes to an upstream origin repository.

The idea of source-code control is simple: Multiple developers commit changes to a single shared code base. How do you preserve code history, know which developer made which change, and prevent developers from stepping on one another's work? Git solves these problems.

Even if your job role isn't development, you should get familiar with Git, because it touches just about every kind of Azure work. You can find plenty of hands-on, interactive Git tutorials online; check them out to see which resonates best with your learning style. You also could read *GitHub For Dummies*, by Sarah Guthals and Phil Haack (John Wiley & Sons, Inc.).

Git fits in perfectly with Azure App Service; in fact, App Service apps can host their own Git repository, as shown in Figure 7-4.

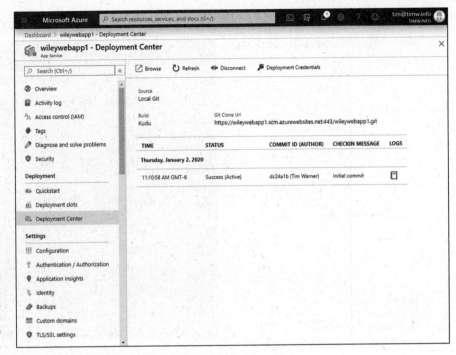

FIGURE 7-4:
Git version control integrates seamlessly with Azure App Service.

I want to show you how you can combine Git with App Service. Visual Studio 2019 Community Edition includes a Git client. To use it to set up Git for use with App Service, follow these steps:

1. **Open Visual Studio, and click the Continue Without Code button in the Startup window.**

2. **Choose View ⇨ Team Explorer to open the Team Explorer Visual Studio extension.**

3. **From the Project list at the top of the extension, choose Settings.**

4. **In the Settings pane, Click Global Settings.**

5. **In the Git Settings pane, fill out the User Name and Email Address fields. Click Update to commit your changes.**

6. **(Optional) Change the location where Visual Studio saves your Git repositories.**

7. **Leave the other Git options at their default settings, and click the Home button to see Git project settings.**

TIP

If you don't see the elements that I describe in this procedure, you may need to choose Git as Visual Studio's source-control provider. To do so, choose Tools⇨Options, and find the Source Control⇨Plug-in Selection option. Choose Git as your source-control plug-in, and click OK to confirm. Figure 7-5 shows the interface.

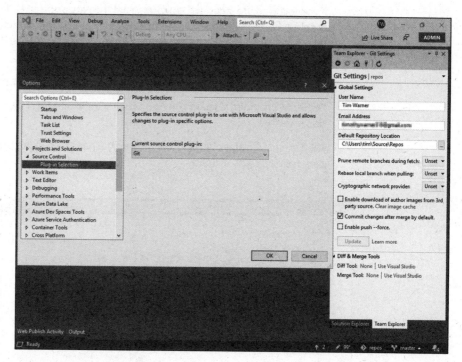

FIGURE 7-5: Ensuring that Visual Studio will use Git for source code version control.

Connecting to a web app from Visual Studio

You use Visual Studio to connect and work with your new Azure-based web app.

This is the workflow:

1. Create a local Git repository for the app in Azure.

2. Clone the Azure-based repository to your local workstation.

3. Work with the app locally, and periodically push changes up to Azure.

It's outside the scope of this book to go into Git in depth, but I'll do my best to ensure that you don't get lost.

Creating a Git repository for a web app

Follow these steps to create a local Git repository for your web app's sample source code:

1. In your web app settings in the Azure portal, select Deployment Center.

If you followed the steps in "Deploying from the Azure portal" earlier in this chapter, the Azure Marketplace template you chose has already created a Git repository. Handy! But click `Disconnect` so that you can create a local Git repository.

2. In Deployment Center, choose Local Git as your source-code provider.

3. For Build Provider, choose the App Service build service. Figure 7-6 shows this interface.

The K stands for *Kudu*, which is the engine that handles building your code and performing publish actions.

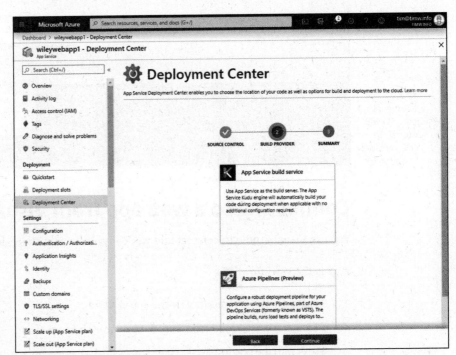

FIGURE 7-6: Adding a local Git repository to an Azure App Service web application.

4. **On the Deployment Center blade, copy the clone URL in the Repository field.**

Typically, Git clone URLs end with the `.git` file extension. My wileywebapp1 Git clone URL, for example, is

```
https://wileywebapp1.scm.azurewebsites.net:443/wileywebapp1.git
```

5. **Open Azure Cloud Shell and create a Git deployment credential.**

This credential is the identity you'll use to authenticate to the Azure-based Git repository. I recommend using Azure Cloud Shell for this purpose. When you're in the session, run the following command from the command line, substituting your own username and (strong) password:

```
az webapp deployment user set --user-name wileydev --password P@$$w0rd111
```

Make a note of both the username and password, because you'll need them for the next step.

6. **On the Team Explorer pane of Visual Studio, select Manage Connections (the power-plug icon).**

7. **Select Clone in the Local Git Repositories section.**

Paste in your App Service clone URL (Step 4), and verify the local directory path and folder name.

8. **Click Clone.**

A clone operation is simply a file copy; in this case, you're copying the Azure-based code based to your local computer.

REMEMBER

9. **Enter your Git deployment credentials when Visual Studio prompts you for them.**

You see the cloned repository on the Solution Explorer pane.

10. **On the Team Explorer pane, choose File ➪ New ➪ Project from Existing Code.**

The Create a New Project dialog box opens.

11. **Locate the closest match to your existing web app.**

You deployed an ASP.NET web application in App Service, so the logical choice is ASP.NET Web Application (.NET Framework).

12. **Give the local version a name, such as 1.0, and a save location.**

13. **Select the Empty template.**

14. **Leave all the other settings at their default values and click OK.**

As shown in Figure 7-7, clicking the Switch Views button in Solution Explorer (circled in the figure) toggles between Git repository view (the folder on the right side) and Visual Studio view (the solution view on the left side).

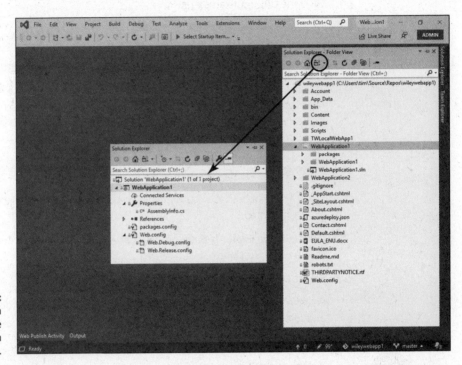

FIGURE 7-7:
Working with
an App Service
web app in
Visual Studio.

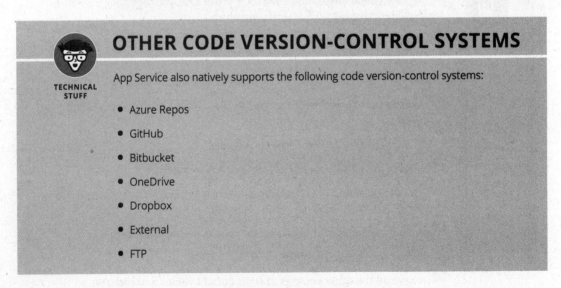

OTHER CODE VERSION-CONTROL SYSTEMS

TECHNICAL STUFF

App Service also natively supports the following code version-control systems:

- Azure Repos
- GitHub
- Bitbucket
- OneDrive
- Dropbox
- External
- FTP

Pushing a code change to Azure

Without writing a single character of C#, you substantially changed the structure of the ASP.NET Starter Web App when you turned it into a Visual Studio solution. Verify this by switching to the Team Explorer pane's Home page and clicking Changes. You'll see a detailed list of any files containing changes.

After you've made a change in Visual Studio, you need to push that code change to Azure. Follow these steps to change the web app's home page and push all the changes to Azure:

1. **In Solution Explorer, click the Switch Views button (refer to Figure 7-7) to switch to Folder view.**

2. **Open** `Default.cshtml`.

3. **On line 3, change the code to the following:**

   ```
   Page.Title = "Production Slot Home Page"
   ```

4. **Switch to Team Explorer, and click the Home button.**

5. **Click the Changes button.**

   You'll see a lot of changes because you converted the code base to a Visual Studio project and solution.

6. **Enter a meaningful commit message, and choose Commit All and Push from the drop-down list.**

   Figure 7-8 shows the interface in Figure 7-7.

TIP

   If you receive a `permission denied` error on `db.lock`, as I did on my development system, find the affected file in the Changes list, right-click it, and choose Ignore This Extension from the shortcut menu.

TECHNICAL STUFF

   How to compose a quality code-commit message is a fervent discussion among developers. What's most important, in my opinion, is that your message concisely describe the effect of your change.

7. **Verify that the Azure web app is current.**

   When you load the page in your web browser (do a hard refresh if you see a cached page copy), you should see Production Slot Home Page instead of Home Page.

TIP

   Alternatively, you can inspect the source code by using the App Service Editor. Select App Service Editor in your web app's Settings list and then click Go to view your source files in App Service Editor (see Figure 7-9). The ability to edit your app's source code directly in the browser is convenient and potentially job-saving during a troubleshooting emergency.

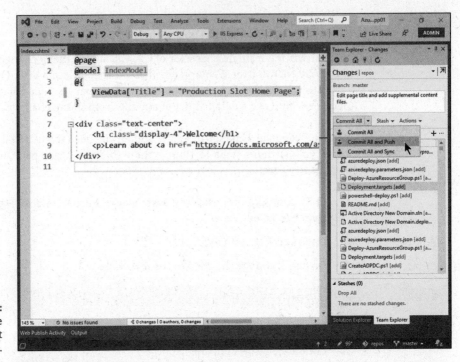

FIGURE 7-8:
Committing code changes using Git and Visual Studio.

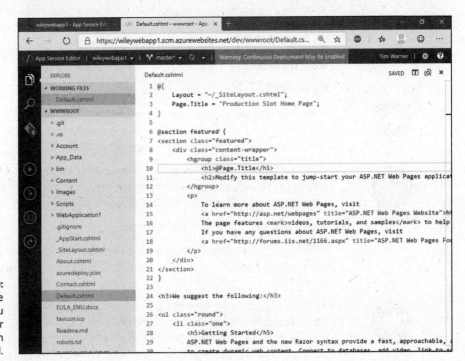

FIGURE 7-9:
App Service Editor allows you to edit your source code in the Azure portal.

Deploying from Visual Studio

I'd be remiss if I didn't show you how to start your web app from your local computer and Visual Studio and then publish directly to App Service. This section explains how to create another simple ASP.NET web app, publish it to Azure, and publish again to a second deployment slot.

Creating a new web app project in Visual Studio

Follow these steps to create a solution in Visual Studio:

1. **Close any existing folders or solutions.**

You can close recent file and solutions from the File menu. Close the Start window if it appears automatically.

2. **Choose File ⇨ New ⇨ Project.**

3. **Choose ASP.NET Core Web Application.**

In the previous exercise, you used a .NET Framework web app. Target .NET Core this time around in the name of forward thinking and cross-platform compatibility.

4. **Give your project/solution a short name and a save location.**

Make sure to keep Azure global uniqueness in mind. The project name has little or nothing to do with the ultimate DNS name under which users will reach the app.

5. **Click Create to move to the template selection process.**

6. **Select the Web Application template, and click Create.**

7. **Deselect the Configure for HTTPS option, and ensure that Authentication is set to No Authentication.**

8. **Run the web application by choosing Debug ⇨ Start Debugging.**

Visual Studio includes a built-in web server called IIS Express. Debugging is the process of running your app in a local environment and resolving any errors or performance issues that arise. In this example, you simply start and stop debugging so you can see what the process looks like.

If you're prompted to accept the application's self-signed digital certificate, do so.

9. **To end the debugging session, close the browser tab that hosts the app.**

Publishing to App Service

The Git publishing workflow is one of many ways to publish a web app to App Service. You can also publish to Azure directly from Visual Studio. To do so, follow these steps:

1. In Solution Explorer, right-click your project, and choose Publish from the shortcut menu.

A wizard opens, allowing you to choose among the following publishing targets:

- App Service (Windows VM)
- App Service (Linux VM)
- Azure IaaS VM
- IIS, FTP
- Folder

2. Select App Service as your publishing target, select Create New, and then click Publish (see Figure 7-10).

You'll be prompted to authenticate to Azure if you aren't already signed in.

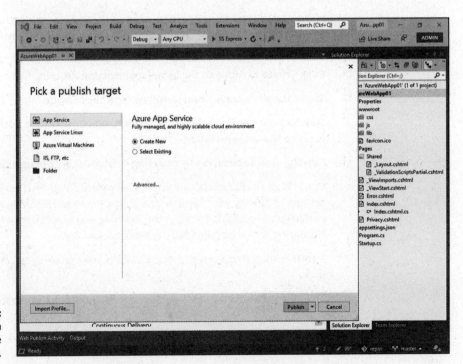

FIGURE 7-10: Publishing a web app to Azure App Service.

3. **Complete the App Service - Create New form.**

I want to draw your attention to two deployment properties:

- *Hosting Plan:* This means App Service plan.

- *Application Insights:* Select None.

    Application Insights is a robust web app monitoring platform that I talk about in the "Monitoring a Web App" section later in this chapter.

TIP

Visual Studio uses a method called Web Deploy to perform the web app publication. Essentially, Visual Studio packages your app and its dependencies into a ZIP archive; transfers the package to Azure; and hands it off to the Kudu build service, which deploys the web app into App Service.

TECHNICAL
STUFF

Understanding deployment slots

Your development team may want to maintain your App Service app throughout its life cycle directly in Azure. In other words, they may want to perform development and testing in one app instance while simultaneously keeping the production instance online.

Deployment slots give you this capability. As long as your App Service plan runs in at least the S tier, you can create one or more additional deployment slots to suit your app-staging needs. Figure 7-11 shows how deployment slots work.

Every App Service app starts with a deployment slot called (appropriately enough) Production. On the Deployment Slots blade, you can create another slot and clone the app settings from the production slot.

It's crucial to understand is that each deployment slot contains a full instance of the application. Keep this fact in mind with regard to your App Service plan; the more slots you have, the heavier the burden on the plan.

REMEMBER

FIGURE 7-11:
Deployment slots allow you to move among development, staging, and production environments seamlessly.

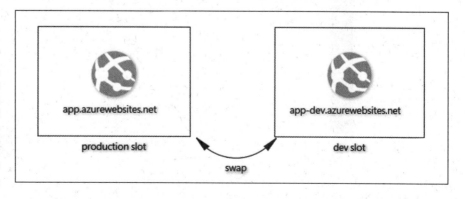

Compare the URLs shown in Figure 7-11. Notice that Azure creates a slightly different host name for the named deployment slots. Specifically, Azure appends a hyphen and the slot name to the original web app's host name.

When I'm working with the web app's production slot, the URL I use is

```
https://app.azurewebsites.net
```

When I'm working with my dev slot instance, the URL is

```
https://app-dev.azurewebsites.net
```

You can see this behavior in the Azure portal by inspecting Figure 7-12. Azure puts a strong emphasis on PRODUCTION — the default deployment slot. This is your default slot, and it cannot be deleted.

Remember, the main reason you use deployment slots is to perform phased roll-outs of your App Service app. Your developers work on the dev slot, for example, and then you perform a slot swap to move the changed code to the public-facing production slot.

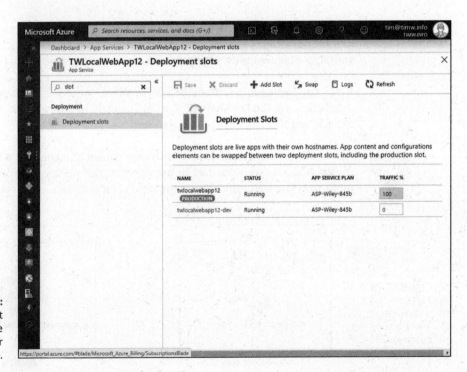

FIGURE 7-12:
Each deployment slot is a separate instance of your web app.

Figure 7-12 shows a Traffic % field, which is useful when you need to perform testing with your live users. Azure sends end-user traffic to the slots based on the percentages you specify on the Deployment Slots blade.

As shown in Figure 7-13, you can perform a slot swap in any direction from the Deployment Slots blade of your web application. What's cool about this process is that the Azure portal shows you which settings will change after the swap. You may have different database connection strings stored in each slot, for example; in that case, you wouldn't want the swap to affect slot-specific settings.

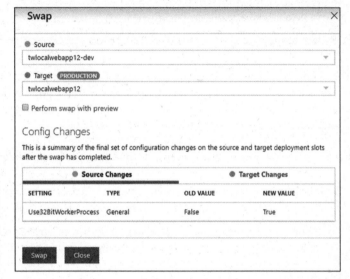

FIGURE 7-13:
The Azure portal gives you visibility into the ramifications of a deployment-slot swap.

Speaking of which, the Perform Swap with Preview option makes the swap a two-phase operation. In the first phase, you see which slot-specific settings will change if you complete the swap operation. In the second phase, you can cancel or proceed with the slot swap.

Configuring a Web App

In this section, I show you some of the most common configuration choices for App Service web apps.

Customizing app settings

If you visit the Configuration blade of your App Service app, you'll see four application settings tabs:

>> **Application Settings:** Application-related key/value pairs; data source connection strings

>> **General Settings:** The application run-time environment(s); whether FTP is allowed; HTTP version

>> **Default Documents:** Which file types Azure should look for when determining default web app display document(s)

>> **Path Mappings:** Mapping handlers (script processors) for different file types

The primary theme of PaaS is you give up full-stack control of the underlying VM in exchange for massive scale and agility. These configuration settings, along with any configuration-related source code that your developers add, are about as close as you can get to server configuration under the hood.

Keep two key factors in mind when you configure these app settings:

>> You store your application key/value settings and database connection string data here instead of in text files (such as web.config for ASP.NET applications).

>> Be sure to mark deployment-slot settings that shouldn't travel with the application during a deployment-slot swap. When you edit a setting or connection string, you'll see the Deployment Slot Setting check box.

Adding a custom domain

Microsoft defines all your App Service apps in its own azurewebsites.net Domain Name System (DNS) domain. That's convenient inasmuch as you can leverage HTTP connections courtesy of Microsoft's *.azurewebsites.net wildcard TLS/SSL digital certificate. But you'll likely want to add your own DNS domain.

TIP

Don't even think about attempting to unbind your web app from the azurewebsites.net domain. Because this domain is how Azure recognizes your web app, you're stuck with that DNS name unless and until you delete the web app. Sorry!

Follow these steps to add your own DNS domain to your web app:

1. In your web app settings, browse to the Custom Domains blade, and set the HTTPS Only setting to Off.

To get to your web app settings, open the web app's settings in Azure portal and select Configuration.

Unless or until you're using your own Secure Sockets Layer (SSL) certificate that matches your custom domain, you don't want to enforce HTTPS.

2. **Click Add Custom domain, add your domain name, and click Validate. The Add Custom Domain blade appears.**

I'm stating the obvious, I think, but this domain needs to be a DNS domain that you own, or at least one for which you have access to the zone file.

3. **Edit your DNS zone file to add a verification/mapping resource record.**

What you're doing is proving to Microsoft that you own the domain in question. This process requires you to log in to your domain registrar's website and add a resource record to your zone.

To prove domain ownership, you need to create a temporary DNS resource record. Azure checks your domain to see whether the record exists. If it does, then Azure "knows" that you must own the domain because only owners can add resource records to their own domain.

- *Host (A) Record:* I advise against selecting this option, which maps your custom domain to your web app's public Internet Protocol (IP). The issue is that your name resolution will break if Microsoft hands your app a new public IP address.

- *CNAME Record:* I recommend selecting this option because you're mapping your custom domain's DNS to point to your web app's DNS host name under azurewebsites.net. The mapping remains valid even if Microsoft changes your app's public IP address.

In my environment, for example, I want to map zoeywarner.info to twlocalwebapp12.azurewebsites.net. After I make that change in my DNS zone file and click Validate, it's just a waiting game. The Azure portal may say it could take up to 48 hours for DNS propagation to kick in, but I find that verification normally occurs within minutes.

Of course, you need to purchase your own domain to take these actions on your own.

4. **When validation completes, click Add Custom Domain to complete the process.**

Figure 7-14 shows a completed domain configuration. Take note of the following important elements:

>> The domain is ready for use, but it's not usable with SSL until you bind a matching SSL certificate. Azure portal throws all sorts of scary warnings, as you see.

>> The site remains accessible with HTTP or HTTPS when you use the original DNS name (such as twlocalwebapp12.azurewebsites.net).

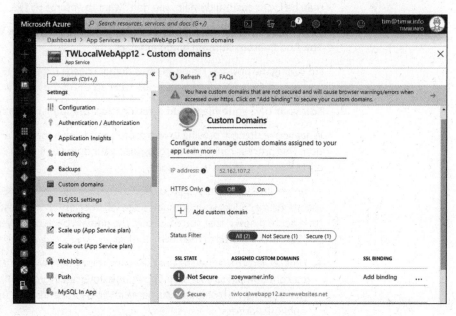

FIGURE 7-14: Adding a custom domain to your App Service app is nice, but you want an SSL certificate to go with it.

Binding a TLS/SSL certificate

A publicly trusted Transport Layer Security/Secure Sockets Layer (TLS/SSL; I'll use just SSL from now) digital certificate provides your web app confidentiality, data integrity, and authentication. I almost always recommend that my customers bind their website certificate to their App Service app as soon as they've added their custom DNS domain.

To bind your certificate to your App Service app, follow these steps:

1. **In your web app settings, navigate to the TLS/SSL Settings blade, and click Add TLS/SSL Binding.**

The TLS/SSL bindings blade appears.

2. **On the TLS/SSL Binding blade, select your custom domain.**

You should see the message No certificates match the selected custom domain.

3. **On the TLS/SSL Bindings blade, select Upload PFX Certificate.**

4. **Browse to your exported PFX certificate, which contains both the public and private key components.**

5. Decrypt the archive with your password, and click Upload.

TECHNICAL
STUFF

For dev/testing purposes, you can create your own self-signed certificate by using the New-SelfSignedCertificate PowerShell cmdlet. You can also use free, publicly trusted certificates by using Let's Encrypt. Microsoft employee Scott Hanselman wrote an excellent document on using those certificates with App Services; you can read it at https://timw.info/ssl.

6. On the TLS/SSL Binding blade, select the private certificate thumbprint and TLS/SSL type, and click Add Binding to complete the configuration.

In most cases, you'll choose IP-based SSL as your TLS/SSL type. You'll use the Server Name Indication SSL when your digital certificate protects more than one explicitly defined DNS name.

7. Test connectivity to the web app by using HTTPS and your custom domain name.

Figure 7-15 shows a completed configuration.

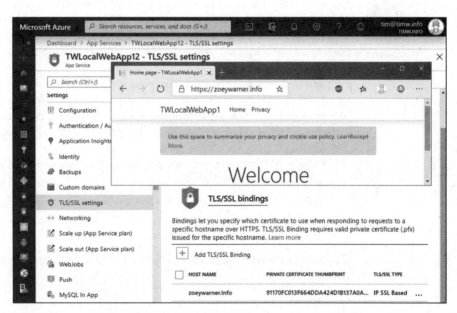

FIGURE 7-15:
This web app is ready to rock with both custom DNS and TLS/SSL in operation.

Configuring autoscaling

Back in the bad old days, if you wanted your on-premises public web servers to handle a predicted usage spike, you normally purchased new hardware. This kind of capital expenditure is a giant waste if the hardware isn't necessary when the spike subsides.

TECHNICAL STUFF

APP SERVICE DOMAINS

As a convenience to its customers, Microsoft partnered with GoDaddy to sell public DNS domains directly from Azure through a service called App Service Domains. Adding domains to Azure products is almost turnkey if you buy the domain from this service. The Azure DNS service allows you to host DNS domains you purchased elsewhere in Azure.

Along the same lines, the App Service Certificates service enables you to purchase and manage publicly trusted SSL certs from the Azure portal. Azure stores the certs in Key Vault and makes it simple to create SSL bindings for your App Service apps.

Instead of purchasing new hardware, you can configure manual or autoscaling for App Service apps.

REMEMBER

You may need to scale up (vertically) your App Service plan before advanced features such as custom domains, SSL certificates, and autoscaling rules become available to you. As this writing, for example, you need at least the S1 plan to use custom domains and SSL and to be able to autoscale up to ten identical instances.

Suppose that you want to configure your web app to scale out from one to three instances, depending on the App Service plan's CPU load over a 10-minute window. Just as important, you want to scale down to your minimum number when the usage spike settles. To complete that configuration, follow these steps:

1. **In your web app settings, select Scale Out (App Service plan) and then click Custom Autoscale.**

   The Custom autoscale options appear. Also notice the Manual Scale option, which instructs Azure Resource Manager to spawn identical web app instances without messing with VMs, DNS, or app configuration — PaaS at its best.

2. **For Scale mode, select Scale Based on a Metric, and configure instance limits.**

   It's important to understand the difference among the three instance limit options:

   - *Minimum:* The smallest number of instances you want running. Note that you're charged for each instance.

   - *Maximum:* The largest number of simultaneous instances you envision needing.

   - *Default:* The value that Azure uses as a fallback if it can't calculate a metric.

3. **Select Add a Rule to define a scale rule.**

   A scale rule is also called a *scale condition*. Use the following settings as a baseline, but feel free to experiment:

- *Time Aggregation:* Average

- *Metric Name:* CPU percentage

- *Dimension Name, Operator, Values:* Instance: = All Values

- *Time Grain Statistic:* Average

- *Operator and Threshold:* Greater than 70

- *Duration:* 10 minutes

- *Action:* Increase count by one instance, with 5-minute cool-down

The cool-down value specifies the amount of time that Azure waits before scaling again.

4. **Click Add.**

You should see your scale condition in the Custom autoscale settings now. You've created one scale condition to define web app scale out, but don't forget about scale in.

5. **Select Add a Scale to create a new metric rule that scales down the cluster when CPU use reaches 40 percent or less.**

TIP

I advise you to rename the scale condition entries so that they're meaningful to you and your team. Click the pencil icon next to an entry to edit it.

Monitoring a Web App

In this section, I briefly explain how to monitor your App Service apps by using Application Insights, an Azure-hosted application performance management platform that provides rich, deep insight into just about any application, whether the app exists in Azure, on-premises, or in another cloud.

Instrumentation refers to adding the Application Insights software development kit (SDK) to your application's source code. You then link the client-side SDK to an Application Insights resource in your Azure subscription.

Some of the intelligence Application Insights can give your developers include the following:

>> **Request and response times and failure rates:** You can see which web app pages are most or least popular at different times of day, as well as where your users connect from.

» **Dependency rates:** You can visually plot any dependencies of your app on external components, which can ensure uptime when you need to perform maintenance or migrations.

» **Exceptions with source-code analysis:** You can follow stack trace output to actual lines in your source code because Application Insights telemetry embeds directly in your Visual Studio project.

» **Performance counters:** You can observe performance statistics gathered from your web app's underlying VM infrastructure.

» **Dashboards:** You can plot your telemetry data in easily digestible formats.

» **Profiler:** You can follow web application requests and responses operation by operation.

Adding the Application Insights resource

Follow these steps to create a new Application Insights resource in your Azure subscription:

1. **In the Azure portal, browse to the Application Insights blade, and click Add.**

    The Application Insights Configuration blade appears.

2. **Configure the resource details.**

    These details are pretty self-explanatory:

    - Subscription

    - Resource group

    - Instance name

    - Region

    The main point I want to make is that to ensure lowest latency, locate your Application Insights resource in the same Azure region as the web app with which it'll be associated.

    Sadly, at this writing, Application Insights isn't available in every public region. You may have to choose the region closest to your app's region.

3. **Submit the deployment by clicking Review + Create, and then Create.**

Enabling instrumentation in a web app

In Azure nomenclature, instrumentation refers to linking your Azure App Service app to an Application Insights instance. Application Insights goes into immediate action gathering details about your application's environment and performance.

Follow these steps to connect your Application Insights instance to an Azure web app:

1. **Switch to Visual Studio, and load the last ASP.NET web application you worked with in this chapter.**

2. **In Solution Explorer, right-click your project, and choose Add ⇨ Application Insights Telemetry from the shortcut menu.**

   The Application Insights Configuration window opens.

   TIP

   If you don't see the Application Insights option, you probably don't have the Application Insights SDK installed. Choose Tools ⇨ Get Tools and Features to open the Visual Studio Installer, where you can install Application Insights.

3. **In the Application Insights Configuration window, click Get Started.**

   The Register Your app with Application Insights window opens.

4. **Complete the form.**

   You provide your Azure account, subscription, resource name, and pricing tier.

   Be sure to specify the Application Insights resource you created earlier.

5. **Click Register.**

Viewing Application Insights telemetry data

You can take advantage of Application Insights telemetry streams in any of the following locations:

» **Visual Studio:** Open the Application Insights toolbar to explore the features. If you don't see the toolbar, choose View ⇨ Toolbars ⇨ Application Insights.

» **The Azure portal:** Open your Application Insights resource, and click Application Dashboard on the Overview blade.

» **Azure Log Analytics:** Log Analytics is a universal query and reporting platform that uses its own SQL-like query language called Kusto (pronounced COO-stow) Query Language. You can query Application Insights in combination with just about any other resource in Azure from one central point. On the toolbar of your Application Insights resource's Overview blade, click Logs (Analytics).

Figure 7-16 and Figure 7-17 show the telemetry data viewed in Visual Studio and the Azure portal, respectively.

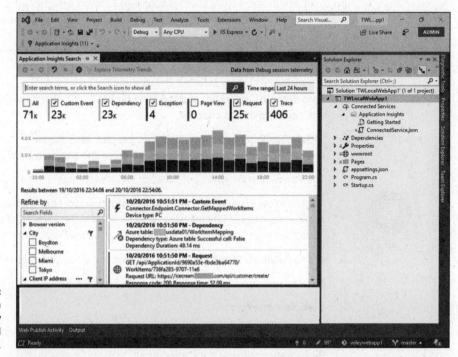

FIGURE 7-16: Application Insights telemetry data in Visual Studio.

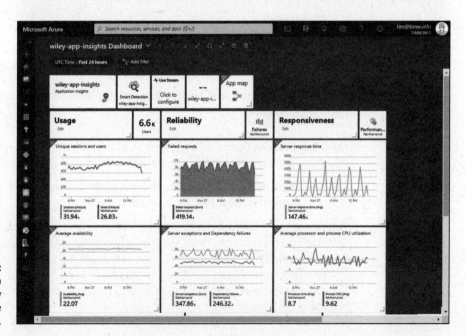

FIGURE 7-17: Application Insights telemetry data in the Azure portal.

Chapter **8**

Running Serverless Apps in Azure

This chapter moves into the wonderful world of serverless computing in Azure. I begin by demystifying the buzzword *serverless* and then discuss how to create Function Apps and Logic Apps in Azure.

Defining Serverless

The term *serverless* gets a lot of attention nowadays. What does it mean? I'll try to cut through marketing jargon and explain the concept succinctly.

App Service apps provide lots of flexibility, in that you don't have to manage the underlying infrastructure, but you still have an entire application to deal with.

The idea behind serverless apps is that Microsoft abstracts almost the entire environment from you. You can pretty much upload a single source-code function and instruct Azure to run it based on a predefined trigger event.

You and I both know that there's no such thing as *serverless* in a physical sense. All App Service apps rely on Linux or Windows Server virtual machines (VMs) under the hood. The term simply denotes an increased abstraction layer for Azure developers, administrators, and solution architects.

Getting to know Azure Functions apps

You can think of Azure Functions as being code as service, by which you upload your source code, and Azure runs it for you. Specifically, Azure runs your function based on a trigger, which is a type of event. The event could be a manually initiated trigger, a scheduled trigger, or some action that takes place elsewhere in Azure.

A *function app* is a container object; you can enclose one or more individual Azure Functions within the function app. The compute and application run time exist at the function-app level and are shared by all enclosed Functions.

TECHNICAL STUFF

A *function* is a named section of a program that performs a specific task. Normally, applications consist of multiple functions. By contrast, Azure Functions are individual, named code blocks that are scoped to perform one action very well.

You have two ways to pay for an Azure Function:

» **Consumption plan:** Azure allocates compute dynamically whenever your function runs. You're charged for the number of function executions per month; Microsoft has a generous free tier. The downside is that the consumption-cost model can be much slower than the App Service plan model.

» **App Service plan:** This pricing model mirrors that of App Service web apps. The benefit is more-predictable performance because you have control of the underlying compute power.

TIP

I don't provide much detail about Azure pricing in this book because Microsoft alters prices and pricing models often. To get the latest details, visit `https://azure.microsoft.com/en-us/pricing/`.

By default, Functions operate in a stateless way — that is, a Function is triggered, the source code runs, and the Function App platform pays no attention to maintaining persistence.

To suit longer-running tasks that do involve state, the ability to set and resume execution at checkpoints, and survive VM restarts, Microsoft offers Durable Functions, which are extensions to Azure Functions. They integrate with many common application architectural patterns, and at this writing, they support the programming languages C#, F#, and JavaScript.

Getting to know Azure Logic Apps

I like to describe Azure Functions as Swiss Army knife–style utilities with which programmers can automate repetitive work without the overhead of an entire application programming interface (API) web application. Azure Logic Apps solve a somewhat different problem, which is creating business workflows that integrate different third-party Software as a Service (SaaS) apps without requiring developers to know disparate APIs.

If you've ever heard of Microsoft BizTalk Server, Logic Apps is essentially a cloud variant of BizTalk. Both BizTalk and Logic Apps include an enormous connector library for all sorts of first- and third-party apps.

Suppose that your human resources department needs to move employee data from one database platform to another and then export selected results to another SaaS platform. Chances are good that Logic Apps has built-in connectors for each platform. Logic Apps Designer is a graphical control surface on which you can build your workflow.

Figure 8-1 illustrates Logic App behavior using a different business scenario.

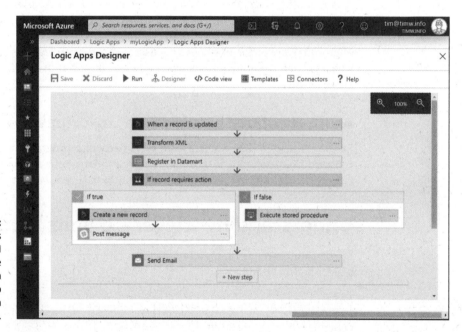

FIGURE 8-1: Logic Apps requires no API knowledge and uses a drag-and-drop workflow design surface.

Figure 8-1 shows that you can add conditional logic to your Logic App workflows. You can successfully mirror any desired business logic, no matter how simple or complex, without understanding different vendors' APIs.

Custom connectors

All Logic Apps, as well as their connectors, are described in JavaScript Object Notation (JSON). Therefore, it's not terribly difficult for your developers to define custom Logic Apps connectors if Microsoft's built-in library doesn't have a particular app. The restriction is that the app in question should expose a RESTful API that supports the OpenAPI standard.

Representational State Transfer (REST) is a programming methodology in which applications send and receive data by using the HTTP protocol. What's cool about REST is you need no special software to use it, and the data transfer occurs over firewall-friendly ports and protocols.

Microsoft Flow versus Azure Logic Apps

Microsoft Flow is an Office 365 member, an SaaS platform built on Logic Apps. Stated another way, Flow is a simpler version of Logic Apps aimed at end users instead of developers.

Microsoft Flow is for business end users whose organizations aren't in Azure, whereas Logic Apps are for business end users or power users whose organization are in Azure.

Azure Functions versus Azure Logic Apps

Functions require development skill with particular programming languages; by contrast, Logic Apps are no-code solutions. Also, Functions are for general-purpose CaaS, whereas Logic Apps are aimed squarely at business workflow development.

Understanding triggers, events, and actions

Interestingly, you can integrate Functions and Logic Apps, using either app as a trigger and/or action.

- » In the realm of the Azure serverless compute platform, a *trigger* defines how an Function or Logic App is invoked. Each serverless app has only one trigger.

- » "But what constitutes a trigger?" you ask. That's the *event*: a lightweight notification of a state change.

- » Finally, the *action* is the response you've configured to occur automatically when the app's trigger is activated.

Working with Azure Functions

The first step in designing a Function is deciding what you want it to do. Suppose that you created a web application in App Service that allows users to upload image files. Your fictional app's source code places the user's uploaded image files in a container named (appropriately enough) images, inside an Azure storage account blob (binary large objects) service container.

What if you want to take automatic action on those uploads? Here are some examples:

>> Automatically converting and/or resizing the image

>> Performing facial recognition on the image

>> Generating notifications based on image type

As it happens, it's possible to trigger a Function based on a file upload.

At this writing, Azure Functions includes the following trigger, among others:

>> **HTTP:** Triggers based on a web hook (HTTP request)

>> **Timer:** Triggers based on a predefined schedule

>> **Azure Queue Storage:** Triggers based on a Queue Storage message

>> **Azure Service Bus Queue:** Triggers based on a Service Bus message

>> **Azure Service Bus Topic:** Triggers based on a message appearing in a designated topic

>> **Azure Blob Storage:** Triggers whenever a blob is added to a specified container (the trigger you need for the example)

>> **Durable Functions HTTP Starter:** Triggers when another Durable Function calls the current one

Creating an Azure Function

I mentioned that a Function App is a container object that stores one or more individual functions. Figure 8-2 shows the Function workflow.

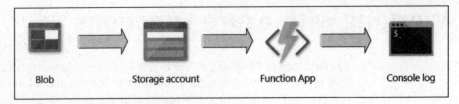

FIGURE 8-2:
Azure Function
for taking action
on uploaded
image files.

Blob   Storage account   Function App   Console log

First, you need to create the Function App. Next, you define the Function itself. Finally, you test and verify that your function is triggered properly.

Creating the Function App

Follow these steps to deploy a new Function App in the Azure portal:

1. **On the Function App blade, click Add.**

   The Basics tab of the Function App blade appears.

2. **Complete the Function App Deployment form (see Figure 8-3).**

   Here are some suggested values:

   - *App Name:* This name needs to be unique because Function Apps are part of the App Services family and have DNS names within Microsoft's public azurewebsites.net zone.

   - *OS:* Choose the type of operating system you have.

   - *Hosting Plan:* Consumption Plan is a good place to start. You can change this setting later if you want or need to do so.

   - *Runtime Stack:* Your choices include .NET Core, Node.js, Python, Java, and PowerShell Core.

   - *Storage:* A general-purpose storage account is necessary to store your code artifacts.

   - *Application Insights:* It's a good idea to enable Application Insights to gain as much back-end telemetry as you can from your Function App.

3. **Click Create to submit the deployment.**

TIP

As of this writing, Microsoft is previewing a new creation experience for Azure Function Apps. Therefore, don't be surprised if you see the new experience instead of what I show in Figure 8-3. The configuration options are the same, but they're presented differently. Change in the Azure portal is one thing in life you can always depend on.

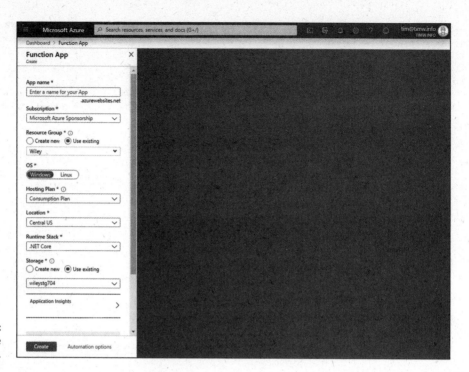

FIGURE 8-3:
Creating an Azure
Function App.

Defining the Function

The next step in the Azure Function creation workflow is defining the Function itself. In my experience, not too many people find the Function App's nonstandard user interface to be intuitive. At all. Figure 8-4 explains what's going on.

> A single Function App (A) contains one or more Functions.

> Each Function that runs in the Function App's run space is stored here (B).

> A Function Proxy (C) allows you to present a single API endpoint for all Functions in a single Function app to other Azure or non-Azure API services.

> Function Apps support deployment slots (D); they serve the same purpose as deployment slots for App Service web apps, and they support slot swapping.

> Function App Settings (E) is where you specify settings for a Function App, Function, or Proxy, depending on the context.

Before you create the function, you should create the images blob container you'll need for this website-upload example. If you have Azure Storage Explorer installed, proceed! If not, refer to Chapter 3 for details on installing it.

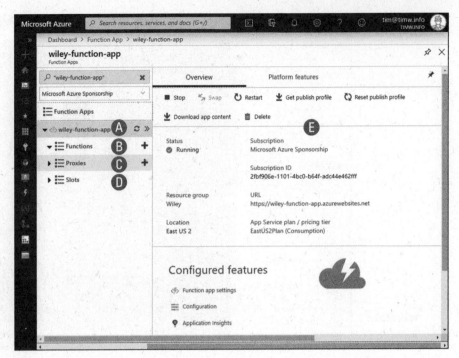

FIGURE 8-4:
Whoever
designed the
Function App's
user interface
wasn't paying
attention to how
the rest of the
Azure portal
behaves.

REMEMBER

Azure Storage Explorer is a free, cross-platform desktop application that makes working with Azure storage accounts a snap. Obtain the tool at `https://azure.microsoft.com/en-us/features/storage-explorer/`.

Follow these steps to create a blob container for the new Function:

1. **Open Azure Storage Explorer, and authenticate to your Azure subscription.**

2. **Expand the storage account you created for your Function App, right-click Blob Containers, and choose Create Blob Container from the shortcut menu.**

   Azure creates the container and places your cursor next to it, all ready for you to name the new object.

3. **Name the container images, and press Enter to confirm.**

Creating the Function

Excellent. You're almost finished. Now you need to create a function. Follow these steps:

1. **Open your Function App in the Azure portal.**

2. **In the Functions row, click the plus sign.**

   The details pane on the right leads you through a Function Wizard, the first step of which is choosing a development environment.

3. **Choose In-Portal as your development environment, and click Continue.**

   Both Visual Studio and Visual Studio Code have native support for writing Functions.

4. **In the Create a Function pane, More Templates, and click Finish and view templates.**

   I show you this in Figure 8-5.

FIGURE 8-5:
Creating a
Function inside
the Azure portal.

5. **Click View Templates to view the Azure Function trigger gallery.**

6. **In the gallery, select the Azure Blob Storage trigger.**

   You'll probably be prompted to install the Azure Storage extension; click Install, and let the process complete.

7. Complete the New Function blade.

Complete the following fields:

- *Name:* I called mine BlobUploadFx. This is the name of the Function that will be contained inside the Function App. The name should be short and descriptive.

- *Azure Blob Storage Trigger Path:* This setting is important. You want to leave the {name} bit alone because it's a variable that represents any uploaded blob. The path should look like this:

```
images/{name}
```

- *Storage Account Connection:* Click New, and select your Function's storage account.

8. Click Create when you're finished.

When you select your function on the Function App's left menu, you can see your starter C# source code. For this example, the code should look like this:

```
public static void Run(Stream myBlob, string name, ILogger log)
{
    log.LogInformation($"C# Blob trigger function Processed blob\n
            Name:{name} \n Size: {myBlob.Length} Bytes");
}
```

This code says "When the function is triggered, write the name and size of the blob to the console log." This example is simple so that you can focus on how Functions work instead of getting bogged down in programming-language semantics.

The new Function contains the following three settings blades:

» **Integrate:** This blade is where you can edit your trigger, inputs, and outputs.

» **Manage:** This blade is where you can disable, enable, or delete the Function, as well as define host keys that authorize API access to the Function.

» **Monitor:** Here, you can view successful and failed Function executions and optionally access Application Insights telemetry from the Function.

Testing

All you have to do to test your function is follow these steps:

1. **In Azure Storage Explorer, upload an image file to the images container.**

   To do this, select the container and then click Upload from the Storage Explorer toolbar. You can upload individual files or entire folders.

   Technically, you can upload any file, image or otherwise, because all files are considered to be blobs.

2. **In the Azure portal, select your Function App, switch to the Logs view, and watch the output.**

   Figure 8-6 shows the output from a test.

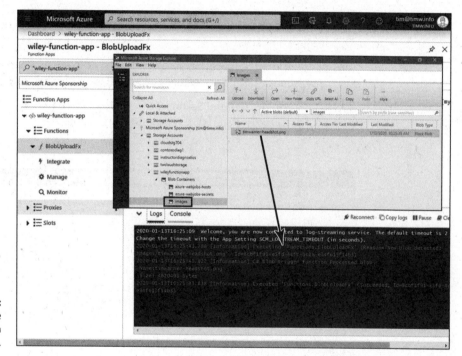

FIGURE 8-6:
Our Azure
Function in
action.

Configuring Function App settings

Before I discuss Logic Apps, I want to make sure that you understand how to tweak Function App settings. You may want to switch from Consumption to App Service plan pricing, for example, or vice versa. Or maybe you want to test a different run-time environment.

I have a difficult time navigating the Function App configuration blades, mainly because they're completely different from the rest of the Azure portal UI. I also think there's some redundancy in the places where some settings controls are located. To make things easier, here's a summary of the major capabilities of each settings blade in the Function App:

REMEMBER

You need to be at the Function App scope (above Functions in the navigation UI). You can see this convention in Figure 8-7.

» **Overview:** Use this blade to stop, start, and restart the Function App. You also can download all site content for use with a local integrated development environment.

» **Platform Features:** This blade is where most Function App settings categories reside.

» **Function App Settings:** From this blade, you can view usage quota and manage host keys.

» **Configuration, Application Settings:** This blade is where you manage application key/value pair settings and database connection strings.

» **Configuration, General Settings:** This blade is where you can configure Architecture; FTP state, HTTP version; Remote debugging.

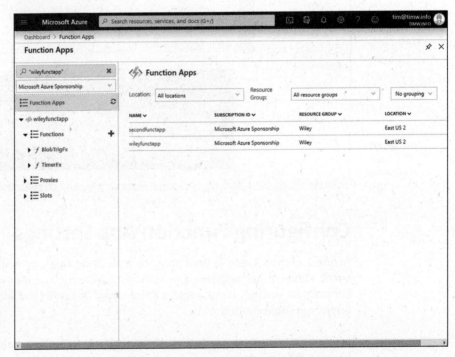

FIGURE 8-7:
Understanding the relationship between the Function App and its enclosed Functions.

Building Workflows with Azure Logic Apps

Suppose that your company's marketing department wants to be notified any time a current or prospective customer mentions your corporate handle on Twitter. Without Logic Apps, your developers would have to register for a developer Twitter account and API key, after which they'd need to immerse themselves in the Twitter API to understand how to integrate Twitter with your corporate notification platform.

Instead, your developers can configure a Logic App to trigger on particular Twitter tweets and send an email message to an Outlook mailbox without knowing Twitter or Office 365 APIs. Figure 8-8 shows a workflow for this Logic App.

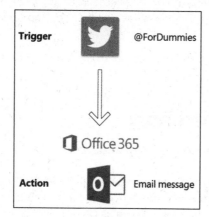

FIGURE 8-8:
The workflow for an Azure Logic App.

Creating an Azure Logic App

You're going to create a Logic App that triggers on mentions of the keyword *Azure* in public tweets. The resulting action sends email notifications to a designated email address. You'll develop your Logic App in three phases:

>> Deploying the Logic App resource

>> Defining the workflow

>> Testing the trigger and action

Deploying the resource in the Azure portal

Follow this procedure to create the Logic App resource:

1. **In the Azure portal, browse to the Logic Apps blade, and click Add.**

   The Create blade opens.

2. **Complete the Logic App Create blade.**

   There's not much to creating the resource. Provide the name, subscription, resource group, and location, and specify whether you want to monitor with Log Analytics.

3. **Click Create to submit the deployment.**

   When deployment is complete, click Go to Resource in the Azure notification menu to open the Logic App. You'll be taken to the Logic Apps Designer by default.

4. **Click the X button in the top-right corner of the interface to close the blade.**

Defining the workflow

Follow these steps to define the Logic App workflow:

TIP

If you want to follow along with this exercise, you need Twitter and Office 365 accounts. Twitter accounts are free, but Office 365 typically is a paid SaaS product. If you like, use another email account (such as Gmail). The Logic Apps connector library is so vast, chances are good that you'll find a service that works for you.

1. **Go to your new Logic App's Overview blade.**

2. **Choose Logic App Designer from the Settings menu.**

   This command takes you to the view you saw the first time you opened the Logic App.

3. **Scroll to the Templates section, and select Blank Logic App.**

   Starting with a blank Logic App enables you to become more familiar with the workflow design process, but Azure provides lots of templates and triggers that you can use for other purposes.

4. **In the Search Connectors and Triggers field, type** Twitter.

5. In the search results, select the Twitter trigger category and then click the When a New Tweet Is Posted trigger.

6. Click Sign In, and log in to your Twitter account.

7. Complete the When a New Tweet Is Posted form.

For the example I outlined earlier, you want the Logic App to trigger whenever someone mentions the keyword *Azure* in a tweet, so you complete the options this way:

- *Search Text:* "Azure"

- *Interval:* 1

- *Frequency:* Minute

WARNING

Configuring a Logic App to trigger on the keyword *Azure* generates *lot* of trigger events and creates a potentially bad signal-to-noise ratio in your results. If you're creating a Logic App for this purpose, experiment with writing more-granular trigger keywords to produce the results you desire.

8. Click New Step.

9. Scroll through the connector library list and look for Outlook.

10. When you find the Outlook connectors, click the Office 365 Outlook connector.

11. Search the actions list for Send, and select the Send an Email action.

12. In the Office 365 Outlook connector dialog box, click Sign In, and authenticate to Office 365.

13. Complete the Send an Email dialog box, preferably using dynamic fields.

This step is where the procedure can get a bit messy.

(a) Put your destination Office 365 email address in the T: field.

(b) Place your cursor in the Subject field.

(c) Click Add Dynamic Content to expose the dynamic content pop-up window.

Dynamic fields allow you to plug live data into your workflow. Figure 8-9, for example, shows a customized email notification message.

14. Click Save.

WARNING

Don't overlook this step! In my experience, it's easy to miss.

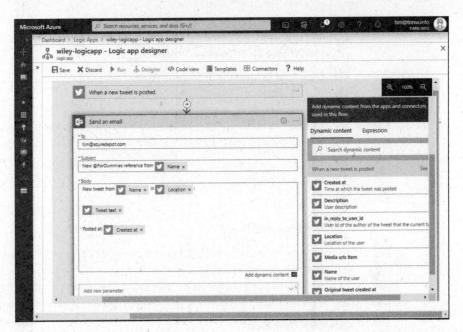

FIGURE 8-9:
Dynamic content
in a Logic App.

GET COMFORTABLE WITH THE LOGIC APP DESIGNER TOOLBAR

You've defined the workflow. Before you test, look at these five toolbar buttons, shown in Figure 8-9:

- **Run:** Click this button to start the Logic App. Keep in mind that a Logic App, as a member of the App Service family, has one or more VMs that power your workflow.

- **Designer:** Click this button when you want to go back to the graphical Designer view from Code view.

- **Code View:** Click this button to see the JSON source code. One of the benefits of Logic Apps, however, is that you don't have to be an API programmer to build high-impact business integration workflows.

- **Templates:** Click this button to view the Logic Apps template gallery.

- **Connectors:** Click this button to view the Logic Apps connector gallery.

Testing the trigger and action

To trigger the action, follow these steps:

REMEMBER

1. **On the Logic App workflow toolbar, click Run.**

   You must— I repeat, *must* — switch the Logic App to a running state for it to catch the trigger.

2. **On Twitter, post a tweet that includes a reference to Azure.**

3. **Await notification.**

   The tweet should trigger an email to the address you designated. Figure 8-10 shows such a notification.

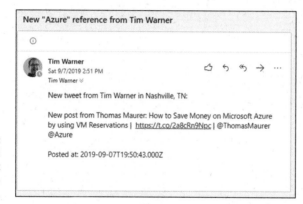

New "Azure" reference from Tim Warner

Tim Warner
Sat 9/7/2019 2:51 PM
Tim Warner

New tweet from Tim Warner in Nashville, TN:

New post from Thomas Maurer: How to Save Money on Microsoft Azure by using VM Reservations | https://t.co/2a8cRn9Npc | @ThomasMaurer @Azure

Posted at: 2019-09-07T19:50:43.000Z

FIGURE 8-10: An email indicating that the Logic App works.

TIP

Another place to check workflow run status is the Overview page, which shows how many times the trigger was tripped, the workflow run, and/or any errors.

IN THIS CHAPTER

» **Evaluating Azure IaaS and PaaS for your application's data tier**

» **Investigating relational and nonrelational database systems in Azure**

» **Working with Azure SQL Database**

» **Working with Cosmos DB**

Chapter **9**

Managing Databases in Microsoft Azure

ost line-of-business applications require a data tier to support data persistence, querying, and reporting, so the time has come for you to see how to implement databases in the Microsoft Azure public cloud.

Databases in the cloud aren't new: SQL Data Services was the first cloud service that Microsoft made generally available. The year was 2008.

By the end of this chapter, you'll be up to speed on both relational and nonrelational database options in Azure, and you'll know the basics of their deployment and configuration.

Revisiting the IaaS versus PaaS Question

A common push–pull issue with customers in an Azure cloud solution architect's life is making sure that a given workload belongs in Azure VMs rather than in various hosted Platform as a Service (PaaS) services. The data tier is an excellent example of this dynamic.

The classical consultant's answer to questions such as "Should I host our app's SQL database in an Azure VM or Azure PaaS?" is "It depends." The answer typically isn't black-and-white. The following sections describe aspects Azure customers need to consider when making their decision.

Controlling the environment

When you host your database on Azure virtual machines (VMs) in a virtual network, you have full-stack control of the entire environment. If you need to tweak your SQL Server's memory allocation, you're free to do that. If you want to make a Windows Registry-based performance enhancement, the VM enables you to accomplish that goal.

By contrast, you lose that degree of administrative control when you use a hosted PaaS product such as Azure SQL Database. With PaaS, Microsoft strictly controls the degree to which you can access your database's underlying virtual server(s).

Running any version of any database

The main reason why some customers opt to run their data tiers on VMs is that a hosted version of their database isn't available. At this writing, Microsoft supports the following versions of Azure SQL Database for MySQL Servers:

>> MySQL Community Edition 5.6

>> MySQL Community Edition 5.7

>> MySQL Community Edition 8.0

What if your app requires an earlier or later version, or you've already paid for MySQL Enterprise Edition? In cases such as these, a VM is most appropriate.

By contrast, as long as your app supports an Azure-hosted PaaS database option, you can immediately take advantage of Azure's massive global scale and elastic compute power.

Using preinstalled VMs from Azure Marketplace

The Azure Marketplace is stocked with preinstalled VM images that run just about every relational or nonrelational database on the market.

The business advantage is you don't have to spend additional time installing, licensing, and configuring the database server software because it's already installed on the image. Furthermore, SQL Server licensing is included in the per-minute VM run-time costs.

By contrast, with PaaS database options, the underlying server infrastucture is abstracted away from you. Thus, you don't have to worry about server performance tuning, backups, and the like. Instead, you can focus more squarely on your line-of-business applications and their back-end data.

Figure 9-1 shows a sample of the templates available in the Marketplace. Some partners offer "pay as you go" licensing that integrates with your Azure subscription costs.

FIGURE 9-1: You can save time by deploying a preinstalled VM from the Azure Marketplace.

Comparing Relational and Nonrelational Databases in Azure

This section goes deeper on Azure-hosted databases, starting with the difference between relational and nonrelational database systems. A full treatment of this subject is beyond the scope of this book, of course, but I can cover the essentials here.

TIP

For further information, please check out *SQL For Dummies*, 8th Edition, by Allen G. Taylor, and *NoSQL For Dummies*, by Adam Fowler (both John Wiley & Sons, Inc.). Fowler's book is a bit older than Taylor's, but between the two volumes, you'll gain wide skills in modern database systems.

Table 9-1 breaks down the biggest differences between relational and nonrelational database systems.

TABLE 9-1

Relational and Nonrelational Databases

	Relational	Nonrelational
Type of data	Large, unrelated, and volatile	Predefined schema
Uses	Mobile apps, real-time analytics, and Internet of Things (IoT) apps	Accounting, finance, banking, transaction processing
Scaling	Horizontal scaling across a cluster	Vertical scaling by adding more resources to VM
Data model	Key/value and wide-column	Related tables, with each table heavily constrained
Query languages	Various, including SQL-like	SQL

The following sections introduce Azure's relational-database PaaS products.

SQL Database

With SQL Database, Microsoft abstracts most of the server platform and allows you to focus nearly exclusively on the database itself.

Table 9-2 describes the members of the SQL Database family.

TABLE 9-2

SQL Database Products

Product	Use
Azure SQL Database	Online transaction processing
Azure SQL Data Warehouse	Online analytical processing
Azure SQL Database Managed Instance	Online large-scale parallel processing

Generally, your selection of the appropriate product falls along the following lines:

> » If you need full control of the environment, choose SQL Database.

> » If you need a balance between Infrastructure as a Service (IaaS) and PaaS flexibility, choose SQL Database Managed Instance.

> » If you need massively parallel processing for intensive query workloads, choose SQL Data Warehouse.

SQL Database for MySQL Servers

For businesses with apps that run MySQL, SQL Database for MySQL Servers — a fully managed, enterprise-ready MySQL Community Edition instance that's natively integrated into Azure — is a good fit.

This solution enables your developers to continue using the MySQL data platform with native tooling and to take advantage of the Azure platform's geoscale, security, and performance features.

Azure Database for MariaDB Servers

Since Oracle purchased MySQL in 2008, some businesses have moved their apps' data platform to another product or embraced the MariaDB project: an open-source fork of Oracle's proprietary MySQL relational database management system.

Azure Database for MariaDB Servers operates almost exactly like Database for MySQL Servers, except that you use MariaDB instead of MySQL. Otherwise, both database servers read and write the same files and even work in parallel versions.

Azure Database for PostgreSQL Servers

PostgreSQL (officially pronounced *post-gres-cue-el*) is a free open-source relational database system that ranks alongside MySQL in its popularity for use with open-source n-tier web application projects.

Azure's support for MySQL and PostgreSQL is a big deal; it wasn't too many years ago that it was unthinkable Microsoft would support any product besides its own SQL Server and Microsoft Access database products.

Implementing SQL Database

This section gets some real work done with SQL Database.

Understanding service tiers

SQL Database has two service tiers and an elastic pool pricing model, all described in the following sections.

DTU-based service tier

In Chapter 5, I briefly mention the Azure Compute Unit (ACU), which is Microsoft's standardization metric for VM compute power. This value is a way to account for Microsoft's use of different hardware across its worldwide data-center network. Similarly, the Database Transaction Unit (DTU) is the SQL Database performance metric. The DTU is a composite value that takes into account server central processing unit (CPU), disk input/output (I/O), and memory allocation. The trick to the DTU model, of course, is forecasting the right service level for your database.

TIP

To help you determine how many DTUs you need for your SQL Database workload, Microsoft employee Justin Henriksen created the Azure SQL Database DTU Calculator, which you can find at https://dtucalculator.azurewebsites.net. Check it out!

vCore service tier

The vCore service tier enables you to specify discrete Azure VM instance sizes to power your Azure SQL Database databases. The advantage here is you have much more granular control over the compute layer than you do with the DTU tier.

With the Serverless option, your compute resources are autoscaled, and you're billed per second based on the number of vCores your database consumes.

Elastic pool model

The DTU and vCore service tiers pertain to single databases. Which pricing model should you choose if your business has several databases, each with its own usage patterns?

That's where SQL elastic pools come in. You populate your databases into an elastic pool, and the databases share an allocation of elastic DTUs. That way, quieter databases can help more active databases by surrendering DTUs that you would have paid for but not used.

Deploying an SQL Database virtual server

This section takes you through the process of deploying an SQL Database virtual server along with the AdventureWorks sample. First, you create the virtual server; then you add the database.

Log in to the Azure portal with your administrative account and then follow these steps:

1. **In the Azure portal, browse to the SQL Servers blade, and click Add.**

   The Basics tab of the Create SQL Database Server blade appears.

2. **On the Create SQL Database Server blade, complete the Basics tab (shown in Figure 9-2) and click Next to continue.**

   Use the following details to complete the fields:

   - *Server Name:* The name needs to be unique because Microsoft puts the virtual server in its database.windows.net DNS domain.

   - *Server Admin Login:* Use a generic account name. You aren't allowed to use common logins such as sa, root, and admin.

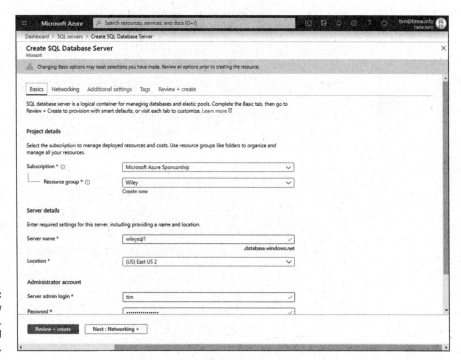

FIGURE 9-2: Deploying a new Azure SQL Database virtual server.

- *Password:* Your password needs to be between 8 and 128 characters long. It can't contain any part of the login name and must possess complexity characteristics such as a mixture of uppercase and lowercase letters, numbers, and nonalphanumeric characters.

3. **On the Networking tab, select Allow Azure Services and Resources to Access This Server.**

   This setting is controversial but crucial. When it's enabled, all Azure IP addresses share a connectivity path to your virtual SQL Server. The setting in no way grants access but provides the possibility.

   Many admins require this setting when they need to integrate SQL Database with services such as Azure Key Vault, storage accounts, HDInsight, and Azure Data Factory.

   You can leave the Additional settings and Tags tab settings at their defaults.

4. **Click Review + Create, and click Create to submit the deployment to Azure Resource Manager (ARM).**

TECHNICAL
STUFF

Azure doesn't charge you for the virtual server. The SQL Database charge comes from the database(s) you place on the virtual server rather than the virtual server itself.

Deploying SQL Database

Next, you need to deploy an Azure SQL Database virtual server along with the AdventureWorks sample database, which gives you some preexisting data to play with. First, you create the virtual server; then you add the database.

TECHNICAL
STUFF

The AdventureWorks sample database has a long, storied history. For more information, visit `https://www.microsoft.com/en-us/download/details.aspx?id=10331`.

Log in to the Azure portal with your administrative account, and follow these steps:

1. **In the Azure portal, browse to the SQL Databases blade, and click Add.**

2. **On the Create SQL Database blade, complete the Basics tab (shown in Figure 9-3).**

   Complete the fields with this information:

   - *Database Name:* This name doesn't need to be globally unique.

   - *Server:* The list should include the virtual server that you created in the preceding section ("Deploying an SQL Database virtual server").

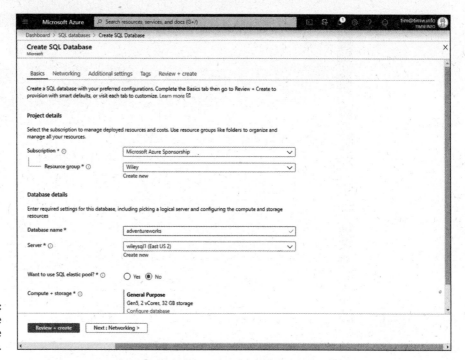

FIGURE 9-3:
Creating an Azure
SQL Database
database.

- *Want to Use SQL Elastic Pool?:* For this example, answer No.

- *Compute + Storage:* Select Configure Database, and on the Configure blade (see Figure 9-4), select Looking for Basic, Standard, Premium?. Then select the Standard tier.

  Because you're just testing, there's no need to "supersize" your database compute layer. Choosing Standard is a good idea because it unlocks most of the administrative and security features you need.

TIP

3. **Click Apply to confirm your choices.**

4. **Complete the Additional Settings page.**

- *Datasource:* Sample. This option instructs Azure to restore the AdventureWorksLT sample database. (*LT* is short for *light,* referring to a stripped-down version of the database.)

5. **Click Review + Create and then click Create to submit the deployment to ARM.**

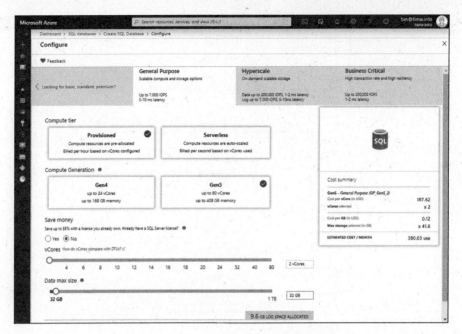

FIGURE 9-4:
The SQL
Database service
tier blade.

Configuring the database

This section covers some of the most common SQL Database configuration settings.

TIP

Check out the Quick Start blade from a resource's Settings list whenever you need to familiarize yourself with a new Azure resource. This blade provides tips, procedures, and documentation links.

TECHNICAL
STUFF

MAKING RESERVATIONS

The Reservations button on the Virtual Machines and SQL Databases blades allows you to prepay for a specified VM and/or SQL Database compute capacity over a yearly term. If you've already done due diligence and determined your compute needs, plus you know you'll need the VM and/or database for that time period, you can save quite a bit of money over the agreement term as opposed to paying per-minute as usual. You can pay for the reservations either up-front or monthly; learn more by reading the "What are Azure Reservations?" Azure docs article at https://docs.microsoft.com/en-us/azure/billing/billing-save-compute-costs-reservations.

Firewall

The SQL Database firewall is a software-defined networking component that protects your database from unauthorized inbound connections.

You configure the firewall at either virtual-server or database level. The advantage of setting the server firewall is you can protect multiple databases with a single configuration.

To configure it, open the server firewall from the database by browsing to the Overview blade and clicking Set Server Firewall on the toolbar.

The SQL Database firewall consists of three components:

>> **Allow Access to Azure Services:** This option enables connectivity traffic from all Azure-sourced public and private IP addresses. This setting doesn't constitute authorization, which you need to configure separately.

>> **Client IP Address and IP Rules:** These settings allow database connectivity from your local workstation's public IP address. You can also define a list of public IP address ranges that should be allowed to connect to the database.

>> **Virtual Networks:** If you defined a SQL Database service endpoint in your virtual network, you can complete the configuration here to constrain access to the virtual server from that network.

Connection strings

The database connection string represents the interface between your application and the database itself. SQL Database provides four driver choices:

>> **ADO.NET:** Generally used for .NET applications

>> **JDBC:** Generally used for Java applications

>> **ODBC:** General-purpose driver

>> **PHP:** Generally used for PHP applications

Choose the connection string that makes the most sense for your application and your development team's skill set.

Georeplication

In my opinion, the ability to configure asynchronous replication for SQL Database is one of the standout features of PaaS. Few businesses have the resources to do this configuration on their own.

You might replicate the database to another region for failover; this means that if the primary database goes offline, you can redirect connections to the secondary standby database copy. Another benefit of georeplication is the ability to run read-only queries against the replica database without creating blocking issues for your users.

Follow these steps to enable georeplication for SQL Database:

1. On your database's Settings blade, click Geo-Replication.

A global map appears.

2. In the Target Regions list, select the region you'd like to use to host your secondary database. Figure 9-5 shows this interface.

TIP

Consider choosing the region designated as your primary region's pair. Microsoft puts additional high-speed network connectivity between paired regions to reduce latency. You don't have to use a paired region, but doing so is a good idea because of the reduced inter-region network latency.

FIGURE 9-5: Configuring georeplication for Azure SQL Database.

TECHNICAL
STUFF

View the mapping of Azure primary and secondary regions in the Azure documentation at `https://docs.microsoft.com/en-us/azure/best-practices-availability-paired-regions`.

3. **Complete the Create Secondary configuration blade, and click OK to save your changes.**

   You need to create a virtual server in the secondary region. Creating a secondary database has pricing implications, but to save money, you can run the secondary database on a lower pricing tier than the primary one.

4. **Above the map, click the banner text** `You can now automatically manage replication, connectivity, and failover of this database by adding it to a failover group` **banner.**

TIP

   The Azure portal changes all the time, so if you don't see this banner, navigate to your virtual server, select the Failover Groups setting, and click Add Group.

5. **Complete the Failover Group configuration blade as follows:**

   - *Read/Write Failover Policy:* Select Automatic.

   - *Read/Write Grace Period (Hours):* This setting is the amount of time Azure waits before automatically failing over to your secondary database when data loss might occur. The decision here is setting a short enough grace period to uphold your service-level agreements, but not long enough to cause undue denial of service.

6. **Click Create to submit the deployment to Azure Resource Manager.**

TECHNICAL
STUFF

Although these steps configure Azure to fail over a database automatically, you're responsible for changing the connection string in your application source code to point to the secondary instance. Azure may be smart, but it isn't that smart. To fetch your database's connection strings, open the database's settings in the Azure portal and browse to the Connection strings blade.

Figure 9-6 shows a completed georeplication configuration.

Configure

The Configure blade is where you can change your service tier. If you're using DTU, you can switch among Basic, Standard, and Premium levels. You can also switch between DTU and vCore purchasing models.

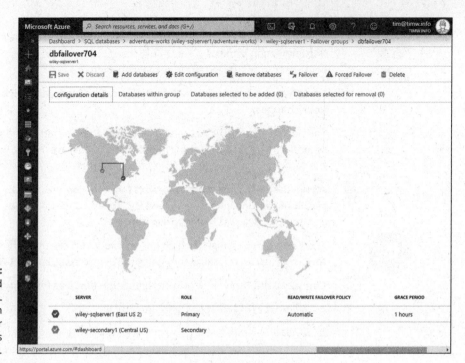

FIGURE 9-6:
Georeplicated
Azure SQL
database with
automatic failover
configured in less
than 5 minutes.

Inspecting the virtual server

This procedure helps you understand the relationship between a new SQL Database and its parent virtual server. Follow these steps:

1. **Navigate to SQL Database's Overview page.**

2. **On the Essentials pane, click the Server Name hyperlink.**

The virtual server name resides on the database.windows.net public DNS zone.

TIP

3. **Make these selections in the Settings list:**

- *SQL Databases:* You should see your database, along with its status and current pricing tier.

- *Manage Backups:* Azure backs up your databases by default. You can select your database and click Configure Retention to adjust how often Azure backs up the database and how long it retains daily (point-in-time restore), weekly, monthly, and yearly backups.

- *DTU Quota:* This setting shows see how many resources your database consumed during the current (monthly) Azure billing cycle.

Connecting to the database

To connect to the SQL database, you need to download and install SQL Server Management Studio (`https://docs.microsoft.com/en-us/sql/ssms/download-sql-server-management-studio-ssms?view=sql-server-2017`), the free SQL Server/Azure SQL Database management interface. When you have that product installed, follow these steps:

1. **On your database's Overview blade, copy your virtual server's Domain Name Service (DNS) name.**

2. **Start SQL Server Management Studio and authenticate with your administrative user account.**

You need to fill in the following information:

- *Server Name:* Your virtual server name in the format *<server-name>*. database.windows.net

- *Authentication:* SQL Server Authentication

TIP

  You can use Azure Active Directory authentication if you've configured it. You learn about Azure AD in Chapter 11.

- *Login/Password:* The administrative credentials you defined for your virtual server

3. **Expand the Databases container, and select the Adventure-Works database.**

4. **Choose File ➪ New Query from Current Connection.**

A new, blank SQL query window appears.

5. **In the query window, type the following Transact-Structured Query Language (T-SQL) query:**

```
SELECT TOP (10) [CustomerID]
      ,[Title]
      ,[FirstName]
      ,[LastName]
      ,[CompanyName]
  FROM [SalesLT].[Customer]
```

6. **Select the query and then click Execute on the SQL Editor toolbar.**

Alternatively, you can right-click your selected query and choose Execute from the shortcut menu.

Figure 9-7 shows the result of a query.

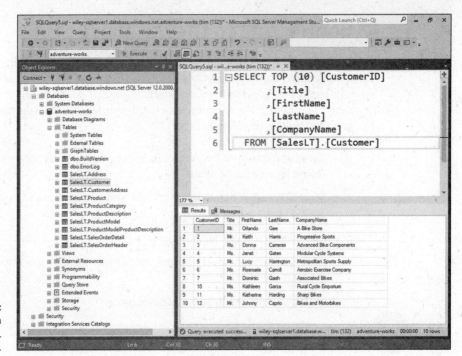

FIGURE 9-7:
Querying an
Azure SQL
Database.

Implementing Azure Cosmos DB

Relational databases are all about *schema*, or structure. I always say that to be a relational database administrator, you should be a micromanager, because every data row needs to be heavily constrained to fit the table, relationship, and database schema.

Although relational databases offer excellent data consistency, they tend to fall down in the scalability department because of all the schema overhead. Enter the nonrelational database.

Rather than call a nonrelational database *schemaless*, it's more accurate to say that NoSQL databases have a flexible schema. At first, you may think that a flexible schema would make querying nearly impossible. But NoSQL databases can overcome this hurdle by partitioning the data set across multiple clustered nodes and apply raw compute power to the query execution.

NoSQL is generally understood to mean *not only SQL*.

TECHNICAL
STUFF

Understanding Cosmos DB

Cosmos DB (originally called Document DB) is Azure's multimodel, georeplicated, nonrelational data store. You can implement Cosmos DB in conjunction or instead of a relational database system.

The following sections give you a tour of Cosmos DB's features.

Multimodel

Originally Document DB was a JavaScript Object Notation (JSON) document-model NoSQL database. Microsoft wanted to embrace a wider customer pool, however, so it introduced Cosmos DB, which supports five data models/application programming interfaces (APIs):

>> **Core (SQL):** This API is the successor to the original Document DB. The data store consists of JSON documents, and Core API provides a SQL-like query language that should be immediately comfortable for relational database administrators and developers.

>> **Azure Cosmos DB for MongoDB API:** This API supports the MongoDB wire protocol. MongoDB, also a JSON document store, allows you to query Cosmos DB as though it were a MongoDB instance.

>> **Cassandra:** This API is compatible with the Cassandra wide column store database and supports Cassandra Query Language.

>> **Azure Table:** This API points to the Azure storage account's table service. It's a key/value data store that you can access with ARM's representational state transfer (REST) APIs.

>> **Gremlin (graph):** This API supports a graph-based data view and the Apache Gremlin query language.

Do you see a theme? The idea is that just about any developer who needs a NoSQL data store should be able to use Cosmos DB without sacrificing original source code or client-side tooling.

Turnkey global distribution

With a couple of mouse clicks, you can instruct Azure to replicate your Cosmos DB database to however many Azure regions you need to put your data close to your users.

TECHNICAL STUFF

Cosmos DB uses a multimaster replication scheme with a 99.999 percent availability service level agreement for both read and write operations.

Multiple consistency levels

Relational databases always offer strong consistency at the expense of speed and scale. Cosmos DB offers flexibility in this regard, allowing you to select (dynamically) any of five data consistency levels:

>> **Strong:** Reads are guaranteed to return the most recently committed version of an item. This level is the slowest-performing but most accurate.

>> **Bounded Staleness, Session, and Consistent Prefix:** These consistency levels offer balance between performance and consistent query results.

>> **Eventual:** Reads have no ordering guarantee. This choice is the fastest but least accurate.

TECHNICAL STUFF

Data consistency refers to the requirement that any database transaction change affected data only in allowed ways. With regard to read consistency specifically, the goal is to prevent two users from seeing different results from the same query due to incomplete database replication.

Creating a Cosmos DB account

This section gets down to business. The first task is getting Cosmos DB off the ground to create a Cosmos DB account. After you have the account, you can define one or more databases.

Follow these steps to create an account:

1. In the Azure portal, browse to the Azure Cosmos DB blade, and click Add.

The Create Azure Cosmos DB Account blade appears.

2. On the Create Azure Cosmos DB Account blade, complete the Basics page, using the following settings:

- *Account Name:* This name needs to be unique in its resource group.

- *API:* Select Core (SQL).

- *Geo-Redundancy:* Don't enable this option. If you do, Azure replicates your account to your region's designated pair.

- *Multi-Region Writes:* Don't enable this option. You can always enable it later if you need multiple read/write replicas of the account throughout the world.

3. **Review the Network page.**

   Chapter 4 shows you how to restrict access to your Cosmos DB account from a designated virtual network.

4. **Click Review + Create and then click Create to submit the deployment.**

Running and debugging a sample Cosmos DB application

In my opinion, the best way to gain general familiarity with a new Azure service is to visit its Quick Start page. I'll now do this with Cosmos DB. Figure 9-8 shows the Cosmo DB Quick Start page.

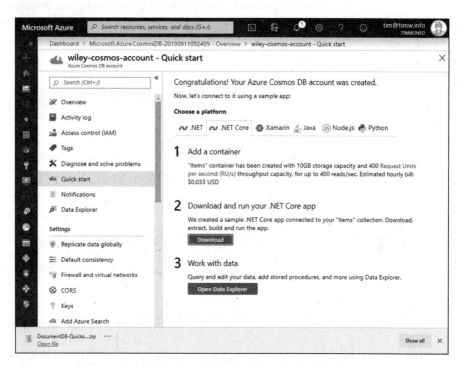

FIGURE 9-8:
The Cosmos DB
Quick Start blade.

If you follow the Cosmos DB Quick Start tutorial, you can accomplish the following goals:

» Create a new Cosmos DB database and container.

» Download a .NET Core web application that connects to the Cosmos DB database.

>> Interact with the container and data store on your workstation by using Visual Studio.

To run a sample application, follow these steps:

1. **On your Cosmos DB account's Quick Start blade, choose the .NET Core platform, and click Create 'Items' Container.**

   Azure creates a container named 'Items' with 10 GB capacity and 400 request units (RUs) per second. As you may rightly guess, the RU is the standardized Cosmos DB performance metric.

2. **Click Download to download the preconfigured .NET Core web application.**

3. **Unzip the downloaded archive on your system, and double-click the** `quickstartcore.sln` **solution file to open the project in Visual Studio 2019 Community Edition.**

4. **In Visual Studio, build and run the solution by choosing Build ⇨ Build Solution.**

5. **Choose Debug ⇨ Start Debugging to open the application in your default web browser.**

6. **In the To-Do App with Azure DocumentDB web application that is now running in your web browser, click Create New, and define several sample to-do items.**

   When you add to-do items, you're populating the Items container in your Azure Cosmos DB database.

7. **Close the browser to stop debugging the application.**

TIP

For extra practice, use the Visual Studio publishing wizard (which you find by right-clicking your project in Solution Explorer and choosing Publish from the shortcut menu) to publish this app to Azure App Service. This exercise is a great test of the skills you've developed thus far.

Interacting with Cosmos DB

To practice interacting with Cosmos DB and your database, return to the Azure portal and look at your Cosmos DB account settings. Here, I highlight some key settings to make sure you know where to find them:

>> **Data Explorer:** Perform browser-based query and database configuration. Figure 9-9 shows Data Explorer.

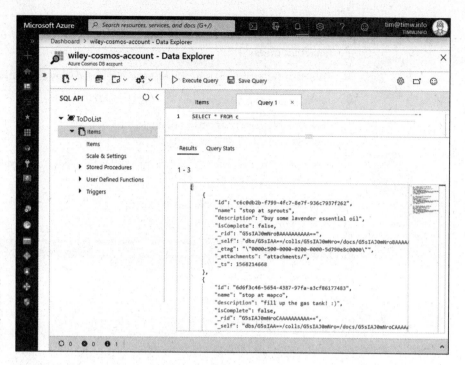

{
    {
        "id": "c6c0db2b-f799-4fc7-8e7f-936c7937f262",
        "name": "stop at sprouts",
        "description": "buy some lavender essential oil",
        "isComplete": false,
        "_rid": "G5sIAJ0mNroBAAAAAAAAA==",
        "_self": "dbs/G5sIAA==/colls/G5sIAJ0mNro=/docs/G5sIAJ0mNroBAAAA/
        "_etag": "\"0000c500-0000-0200-0000-5d790e8c0000\"",
        "_attachments": "attachments/",
        "_ts": 1568214668
    },
    {
        "id": "6d6f3c46-5654-4387-97fa-a3cf86177483",
        "name": "stop at mapco",
        "description": "fill up the gas tank! :)",
        "isComplete": false,
        "_rid": "G5sIAJ0mNroCAAAAAAAAA==",
        "_self": "dbs/G5sIAA==/colls/G5sIAJ0mNro=/docs/G5sIAJ0mNroCAAAA/

FIGURE 9-9:
Cosmos DB Data Explorer is available directly in the Azure portal.

>> **Replicate Data Globally:** Click the map to replicate your Cosmos DB account to multiple regions. (Additional costs apply.)

>> **Default Consistency:** Switch among the five data consistency levels.

>> **Firewall and Virtual Networks:** Bind your Cosmos DB account to specific virtual network(s).

>> **Keys:** View the Cosmos DB account endpoint Uniform Resource Identifier, access keys, and connection strings.

Now follow these steps to interact with your new Cosmos DB database directly from the Azure portal:

1. **In your Cosmos DB account, select Data Explorer.**

2. **Click the Open Full Screen button on the Data Explorer toolbar.**

   This button takes you to https://cosmos.azure.com in a separate browser tab, giving you more screen real estate to run queries.

   The ToDoList planet icon represents the icon, and the Items icon represents the container. The container is the Cosmos DB replication unit.

3. Right-click the Items container and choose New SQL Query from the shortcut menu.

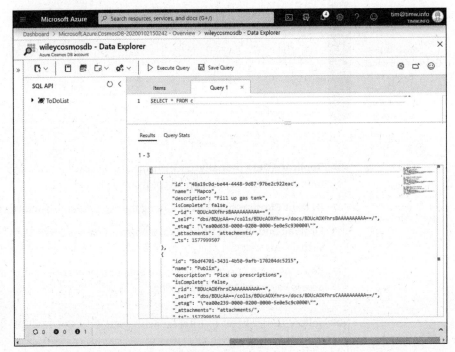

The Save Query button is handy for retaining particularly useful queries.

TIP

4. View your existing items by running the default query.

The default query provided by Azure in the Data Explorer, `SELECT * FROM c`, retrieves all documents from your Items container.

TIP

c is an alias for *container*. You'll find the alias to be super useful when you work with the Cosmos DB Core API.

Figure 9-10 shows example query results.

FIGURE 9-10: Use Azure Data Explorer and SQL to query your Cosmos DB Core API items.

5. Experiment with different `SELECT` queries.

The double dash (--) denotes a one-line comment in Data Explorer. Try entering these queries in Data Explorer.

```
-- select two fields from the container documents
SELECT c.name, c.description from c
-- show only incomplete todo items
SELECT * from c WHERE c.isComplete = false
```

6. Use Data Explorer to update a document.

In the SQL API tree view on the left side of Figure 9-10, expand the Items container, and select Items. Click the document you want to edit, and update the isComplete field on at least one document from "false" to "true," or vice versa (see Figure 9-11).

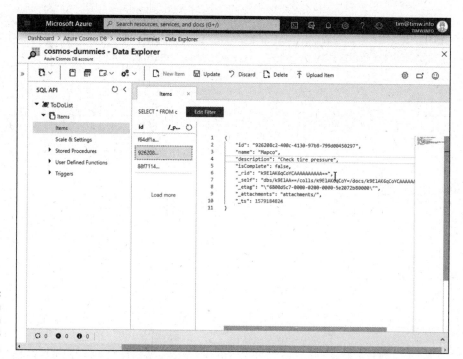

FIGURE 9-11:
Editing a
document in a
Cosmos DB
collection.

7. Click the Update toolbar button to save your changes.

TIP

Bookmark the URL https://cosmos.azure.com so that you can easily access Cosmos DB Data Explorer in a full-window experience. Also, Microsoft offers excellent Cosmos DB SQL query cheat sheets at https://docs.microsoft.com/en-us/azure/cosmos-db/query-cheat-sheet.

TECHNICAL STUFF

CLEANING UP YOUR ENVIRONMENT

The Azure subscription model requires you to pay only for the resources you consume, so you need to understand how to remove your deployments when you don't need them anymore.

You've probably been using the Delete or Remove Azure portal commands to clean up your environments. A faster method is to invoke Azure PowerShell or Azure CLI from Azure Cloud Shell or from your own computer. To force-delete a resource group named `'Wiley'` by using PowerShell, run the following command:

```
Remove-AzResourceGroup -Name 'Wiley' -Force -Verbose
```

To do the same thing with CLI, the command is

```
az group delete --resource-group Wiley --no-wait --yes
```

4

Providing High Availability, Scalability, and Security for Your Azure Resources

IN THIS PART . . .

Backing up and restoring Azure storage accounts,
VMs, App Service apps, and databases

Becoming familiar with Azure Active Directory

Implemeting least-privilege security for your Azure
subscriptions and resources

Applying governance policy to your Azure environment

Chapter **10**

Backing Up and Restoring Your Azure Data

D isaster recovery is your business's ability to recover from an IT-related failure. Before I get into the specifics of disaster recovery, it's important you to understand the shared responsibility model in cloud computing.

The Azure services operate on the shared responsibility model. Microsoft is the cloud provider and gives you access to highly available resources that you use on a pay-per-use basis. Microsoft's responsibility is to provide the infrastructure and specific degrees of high availability as outlined in the service-level agreements (SLAs). A good example is the Azure storage account. Microsoft's SLA for storage accounts, at least as of this writing, claims the following:

We guarantee that at least 99.9% (99% for Cool Access Tier) of the time, we will successfully process requests to read data from Locally Redundant Storage (LRS), Zone Redundant Storage (ZRS), and Geo Redundant Storage (GRS) Accounts.

This statement means that if your storage account's blob service falls victim to a cryptolocker attack, Azure will replicate the encryption to all replica instances of the infected storage account, but that's not the same thing as offering you a disaster recovery plan.

The bottom line is that it's your responsibility as an Azure customer to take control of disaster recovery for your organization's Azure resources. Microsoft provides the disaster recovery tools, but you need to put them into action.

By the end of this chapter, you'll understand how to protect your storage accounts, virtual machines (VMs), app services, Azure SQL Database instances, and Cosmos DB databases.

Protecting Your Storage Account's Blob Data

Well, I have good news and bad news. The good news is that Azure has some options for backing up and restoring individual blobs and even (with manual intervention) for protecting entire blob containers.

The bad news is that the tooling isn't the smoothest or most convenient, in my humble opinion. In the following sections, I show you around so you can decide how you want to approach Azure blob storage disaster recovery in your environment.

Backing up and restoring individual storage blobs

A blob (binary large object) is an unstructured data file. Examples include document files, log files, and media files.

Soft delete in Azure storage accounts is effectively a recycle bin for deleted blobs. Enable the feature postdeployment by navigating to your storage account in the Azure portal, selecting the Soft Delete setting, enabling that feature, and determining your retention policy. The time span for soft-deleted blob retention ranges from 1 to 365 days.

TIP

If you're going to walk through the steps in the next couple of sections, I suggest that you create a container in a storage account and populate it with some unimportant files that you don't mind playing with. I cover creating Azure storage accounts in detail in Chapter 3.

In my environment, I created a storage account with the following properties:

> **Storage account name:** wileyprimstorage

> **Type:** General-purpose v2

> **Blob soft delete:** Enabled

> **Container name:** scripts

> **Container contents:** Several Azure PowerShell script files that I had stored on my workstation

Creating and viewing snapshot backups

You can take manual snapshot backups of your Azure storage account blobs. The term *snapshot* denotes these backups as point-in-time file version that you can download or restore as needed.

Within the Azure portal, follow these steps to take a snapshot backup:

1. Browse to your target container, and select one or more blobs.

The Azure portal allows multiple selection via the check-box controls.

2. On the toolbar, click Create Snapshot.

You won't see any confirmation within the storage account, but you should see a `Successfully created blob snapshot(s)` message in the Azure portal's Notifications menu.

3. Select only one of the blobs you selected in Step 1 and then click View Snapshots on the toolbar.

Figure 10-1 shows my snapshot list for a script file named `arm-deployment.ps1`. I've annotated the following:

- The Download Snapshot button (A) helps when you need a copy of a blob's previous version. This command downloads the blob to your local computer.

- The Promote Snapshot button (B) replaces your current blob copy with the selected snapshot backup. Be careful with this option because you will overwrite the current version of the blob.

- The Delete Snapshot button (C) enables you to selectively remove snapshots that you don't want to use again.

- The Edit Blob tab (D) enables you to modify snapshot contents.

- The Generate SAS tab (E) makes it easy to create a shared access signature Uniform Resource Identifier (URI) for the blob. A shared access signature allows you to provide time-limited public access to a blob; Azure developers use SAS tokens all the time to handle blob uploads and downloads with storage accounts.

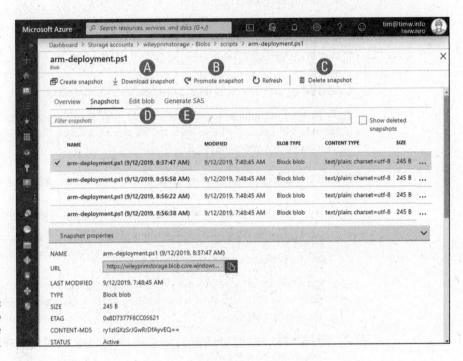

FIGURE 10-1: Managing blob snapshots in the Azure portal.

Deleting and restoring a snapshot

You can clean up your storage account blob list by deleting (and restoring, if you've enabled Soft Delete) any blob. Follow these steps to delete a parent blob and then recover it:

1. **Choose a blob for which you created a snapshot, open its context menu, and choose Delete.**

A confirmation message lets you know that deleting a parent blob also deletes its snapshots. Check the box to proceed.

2. Click OK in the message to confirm.

3. Click Refresh to verify that the blob is gone from the list.

The blob you deleted should no longer appear in the list. That's expected — no big surprise.

4. On the toolbar, select the Show Deleted Blob check box.

This action reveals what is essentially the recycle bin for soft-deleted blobs.

5. Open the item's context menu (...), and choose Undelete.

The success confirmation you're looking for appears on the Notifications menu.

You configure soft delete in the storage account settings. As shown in Figure 10-2, you first navigate to the Data Protection settings blade, toggle the Blob soft delete control to Enabled, and then choose a retention period. Soft delete supports a retention range of 1 to 365 days.

A soft-deleted blob is permanently purged from your storage account after it exceeds your retention policy.

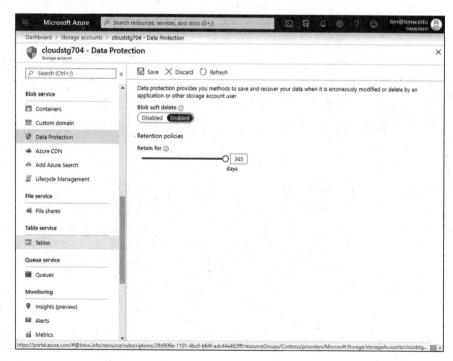

FIGURE 10-2: Configuring soft delete for Azure storage account blobs.

TIP

When I refer to a resource's *context menu* in the Azure portal, I typically mean the ellipsis (...) icon that appears at the right end of the item row.

Backing up storage blobs in bulk

The question we consider now is how to take backups of entire blob containers. Sadly, the Azure platform doesn't have any native features to assist you; I don't have any definitive answer for why this is, but Microsoft may consider that as a feature request in the future. But you can write a shell script that calls AzCopy (see the nearby sidebar) to copy blobs between two storage accounts, preferably in different regions.

First, install AzCopy (see the "AzCopy" sidebar later in this chapter), and then open an elevated command prompt and run the following PowerShell command to set a new environment variable that points to your AzCopy installation directory (in this example, AzCopy is in my C:\azcopy directory). You do this so you can call the AzCopy command from any directory in a command-prompt session or script file:

```
[Environment]::SetEnvironmentVariable("Path",
        $env:Path + ";C:\bin", "Machine")
```

Then restart your computer to enable the new system environment variable.

Here's the AzCopy command I used to copy my scripts container from my wileyprimstorage storage account to my scripts-backup container in my wiley-secstorage storage account:

```
AzCopy /Source:https://wileyprimstorage.blob.core.windows.net/
        scripts /Dest:https://wileysecstorage.blob.core.
    windows.net/
        scripts-backup /SourceKey: 4SXSCKBA==
        /DestKey: ZpuwuCLQ== /S
```

You authenticate to the storage accounts by passing in an access key. If you've been studying this book in chapter sequence, you know what access keys are and how to find them. If not, then I suggest you read Chapter 3 for a formal treatment of Azure storage accounts.

AZCOPY

AzCopy is a command-line tool for Azure storage that allows you to

- Work with Azure blob storage as well as Amazon Web Services S3 storage

- Integrate with Azure Storage Explorer

- Access verbose logging of all copy operations

- Throttle blob-copy speed

You can download AzCopy at https://docs.microsoft.com/en-us/azure/storage/common/storage-use-azcopy-v10). The tool is a stand-alone executable. You can place it in any directory on your system, but I suggest that you add the AzCopy directory path to your PATH system environment variable to ensure that you can start the tool from any command-prompt location.

Protecting Your Virtual Machines

That's enough about storage accounts. This section discusses protecting your precious Azure VM operating system and data disks that currently reside in Managed Disk storage.

Getting to know the Recovery Services vault

The Azure Recovery Services vault has two purposes:

» Backup and recovery: Backing up and restoring individual VMs or VMs in bulk

» Disaster recovery: Configuring warm standby instances of your Azure VMs and switching to them quickly if the primary instance(s) go offline

TECHNICAL STUFF

Both the Managed Disk service and the Recovery Services vault are abstraction layers on top of the Azure storage account. Much of Azure Resource Manager deals with abstracting higher levels of administrative overhead for more-manageable levels.

Deploying a Recovery Services vault

Follow these steps to deploy a Recovery Services vault in the Azure portal:

1. **Browse to the Recovery Services vaults blade, and click Add.**

2. **Complete the Create Recovery Services vault form.**

   The vault name needs to be unique at the Azure subscription level. Keep in mind that your VMs to be backed up need to be in the same region as your Recovery Services vault.

3. **Click Review + Create and then click Create to submit the deployment.**

   The deployment is fast because the Recovery Services vault is essentially a container.

Azure Recovery Services vaults can automate the backups of SQL Server running in Azure VMs as well as storage account file shares, but you need to drill into VM backup.

WARNING

You can back up Azure VMs only to a Recovery Services vault in the same Azure region. If your VMs span regions, you need multiple Recovery Services vaults that do the same.

Creating a backup policy

A *backup policy* determines your backup schedule — that is, how often Azure makes backups and how long it retains them.

Follow these steps to create a simple backup policy to use for your VM backups:

1. **In your Recovery Services Vault settings, click Backup Policies.**

2. **On the Backup Policies page, click Add.**

   The Add blade appears.

3. **In the Add blade under Policy Type, select Azure Virtual Machine.**

   Notice that you can also create policies for SQL Server in an Azure VM and Azure File Share backups.

4. **Complete the Create Policy blade.**

   Here are the major policy options:

   - *Policy Name:* Use a descriptive name. (I chose wiley-windows-policy, for example.)

   - *Backup Schedule:* Select Daily or Weekly.

- *Instant Restore:* Specify a value between 1 and 5 days to keep your latest backup snapshot in the Recovery Service vault staging area. This feature makes restores much faster because the vault doesn't have to unpack the snapshot from the archives to place it in the staging area.

- *Retention Range:* Specify how long Azure archives weekly, monthly, and yearly backup points.

5. **Click Create to commit your changes.**

Backing up VMs

You can configure VM backup from the perspective of the Recovery Services vault or the perspective of an individual VM. In this section, I show you both methods.

Note: To follow along with the exercises in this section, you need two VMs; it doesn't matter whether they run Windows Server or Linux. It's important that the VMs be in a running state so that the Azure VM Snapshot extension can back up files in use and provide for application-consistent backups.

I cover Azure VM creation in Chapter 5.

Backing up a single VM

Follow these steps to back up a running VM in the Azure portal:

1. **In the VM's Settings list, select Backup.**

2. **Complete the Welcome to Azure Backup blade.**

   All you need to do is choose your newly created Recovery Services vault and your new backup policy from the provided drop-down menus.

3. **Click Enable Backup.**

4. **When deployment is complete, return to the VM's Backup blade.**

5. **On the toolbar, click Backup Now.**

   This step initiates a manual backup rather than waiting for the next backup window specified in your policy.

6. **Confirm the backup retention date.**

7. **Click OK to start the backup.**

Backing up multiple VMs

Follow these steps to back up one or more VMs from your Recovery Services vault:

1. **In your Recovery Services vault's settings list, select Backup.**

2. **Complete the following fields as shown here:**

   - *Where Is Your Workload Running?:* Azure

   - *What Do You Want to Back Up?:* Virtual machine

3. **Click Backup to continue.**

4. **On the Backup Policy blade, select your VM policy, and click OK to continue.**

   The Select Virtual Machines blade appears.

5. **On the Select Virtual Machines blade, select the VMs you want to include in the batch backup job configuration.**

   Figure 10-3 shows my environment.

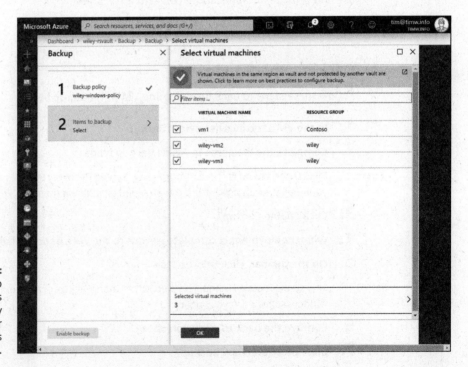

FIGURE 10-3:
You can back up
multiple VMs
simultaneously
from your
Recovery Services
vault.

6. Click OK.

The Backup blade appears.

7. In the Backup blade, click Enable Backup to complete the configuration.

TIP

You can check on the backup job status by clicking the Backup Jobs setting in your vault.

Restoring VMs

Before I explain the "clicky-clicky" procedure, I want to explain the VM restore options.

VM backup consistency levels

Azure offers three guarantees for VM restore, depending on the consistency level of the backup snapshots:

>> **Application-consistent:** This level is the most preferred snapshot consistency level. The guarantee is that the VM will boot up and that you won't suffer data corruption or loss.

>> **File-system-consistent:** The SLA stipulates that the VM will boot up and that you'll suffer no data corruption. You may need to implement manual or automated fixups, however, to ensure that your data is current.

>> **Crash-consistent:** This level is the least-preferred snapshot consistency level. The SLA offers no guarantees. The VM runs a disk check at startup.

VM restore options

Azure offers flexibility in restoring a VM. You may need to perform a trial restore of an entire VM to ensure that the backup operation works, for example, or you may simply need to pluck some files from one of your VM's data disks.

Here are your restore configuration options in a nutshell:

>> **Create New Virtual Machine:** Overwrite the existing VM or restore to an alternative virtual network.

>> **Restore Disks:** Copy the backed-up operating system and data disk(s) to a storage account blob service.

>> **Replace Disks:** Swap out your troubled VM's operating system and data disks for snapshot copies.

>> **File Recovery:** Mount snapshot operating system and data disks on your local workstation through some clever PowerShell scripting magic. Then you can recover individual files from backup quickly and easily.

TECHNICAL STUFF

The File Recovery feature is exceedingly cool and useful. To learn more about it, take a look at the Azure documentation: `https://docs.microsoft.com/en-us/azure/backup/backup-azure-restore-files-from-vm`.

Backup and restoration

Figure 10-4 shows a VM's Backup blade.

Initiate a manual backup

Initiate a restore   Initiate file recovery

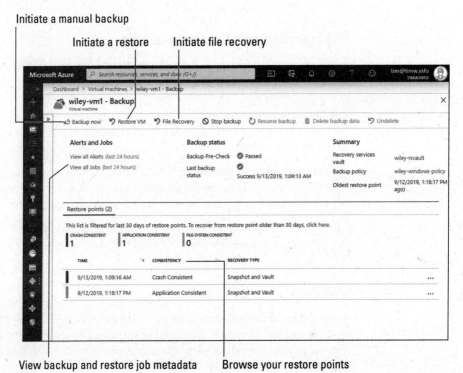

View backup and restore job metadata   Browse your restore points

With no further ado, let me show you how to work with the Azure VM restore experience. Follow these steps:

1. **In your VM's Settings list, select Backup.**

2. **On the Backup blade, click Restore VM.**

3. **On the Select Restore Point blade, choose a restore point.**

   The general guidance here is for you to choose the most recent application-consistent backup.

4. **On the Restore Configuration blade, choose a restore option.**

   You can choose to restore the entire VM or only its disks to their original locations or to an alternative storage account and virtual network.

Protecting Your App Services

One of the conveniences of the built-in backup in Azure App Service is that in addition to backing up the app's source code, Azure also backs up its associated configuration settings and support files:

- » App file system artifacts
- » App configuration data
- » Database connected to the app

Backing up App Service apps

Note: To follow along with this section, you'll need a running App Service app and a general-purpose storage account. At this writing, App Service backup doesn't use the Recovery Services vault.

To back up App Service apps, follow these steps:

1. **On your app's Settings blade, click Backups.**

2. **On the toolbar, click Configure.**

3. **Complete the Backup Configuration blade.**

   Complete the following information:

   - *Backup Storage:* Select a storage account in the same region, and either create or designate an existing container to house your app backups.

   - *Backup Schedule:* Schedule automatic backups every *n* days or hours, and choose your retention period in days.

   - *Backup Database* (optional): Include a database connection in the backup definition.

4. **Click Save to commit your configuration.**

5. **Click Save to submit the deployment.**

   You are returned to the web app's Backups blade.

REMEMBER

Your App Service features depend on your App Service plan's pricing tier. To take advantage of scheduled backups, your App Service plan must run at least the S1 service tier. I present Azure App Service in Chapter 7.

Restoring App Service apps

This section considers the other side of the proverbial coin: restoring apps. Perhaps you want to do a trial App Service restore to make sure that the backup is consistent.

To restore an App Service, follow these steps:

1. **Navigate to the Backups blade in your App Service app.**

2. **In the Backup section, select Restore.**

   The Restore Backup blade appears.

3. **Complete the Restore Backup blade.**

   - **Restore Source:** Choices are App Backup (choose this one), Storage, or Snapshot.

   - **Select the Backup to Restore:** This lists previously taken backups.

   - **Restore destination:** The choices are Overwrite or New or Existing App.

   - **Ignore Conflicting Host Names on Restore:** Choices are No or Yes. Leave this set to No to prevent Azure from restoring an App Service app with a conflicting name to your environment.

   - **Ignore Databases:** Choices are No or Yes. If your web app has a database connection string, you'll want to set this option to No.

4. **Click OK to finish the App Service restore process.**

Figure 10-5 shows the Restore Backup blade in the Azure portal.

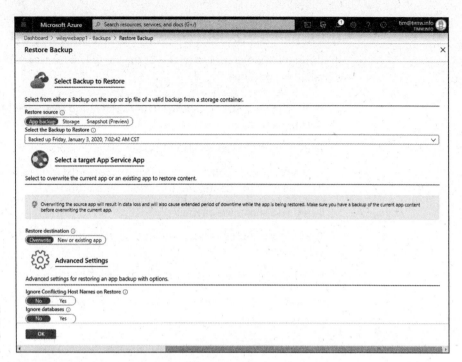

FIGURE 10-5:
Restoring an
Azure App
Service app.

Protecting Your Databases

The last things to back up and restore are Azure SQL Database and Cosmos DB.

Backing up and restoring SQL Database

SQL Database creates full backups of your databases every week, differential backups every 12 hours, and transaction log backups every 5 to 10 minutes. The backups occur automatically with no intervention on your part.

Moreover, SQL Database places the backups in a read-access georedundant storage account to ensure that your backups remain available even if your primary Azure region becomes unavailable.

I teach you how to use Azure SQL Database in Chapter 9.

Configuring SQL Database backup retention

You configure SQL Database backups at the virtual-server level. Follow these steps to manage the backups:

1. **Browse to your SQL Database virtual server, and select the Manage Backups setting.**

   The Configure Policies/Available Backups blade appears.

2. **On the Configure Policies tab, select the desired database in the database list, and click the Configure Retention toolbar button.**

   Figure 10-6 shows the interface.

   The Configure Policies blade appears. This blade has four configurable properties:

   - *Point in Time Restore Configuration:* Range is 7 to 35 days.

   - *Weekly Long-Term Retention (LTR) Backups:* Range is 1 to 520 weeks.

   - *Monthly LTR Backups:* Range is 4 to 520 months.

   - *Yearly LTR Backups:* Range is 1 to 10 years.

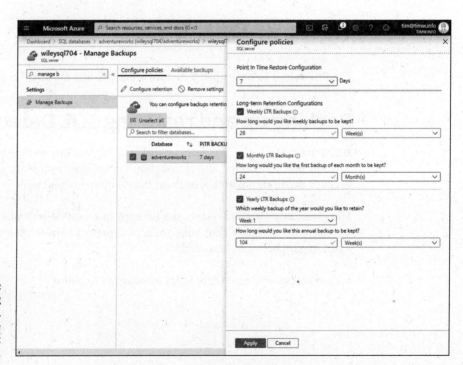

FIGURE 10-6:
Customizing Azure SQL Database automatic backup.

3. Click Apply to submit your retention-policy changes.

4. On the Manage Backups blade, click the Available Backups tab.

5. Browse backups for all databases attached to the virtual server.

Restoring SQL Database

To recover an accidentally deleted database, navigate to your Azure SQL Database virtual server and click the Deleted Databases setting. Next, select the deleted database, choose a restore point, and click Restore to bring back the database. You'll need to provide a new name for the restored database.

TIP

You can also perform SQL Database backups and restores by using native SQL Server client tools such as SQL Server Management Studio and Transact-SQL.

To recover a damaged database, browse to your SQL Database's Overview page, and click Restore. You'll be asked to confirm your desired restore point.

You also can restore the database to another database server and/or elastic pool, and can even change the pricing tier on the fly.

Backing up and restoring Cosmos DB

Like SQL Database, Cosmos DB takes backups of your data automatically, with no customer intervention required. Cosmos DB takes a database backup every 4 hours and keeps the latest two backups. Cosmos DB also retains snapshots for 30 days.

The Azure documentation recommends that you use Azure Data Factory to take manual backups of your Cosmos DB data by copying the data to another Cosmos DB account.

As of this writing, you need to file a support ticket with Microsoft to request any sort of data restore. The Cosmos DB team told me that Microsoft has user-initiated data restore on its new feature backlog. Who knows; maybe the feature will have been added by the time you're reading this chapter! That's Azure for you.

There are four Azure support plans. All pay-as-you-go subscribers start with the Basic support plan, which is free; the other three plans have a fixed monthly cost. Here's a quick rundown of the four plans and the SLAs associated with them:

>> **Basic:** No response-time SLA

>> **Developer:** Less than 8-hour response time SLA for minimal impact support issues

» **Standard:** Less than 1-hour response time SLA for critical business impact support issues

» **Professional Direct:** Shortest response times, plus Azure architecture and operations support

Suppose that you accidentally deleted your Cosmos DB account and need to restore it as quickly as possible. You have to file a support ticket. Here's the procedure:

1. **In the Azure portal, choose Help ⇨ Help + Support.**

The Help + Support tool appears, as shown in Figure 10-7.

2. **Select New Support Request, and follow the prompts.**

In this case, you'd choose your Cosmos DB instance and select the Backup and Restore problem type.

3. **Periodically check the All Support Requests blade for updates.**

Azure support is likely to contact you via email and/or telephone call, depending the preference you indicated when you filed the support request.

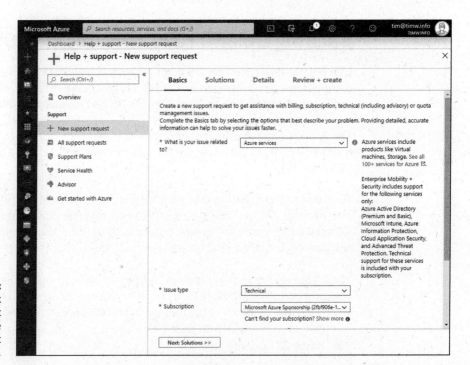

FIGURE 10-7:
Create and track Azure support requests on the Help + Support blade.

IN THIS CHAPTER

» **Differentiating AD products**

» **Describing the relationship between subscriptions and AD**

» **Creating and managing AD users and groups**

» **Implementing role-based access control**

» **Accepting Azure Advisor recommendations**

Chapter **11**

Managing Identity and Access with Azure Active Directory

Every time you do work in Azure, you're interacting with Azure Active Directory (Azure AD), which is a hosted identity service that is relevant to Azure architects, administrators, developers, business analysts, information workers, and even your customers.

The reason why Azure AD is central in Azure is that it forms the identity base for your subscriptions. Any person or process who needs to access your Azure subscription must be defined in Azure AD.

By the end of this chapter, you'll have a strong grasp of the relationship between Azure AD and Azure subscriptions. You'll also have the skills necessary to protect resources with least-privilege security. The IT security principle of least privilege means you should give your users only enough permissions for them to do their jobs and no more.

Understanding Active Directory

Azure AD is a multitenant, hosted identity store used by Azure as well as other Microsoft cloud services, including

» Office 365

» Dynamics 365

» Intune

» Enterprise Mobility + Security

Any computer nowadays — whether it runs Windows, macOS, or Linux — has a local identity store that defines the users authorized to use that computer. Microsoft has offered Active Directory Domain Services (AD DS) in its Windows Server product since 1999; AD DS is a centralized identity store for on-premises networks.

The terms *tenant* and *multitenant* tend to confuse people, so let me clear up the confusion right away. With regard to Azure AD, a *tenant* is simply a single Azure AD instance. A single organization can have one or many Azure AD instances — one Azure AD instance for internal use and another for customers, for example.

Azure AD is called a multitenant identity store because

» You can have more than one Azure AD tenant.

» Each tenant can host user accounts from multiple sources, including other Azure AD tenants.

» One or more subscriptions can trust Azure AD (share a single identity store).

Another term that is often fuzzy is *cloud apps*. With regard to Azure AD, a cloud app is any application (web, desktop, or mobile) that relies on Azure AD as its user identity store.

AD versus AD DS

Azure AD may share part of a name with Active Directory Domain Services (AD DS) in your on-premises network, but these directory services are very different. Table 11-1 provides a high-level comparison.

TABLE 11-1   Azure AD and AD DS Comparison

	AD DS	Azure AD
Access protocol	Lightweight Directory Access Protocol	Microsoft Graph REST API
Forest/tree domain structure	Yes	No
Group policy management	Yes	No
Organizational units	Yes	No
Dynamic groups	No	Yes
Multifactor authentication	No	Yes

Although AD DS and Azure AD are quite different, it's possible to combine them into a hybrid identity solution. You could deploy Azure AD Connect, Microsoft's free identity synchronization engine, to synchronize or federate local AD accounts to AD and thus provide single sign-on to cloud apps.

TIP

For more information on using Azure AD Connect to extend your on-premises Active Directory to Azure AD, see `https://docs.microsoft.com/en-us/azure/active-directory/hybrid/whatis-azure-ad-connect`.

Relationship between subscriptions and AD tenants

You also need to understand clearly how the Azure AD tenant relates to Azure subscriptions. To create an Azure account, you need to use a Microsoft account identity. When you do, your trial subscription is linked to a default AD tenant typically labeled Default Directory.

The Azure AD tenant can exist separately from a subscription, but Azure won't let you deploy any resources unless and until the Azure AD tenant is linked to at least one subscription. Figure 11-1 shows what I mean.

Figure 11-1 depicts a trust relationship that exists between your Azure subscription and a single Azure AD tenant.

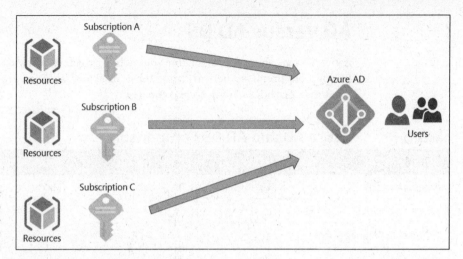

FIGURE 11-1:
Relationship
between Azure
AD and Azure
subscriptions.

Multitenant Azure AD

Although Azure AD can be the identity store for more than one subscription, a single Azure subscription can trust only a single Azure AD tenant at a time. To understand these concepts, follow these steps:

1. **Log in to the Azure portal as the administrative user.**

2. **Select Create a Resource.**

3. **On the Azure Marketplace blade, search and select for Azure Active Directory, and consider the implications of having more than one Azure AD tenant.**

   You can deploy as many Azure AD tenants as you have use cases for, but you can't do anything substantial with them until you bind an Azure subscription to them. Azure AD tenants are resources much like any other resources in Azure Resource Manager (ARM).

4. **Use the global Search box to browse to the Subscriptions blade, and select your subscription in the subscriptions list.**

   If you have only one subscription, this step is an easy one.

5. **On the Overview page toolbar, click Change Directory.**

   Now you're getting somewhere! This control allows you to unplug a subscription from its current Azure AD tenant and plug it into another. Figure 11-2 is a composite screenshot that shows the directory change process in my environment.

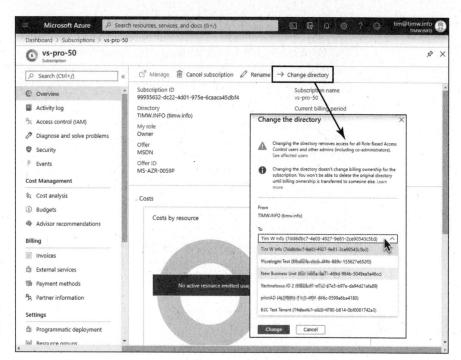

FIGURE 11-2:
Moving an Azure subscription to another Azure AD tenant.

Perhaps your developers want to isolate their environment as they work on their cloud apps. Using a separate Azure AD tenant is great for providing isolation between Azure deployment environments.

WARNING

You'll have to redo all your role-based access control (RBAC) assignments when you move a subscription to another Azure AD tenant. The reason should be pretty obvious: You have a new group of Azure AD user and groups accounts to work with.

The "other" Azure AD Directory family members

Before I dive into the topic of creating Azure AD identities, I'll differentiate among the other members of the Azure Active Directory product family:

>> **Azure AD Business-to-Business (B2B):** This collaboration technology simplifies inviting external users into your Azure AD tenant by allowing them to use their existing email IDs. Use this service when you want to give a contractor or temporary employee limited access to your Azure environment.

>> **Azure AD Business-to-Consumer (B2C):** This portable identity store is aimed at your line-of-business customers. This tenant includes turnkey integration with social media account sign-up and sign-in. Use this service when you want to simplify customer account management for public-facing Azure-based applications.

>> **Azure AD Domain Services:** Azure AD Domain Services is a managed, cloud-hosted Azure AD domain. You can take advantage of LDAP, Kerberos/NTLM authentication, organizational units, group policy, and other features normally reserved only for local AD. Use this service when you want to decommission your local AD DS environment and move entirely to the cloud while preserving your existing Active Directory management tools such as Group Policy.

>> **Azure AD Connect/Connect Health:** The former is a free application you install in your on-premises AD environment to synchronize and/or federate local accounts to Azure AD to support single sign-on. The latter is an Azure portal-based monitoring/reporting layer for Azure AD Connect. Use this product when you've configured hybrid identity between on-premises and Azure, and you need to monitor the connection health.

Creating Users and Groups

This section gets to the good stuff. If you browse to your AD tenant's Properties page, you can change the tenant label from Default Directory to something more meaningful. (You may have noticed in the screenshots in this book that I named my directory timw.info after my DNS domain.)

Generally speaking, you want your users' sign-in names to match their email addresses. The following sections describe how to accomplish this goal.

Adding a domain to your directory

Browse to the Custom domain names setting in your Azure AD tenant. You'll see your original directory name on Microsoft's onmicrosoft.com domain name. The *.onmicrosoft.com domain is the default sign-in suffix for your Azure AD users, but it doesn't make for a good user sign-in experience.

WARNING

You can't delete the *<tenant>*.onmicrosoft.com domain name. This is how Microsoft fundamentally identifies your tenant via the Domain Name System (DNS).

I highly recommend you associate your business DNS domain with your Azure AD tenant. You will then have a choice which sign-in suffix you want your Azure AD users to use.

All you have to do to add your own business DNS domain to your tenant's is verify ownership. Follow these steps:

1. **On the Custom Domain Names blade, click Add Custom Domain.**

2. **In the Custom Domain Name blade, add your custom domain name and then click Add Domain.**

   You're taken to a verification blade.

3. **Add a TXT or MX resource record to your domain's zone file.**

REMEMBER

   You need to have administrative access to your DNS zone to complete this step. It doesn't matter which record type you choose for verification.

   Azure provides you the resource record details.

4. **Click Verify, and wait for Azure to verify the existence of the resource record.**

   The idea is that only the DNS domain owner is able to create the record; thus, you've verified to Microsoft that you own the domain.

5. **When verification is complete, delete the verification record from your domain registrar zone file.**

   You no longer need the record, and now you're free to use your custom domain as a user sign-in suffix.

Figure 11-3 shows my tenant's custom domains list. You can see I have my onmicrosoft.com domain, one verified domain I can use, and a few unverified names I cannot yet use.

Understanding AD user and group types

An identity store is worthless without user and group accounts. User accounts represent individual identities, whereas groups aggregate multiple user accounts for easier management.

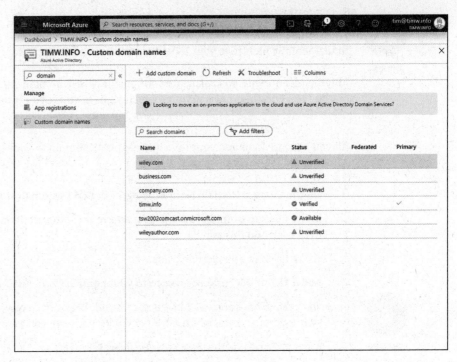

FIGURE 11-3:
Custom domain names in Azure Active Directory.

Next, let me explain how Azure AD users and groups work. In your Azure AD tenant, select the Users blade. Azure AD has two user account types and two group account types:

>> **Member user:** This account is a user created directly in the tenant or a synchronized/federated user from another directory (on-premises or AD).

>> **Guest user:** This account is a user invited into your tenant via AD B2B.

>> **Assigned membership group:** This group is one that you've statically populated with users.

>> **Dynamic group:** This group is one that Azure populates automatically based on predefined user account property values.

The Source column in your AD users list denotes where the user was created and where it is authenticated. This source of authority is important because you may want to treat cloud-native Azure AD accounts differently from federated or synchronized accounts. Options include

>> **AD DS:** These users were created directly in the local tenant.

>> **External Azure AD:** These users were created in a separate Azure AD tenant (yours or somebody else's) and invited into your tenant via AD B2B collaboration.

>> **Microsoft Account:** These users are Azure AD B2B invitees; the account that initially created the tenant/subscription is also a Microsoft account.

REMEMBER

A Microsoft account is a free account that you can use to access several Microsoft services, including Xbox, Office 365, and, of course, Azure. The Microsoft account directory predates Azure; you might remember what used to be called "Windows Live accounts," which are the same thing.

>> **Windows Server AD:** These users are synchronized or federated from a local AD DS domain.

Creating an AD group

For the purposes of this book, I use the Azure portal to create and manage AD user and group accounts. Azure PowerShell and Azure CLI are alternatives you can use; these automation languages make for much shorter work when you need to create accounts in bulk.

You use AD groups in Azure much the same way you use groups in local Active Directory: to simplify administration. Follow these steps to create a sample Azure AD group:

1. **In your Azure AD settings, browse to the Groups blade and click New Group.**

2. **On the New Group blade, complete the form.**

    Following are my recommendations for completing this form:

    - *Group Type:* Choose Security. Office 365 is used for distribution groups in Microsoft Exchange Online. (Office 365 uses Azure AD as well.)

    - *Group Name:* Give the group a meaningful name that's easy to type.

    - *Membership Type:* Choose Assigned. The other options are Dynamic User and Dynamic Device. Dynamic groups instruct Azure to automatically populate these groups based either on user account properties (city, for instance) or their device type (desktop or mobile, for example).

    - *Owners*: These are Azure AD users who will have privilege to edit group membership.

    - *Members*: If you chose Assigned as your group type, then you need to manually add Azure AD users to the group.

3. **Click Create to create the new group.**

Creating an Azure AD user

Now you can create a new Azure AD user account. Follow these steps:

1. **In the Azure AD settings list, select the All Users blade and then click New User.**

2. **In the New User dialog box, click Create User, and fill in the Identity properties.**

   If possible, define the user name and domain parts to match your corporate email ID format. If you haven't added a custom domain, you have no choice but to use the *<tenant>*.onmicrosoft.com suffix.

   I explain how to associate a custom domain with Azure AD in the section "Adding a domain to your directory" earlier in this chapter.

WARNING

   Just because your Azure AD user name matches an email name doesn't mean that Azure validates the address. Azure will send notification messages to this address but doesn't create a mailbox for the user. You have to handle email for your users separately.

3. **Decide how to handle the user's initial password.**

   Users need to supply this initial password the first time they attempt authentication against your AD tenant.

4. **Add the user to an existing group.**

   In the Groups and Roles section, click `0 Groups Selected`, browse your directory, and select the AD group you created. The Groups property should read `1 group selected`.

5. **Leave the other settings at their defaults, and click Create.**

Working with Azure AD user accounts

In this section, I investigate some of the most important actions you can take with your Azure AD user accounts, such as assigning Azure AD licenses to users, logging in as a user, and changing a password.

Assigning licenses to users

All subscription owners start with their Azure AD tenant at the Free pricing tier. Table 11-2 shows a few distinctions among the various editions.

TABLE 11-2   ## Azure AD Edition Comparison

	Azure AD Free	Azure AD Premium P1	Azure AD Premium P2
Maximum directory objects	500,000	Unlimited	Unlimited
AD Connect synchronization	Yes	Yes	Yes
Company branding	No	Yes	Yes
Service-level agreement	No	Yes	Yes
Dynamic groups	No	Yes	Yes
Nonadministrative MFA	No	Yes	Yes

TIP

If you check out the AD pricing page (`https://azure.microsoft.com/en-us/pricing/details/active-directory/`), you'll see an Office 365 Apps edition. I don't address this variant in this book because the focus is Azure.

Keep the following things in mind:

>> Azure AD Premium has a fixed price per user and per month.

>> Each user who will use a premium feature needs to be assigned the appropriate license.

WARNING

You need a native AD account rather than a Microsoft account. The account must also be assigned the Global Administrator directory role. A directory role is a named collection of permissions that give the user greater control over Azure AD.

To purchase Azure AD licenses, follow these steps:

1. **Log in to the Microsoft 365 admin center** (`https://portal.office.com`), **using your Azure AD administrator account.**

2. **Choose Billing ⇨ Products & Services.**

The Purchase Services gallery opens.

3. **Locate Azure Active Directory in the services list, and select P1 or P2.**

Figure 11-4 shows the interface.

4. **Specify your desired license count, and complete the transaction.**

You use your Azure subscription's listed payment method to pay for the licenses.

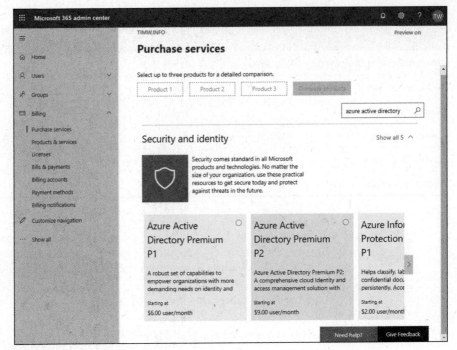

FIGURE 11-4:
You purchase AD Premium licenses in the Microsoft 365 portal rather than the Azure portal.

Distributing licenses

Now that you have some licenses to distribute, this section shows you how to do so in the Azure portal. Follow these steps:

1. **In your AD tenant, choose the Licenses setting.**

   The Get Started with License Management blade appears.

2. **In the Licenses Settings list, select All Products.**

3. **Select the type of license you purchased from the licenses list.**

   If you purchased Azure AD Premium licenses, for example, they show up in this list. You can see how many licenses you've assigned and how many licenses you have available.

4. **On the Licensed Users blade, click Assign from the toolbar.**

5. **On the Assign License blade, select the target user, and click Assign.**

Logging in as an Azure AD user

If you're not familiar with the Azure application access panel (https://myapps.microsoft.com), it's an authenticated site where your AD users can do the following:

>> Log in to Azure cloud apps to which they've been assigned with single-sign on

>> Manage their user accounts, including changing their passwords and/or MFA options

In the example in this section, the fictional user supplies her username (`ginger@timw.info`) and the password she was assigned when her account was created. After she changes her password, she sees her personalized application access panel, shown in Figure 11-5.

FIGURE 11-5:
The application access panel is a one-stop shop that lets Azure AD users access their profile properties and cloud apps.

Changing a user's password

I'm sure that password resets are your support desk's most common user account maintenance operation. To change a password in Azure AD, follow these steps:

1. **Locate and select the user in question in your AD tenant.**

2. **On the user's Profile blade, click Reset Password.**

   The Reset Password blade appears.

3. **In the Reset password blade, click Reset Password.**

   You can copy the temporary password and give it to the user or let Azure notify the user via email message to her sign-in address. The user is forced to change her password at the next sign-in.

You can't reset a Microsoft account's password from AD.

WARNING

Configuring Role-Based Access Control (RBAC)

Microsoft uses a role-based access control (RBAC, typically pronounced *are-back*) authorization model. Authentication refers to credential validation, ensuring that the user is who he or she claims to be. A *role* is a predefined collection of authorizations typically aligned with a job role, so authorization defines the limits of that authenticated user's actions in your system.

Azure RBAC takes advantage of inheritance. In other words, an RBAC role assignment at a higher scope cascades via inheritance to lower scopes. Figure 11-6 shows the five Azure management scopes:

>> **Tenant root:** The highest scope level in ARM.

>> **Management group:** A container that can hold one or more subscriptions. This option is great for businesses that need to apply the same RBAC role assignments to multiple subscriptions at the same time.

>> **Subscription:** The fundamental billing unit in Azure.

>> **Resource group:** The fundamental deployment unit in Azure.

>> **Resource:** Individual Azure assets (virtual machine, database, and so on).

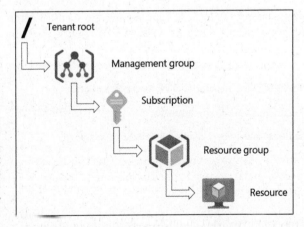

FIGURE 11-6:
Azure management scopes use inheritance to simplify administration.

Implementing built-in RBAC roles

To avoid making a common rookie mistake, understand that Azure has two separate and distinct RBAC roles:

>> **AD roles:** Governing actions within AD

>> **Resource roles:** Governing actions with Azure resources at the tenant root, management group, subscription, resource group, and resource scopes

These roles are discussed in the following sections.

Azure AD roles

When you create an ordinary Azure AD user, that user has no directory roles assigned. The reason is simple: Only selected team members should have privileges in Azure AD itself.

Member-class user accounts can do basic things such as edit their profile properties and perhaps view the properties of other member user accounts. However, you may have people on your team who need the ability to register cloud apps with Azure AD, or to create user and group accounts.

In your Azure AD tenant, select the Roles and Administrators setting to see the full list of built-in Azure AD roles. Some of the most common are

>> **Global administrator:** Role holders can perform all actions within the tenant. This role is the highest-privilege role in your directory, and you need to be extraordinarily careful to whom you assign it.

>> **Application administrator:** Role holders can manage cloud app registrations.

>> **Billing administrator:** Role holders can manage subscription invoicing and payment methods.

>> **Guest inviter:** Role holders can invite external users into your directory via AD B2B collaboration.

>> **Password administrator:** Role holders can reset passwords for nonadministrators.

>> **Reports reader:** Role holders can read Azure auditing reports.

>> **User administrator:** Role holders can manage AD users and groups.

Suppose that a new user, Ginger Grant, should be granted the user administrator role so that she can create and manage Azure AD user accounts. To do so, follow these steps:

1. **Log in to portal.azure.com as the user.**

   Recall that the user is an ordinary user with no Azure AD role assignments.

2. **Browse to the Subscriptions blade.**

   You shouldn't see any subscriptions listed because the new user doesn't have sufficient permissions.

3. **In your Azure AD tenant, open the new user's settings, and click the Directory Role blade.**

   Choose the All Users setting, select the user, and then choose the Directory Role blade from within the user's own settings.

4. **On the Directory Role blade, click Add Assignment.**

5. **In the Directory Roles list for User Administrator, select the role.**

6. **Click Add.**

   The user should be granted membership to the user administrator role.

7. **To test access, sign the user out of the portal and sign in again to refresh the account's access token.**

Figure 11-7 shows that relevant user administration controls — such as adding new users — are unavailable before the user's new role assignment is applied.

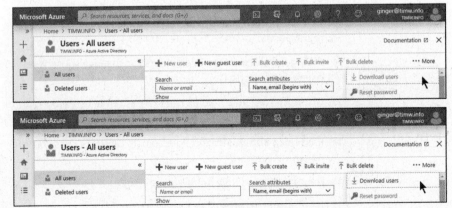

FIGURE 11-7: Before (top) and after (bottom) RBAC role assignment.

TECHNICAL STUFF

The user interface technique of hiding or disabling controls to which the user has no privilege is known as *security trimming*.

Resource roles

Azure AD roles are named permissions collections usable within your Azure AD tenant. By contrast, resource roles are permissions collections that can be associated with your Azure subscriptions and resources. Note that this is an entirely different set of roles from what you've seen thus far in Azure AD.

You can apply RBAC roles to any of the five management scopes discussed in "Azure AD roles" earlier in this chapter, and those assignments cascade via inheritance to lower scope levels.

You add role assignments for a user on the Subscriptions blade. The most common built-in resource roles include

>> **Owner:** Lets you take any action at that scope, including editing the RBAC role memberships

>> **Contributor:** Has the same privileges as Owner except that you can't edit RBAC assignments

>> **Reader:** Lets you view resources but not change them

>> **Virtual Machine Contributor:** Lets you manage virtual machines (VMs) but not their associated network and storage resources

>> **Virtual Machine Administrator Login:** Lets you view VMs in a subscription and log in to them as an administrator

Adding an account to an Azure AD role

Follow these steps to add an account to the Reader role at the subscription level:

1. **To test the "before" state, log in to the Azure portal as a new user, and navigate to the Resource Groups blade.**

Type **resource groups** into the Azure global Search box to find this blade quickly.

You shouldn't see any resource groups listed because the user hasn't been given any privileges yet.

2. **Browse to the Subscriptions blade, select your subscription, and click the Access Control (IAM) setting.**

3. **On the Check Access tab, type the user's sign-in name to view her current access level.**

   The Azure portal should show zero role assignments for this user.

4. **On the Role Assignments tab, choose Add ⇨ Add Role Assignment.**

5. **On the Add Role Assignment blade, assign the user the Reader role.**

   Use the following settings:

   - *Role:* Select the Reader role.

   - *Assign Access To:* Use Azure AD user, group, or service.

   - *Select:* Type the user's sign-in name to resolve the account, and click to select it.

6. **Click Save to commit your changes.**

7. **As your user, sign out of the Azure portal and then sign in again to test access.**

   The Resource Groups blade should show limited access to all resources in the user's subscription scope. Azure prevents you from taking most actions, which you can test by attempting to shut down a VM or upload a blob to a storage account.

At any scope, you can visit the Access Control (IAM) blade and its Role Assignments tab to view which accounts have which degrees of access (see Figure 11-8).

TECHNICAL STUFF

CUSTOM RBAC ROLES

The time will almost certainly arrive when the built-in RBAC roles don't precisely meet your needs. The good news is that you can define custom RBAC roles for Azure AD and for Azure resources. At this writing, you need to use Azure PowerShell or Azure CLI to create a custom RBAC resource role. By contrast, you can create Azure AD custom roles directly in the Azure portal. Learn more about custom roles in Azure by reading the docs article "Custom roles for Azure resources" at https://docs.microsoft.com/en-us/azure/role-based-access-control/custom-roles.

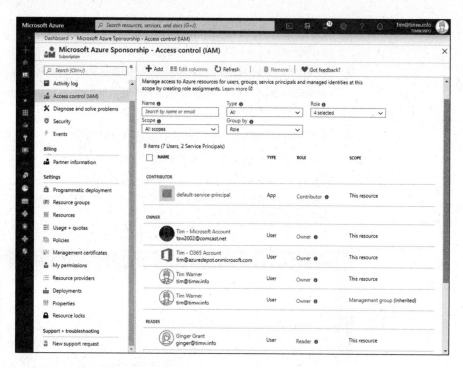

FIGURE 11-8:
Viewing RBAC
role assignments
at a particular
management
scope.

Touring Azure Advisor

I wrap up this chapter by discussing an often overlooked but extremely helpful Azure service called Azure Advisor.

Practically nobody has 100 percent vision in his or her Azure infrastructure's cost, performance, security, and high availability. Azure Advisor uses machine learning algorithms to make recommendations on how you can better optimize your Azure environment for cost, security, availability, and performance.

Azure Advisor is a recommendation engine that scans your subscriptions and provides guidance on high availability, security, performance, and cost. The service is free, so it's an economical way to get feedback on places where you may benefit from making changes in your subscriptions. You can create alerts that fire when Advisor makes particular recommendations, and you can tweak the recommendation engine to better suit your environment.

To work with Advisor, follow these steps:

1. **In the Azure portal, navigate to the Advisor Overview blade.**

From this blade's toolbar, you can download reports in CSV (comma-separated values) or PDF format.

2. **Choose Settings ➪ Recommendations ➪ Security.**

The Security Recommendations blade appears.

Figure 11-9 shows the security recommendations Advisor made for me, listing impact, problem description, affected resources, and the date when it created the recommendations.

FIGURE 11-9: Advisor provides detailed recommendations and sometimes fixes problems automatically.

3. **Select a recommendation to view its details.**

You might select the recommendation titled Secure Transfer to Storage Accounts Should Be Enabled, for example. This recommendation can be remediated automatically. Select the affected resource(s), and click Remediate; Azure enables secure transfer for my selected storage accounts.

Notice the Security Center button at the top of the Advisor security recommendations. Azure Security Center also uses machine learning to make recommendations on your environment; Advisor includes Security Center recommendations as part of its logic. Security Center is covered in Chapter 12.

At this writing, you can't create your own Advisor recommendations, but you can customize the behavior of the built-in recommendations. Follow these steps:

1. **In Advisor, select the Configuration setting.**

2. **Browse to the Rules tab.**

3. **Select a rule and then choose Edit from the pop-up menu.**

   You might choose to customize the Right-Size or Shutdown Low Usage Virtual Machines recommendation, for example.

4. **On the Edit Recommendation Rule blade, make your change.**

   You might change the recommendation threshold from 5 percent CPU to 10, 15, or 20 percent CPU, for example.

5. **Click Apply to finish the configuration.**

Chapter **12**

Implementing Azure Governance

Azure governance is how your organization approaches the management of your various Azure resources. For instance, how can you ensure that resources are deployed only to authorized regions? How can you limit resource sizes so you don't exceed your budget? In this chapter, you see how to use Azure's core governance tools: taxonomic tags and Azure Policy.

Implementing Taxonomic Tags

The resource group is Azure's fundamental deployment unit. The idea is that you place all resources that share a life cycle in the same resource group to simplify management and auditing.

Life is rarely that simple, however. It's just as likely that you'll have deployments that span resource groups, regions, and even subscriptions. Satisfying your accounting and compliance departments to track these loosely coupled resources can be difficult.

Using taxonomic tags is the answer. In Azure, a *tag* is a simple key/value pair. As long as a user has write access to a resource, he or she can add existing tags to that resource or create a new tag.

For example, you may have tags to denote various cost centers in your organization, or perhaps your tags separate different Azure-based projects. Azure presents tags in the format key:value, such as CostCenter:Development.

Taxonomic tags in Azure are a bit fussy. Here are some facts about taxonomic tags to keep in mind as you go along:

>> Each resource group or resource can have a maximum of 50 tags.

>> Tag names are limited to 512 characters; tag values are limited to 256 characters.

>> Tags applied to a resource group don't flow by inheritance to lower management scopes.

>> Not all Azure resources support tags. You can't apply tags to management groups or subscriptions, for example — only to resource groups and most resource types.

>> Tag names can't include the following reserved characters: < > % & \ ? /.

WARNING

Unlike RBAC and Azure Policy assignments, tags applied to a resource group are not inherited to the resources inside that resource group. You can use Azure PowerShell or Azure CLI to work around this limitation, but it's significant and worth noting.

Another pain point to consider is how easy it is to use Azure tags inconsistently. You'll find by bitter experience that some of your colleagues (never you, mind you, but your colleagues) do the following things:

>> Forget to add tags to resources during or after deployment

>> Accidentally use an incorrect tag name or value

>> Misspell a tag name or value

These problems can have big implications if you're using taxonomic tags for cost tracking because inconsistent tagging leads to inconsistent (inaccurate) reporting results. The good news is that you can use Azure Policy to standardize your tag application.

Applying tags to resource groups and resources

One of the most important governance conversations your team needs to have is about which Azure resource naming and tagging standard makes the most sense.

You can refer to the following Microsoft online resources for guidance on resource and tag-naming best practices:

>> Ready: Recommended naming and tagging conventions: `https://docs.microsoft.com/en-us/azure/cloud-adoption-framework/ready/azure-best-practices/naming-and-tagging`

>> Resource naming and tagging decision guide: `https://docs.microsoft.com/en-us/azure/cloud-adoption-framework/decision-guides/resource-tagging/`

Table 12-1 summarizes a few ways to classify taxonomic tags and which tag names to use.

TABLE 12-1   ## Common Azure Taxonomic Tagging Patterns

Tag Type	Example Tags (name:value)
Accounting	`department:legal`
	`region:europe`
	`project:salespromo`
Classification	`confidentiality:private`
	`sla:8h`
Functional	`app:prodsite1`
	`env:staging`
	`tier:web`
Partnership	`contact:jsmith`
	`owner:twarner`
Purpose	`businessproc:development`
	`revenueimpact:high`

Adding tags in the Azure portal

With no further ado, let me walk you through adding tags to resource groups and individual resources. I show you how to create resource groups in Chapter 2.

Make sure that you have a resource group with at least two resources inside and that you're logged in to the Azure portal with your administrator account, and then follow these steps:

1. **In your resource group's settings list, select Tags.**

2. **Type a new tag name and value, and then click Save.**

    You might use the name "project" and the value "learning," for example.

    Don't be surprised if you see other tag names and values, even if you're the only user in your subscription. Sometimes, Azure itself adds tags to resources.

3. **Navigate to the resource group's Overview page, and verify its tag.**

    You should see a Tags field in the Essentials pane.

4. **Click the tag you named in Step 2.**

    Azure transports you to the project:learning blade, which lists any resources to which you've assigned this tag.

5. **Browse to a resource within your resource group, and click Tags from the resource's settings list.**

6. **Reuse the existing project tag, but change the name to testing.**

    The tag now reads `project:testing`.

    Azure tags are modifiable, which is both convenient and dangerous because a misspelling can result in incorrect reporting.

7. **Click Save to commit your changes.**

8. **Associate either tag or both new tags with a few other resources in different resource groups.**

You can (and should) add appropriate tags to new resources during deployment.

Figure 12-1 shows the Create storage account's Tags deployment blade.

Adding tags programmatically

It's super-easy to add tags to resources programmatically with PowerShell. Chapter 2 talks about both Azure CLI and Azure PowerShell. First, use the following code to list existing tags on your resource group (mine is called `'wiley'`):

```
(Get-AzResourceGroup -Name 'wiley').Tags
Name                           Value
----                           -----
project                        learning
```

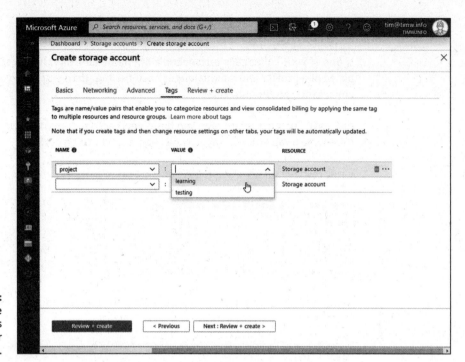

FIGURE 12-1:
It's best practice
to tag resources
during their
deployment.

REMEMBER

Log in to Azure with `Login-AzAccount` and set your default subscription with `Set-AzContext` before you try any of these steps.

Suppose that you want to add a new tag (env:dev) to your resource group. If you use the Set-AzResourceGroup command to add the new tag, PowerShell overwrites any existing tags and replaces them with the new one, so you don't want to do that. Instead, you can first store the `'wiley'` resource group's tags in a variable named $tags:

```
$tags = (Get-AzResourceGroup -Name 'wiley').Tags
```

Next, use the $tags object's Add method to include a new env:dev tag:

```
$tags.Add("env", "dev")
```

Finally, run Set-AzResourceGroup to commit the change:

```
Set-AzResourceGroup -Tag $tags -Name 'wiley'
```

Removing tags

If one of your colleagues misspelled a tag name and/or value, or if your team disposed of a project and you no longer need the tag, then you have yourself an Azure governance problem to solve.

Just as it's easy to create tags and build new tags from existing entries, it's simple to remove a tag you no longer want. Again, you use PowerShell.

First, retrieve the existing tags (mine are on my 'wiley' resource group):

```
(Get-AzResourceGroup -Name 'wiley').Tags
Name                          Value
----                          -----
env                           dev
project                       learning
```

Next, use the following code to try to delete the env tag and all its values with this command:

```
Remove-AzTag -Name env
```

The result is

```
Remove-AzTag : Cannot remove tag/tag value because
               it's being referenced by other resources.
```

Ouch! It looks as though you have to remove this tag from all related resources before you can delete it, which makes sense. You can run the following two commands to locate all resource groups and resources that have a specific tag:

```
(Get-AzResourceGroup -Tag @{ 'env' = 'dev' }).ResourceGroupName
(Get-AzResource -Tag @{ 'env' = 'dev' }).Name
```

TIP

You can leave a tag's name but delete a particular value by using the -Value parameter of Remove-AzTag. In this example, you could remove the 'projektY' value from your 'project' tag by running Remove-AzTag -Name 'project' -Value 'projektY'. That way, any other project values would persist in your subscription.

At this point, it's probably easier to look up the resources in the portal and delete the tag references. After you've cleared the tag from any associated resources, you can retry using the Remove-AzTag command to remove the tag.

Reporting via tags

The simplest way to report on which resources have been associated with a given tag is to open the Tags blade and click the appropriate tag, as shown in Figure 12-2.

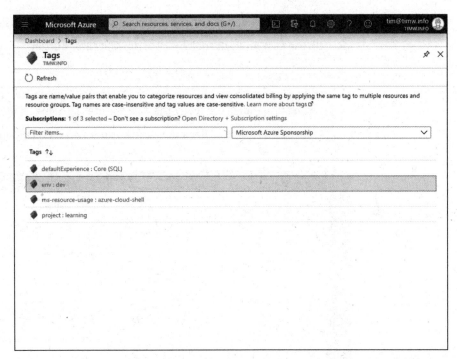

FIGURE 12-2:
Tag reporting in
the Azure portal.

Each name:value pair shows up as a separate row in the Tags list. You might see project:learning or project:testing, for example.

One of the most important use cases for Azure taxonomic tags is cost reporting. As it happens, Azure makes it simple to generate this data in a visually appealing format.

Cost Management + Billing blade

You can see basic resource use/costing information on the Subscriptions blade in the Azure portal. To really dig into your spending and forecast future spend, however, use the Cost Management + Billing blade. Follow these steps to filter the view based on tag name/value:

1. **In the Azure portal, use global search to browse to the Cost Management + Billing blade, and then select the Cost Management setting.**

2. **In the Cost Management blade settings list, click Cost Analysis.**

3. **On the Cost Analysis toolbar, click the Add Filter button.**

   Azure creates a row to hold your filter expression.

4. **From the first drop-down list, choose Tag as your attribute, and from the second drop-down list select the appropriate tag names and/or values.**

   Azure applies the new filter immediately. Figure 12-3 shows my environment.

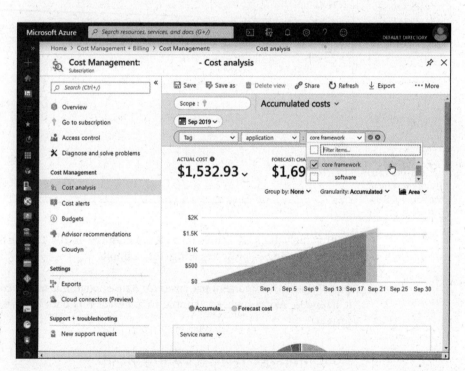

FIGURE 12-3:
Use tags to
perform Azure
cost analysis.

API access to tags and billing

Developers often prefer to use API access to find their answers as quickly as possible. To do this, they can use several billing-related APIs that include tags:

>> **Resource Usage API:** This API reveals your Azure service consumption data.

>> **RateCard API:** This API displays current prices for Azure services based on region.

>> **Cloud Cost Management API:** This API lies behind the Cost Management + Billing Azure portal blade.

Learn more about the Azure consumption APIs by reading the Azure documentation article "Azure consumption API overview" at `https://docs.microsoft.com/en-us/azure/billing/billing-consumption-api-overview`.

Implementing Azure Policy

Azure Policy is a simple JavaScript Object Notation (JSON) document that can protect your entire management group or subscription against deployment actions that violate your company policy. Policy limits what authorized users can do within their deployment scopes. You may deploy a Policy that prevents users from deploying virtual machines (VMs) outside your allowed Azure regions, for example.

TIP

Fundamental differences exist between role-based access control (RBAC) roles and Policy. RBAC roles enable your Azure users to perform particular actions on your Azure resources, such as deploying a VM.

You can define your own policies, but Microsoft offers existing policies you can use. Here are some examples of built-in Policy definitions:

>> **Allowed locations:** Restrict the locations that your organization can specify when deploying resources.

>> **Disk encryption should be applied on VMs:** Apply whole-disk encryption to your Azure VM operating system and data disks.

>> **Add a tag to resources:** Add the specified tag and value when any resource missing this tag is created or updated.

>> **Allowed virtual machine SKUs:** Restrict which VM sizes users can deploy.

Policy definition structure

Like just about everything else in Azure Resource Manager (ARM), Policy definitions are JSON documents. It's a great idea to add parameters to your policies to make them more flexible. Consider the following example, which defines a parameter named `listOfAllowedLocations`:

```
"parameters": {
  "listOfAllowedLocations": {
    "type": "Array",
    "metadata": {
      "description": "The list of locations that can be specified when
          deploying resources.",
      "strongType": "location",
      "displayName": "Allowed locations"
    }
  }
}
```

TIP

You can learn more about Azure Policy JSON syntax by reading the Azure documentation article "Azure Policy definition structure" at `https://docs.microsoft.com/en-us/azure/governance/policy/concepts/definition-structure`.

At policy deployment, you specify a value for the `listOfAllowedLocations` parameter. The `strongType` element is a bit of ARM magic that creates a drop-down list containing all Azure regions. It's a handy trick to use in your ARM templates and Policy definitions.

Recall that Azure Resource Manager (ARM) is the API that underlies anything and everything you do in Azure.

As an alternative, you can create an enumeration of allowed values by substituting the `allowedValues` array:

```
"allowedValues": [
  "EastUS",
  "EastUS2",
  "CentralUS"
]
```

The guts of a policy is the condition statement. The next code block uses an `if` block with one or more constraints. In this example, all the conditions must evaluate to `true` for the policy to take effect. The policy evaluates the location specified in the deployment. If the target location isn't in the list of allowed locations, then the policy denies the deployment.

```
{
    "if": {
        "allOf": [
            {
                "field": "location",
                "notIn": "[parameters('listOfAllowedLocations')]"
            }
        ]
    },
    "then": {
        "effect": "Deny"
    }
}
```

Policy includes quite a different policy effects. In Azure Policy, an effect determines what Azure does if a given policy evaluates to true.

With the Audit effect, you can allow deployments but track them closely for auditing purposes. The DeployIfNotExists effect is super-powerful because the policy can execute an ARM template deployment to enforce the policy. For example, you can have a policy automatically reenable resource diagnostics if a colleague accidentally or intentionally turns them off on a resource.

TIP

If you'd like to dive deeper on Policy, see "Understand Azure Policy Effects" at https://docs.microsoft.com/en-us/azure/governance/policy/concepts/effects.

Policy life cycle

Deploying a policy occurs in three phases:

>> **Authoring:** Typically, you make a copy of an existing policy definition, attach it to a management scope, and edit it to suit your requirements.

>> **Assignment:** You link a policy to a management scope.

>> **Compliance:** You review and report on Azure resource compliance and take authoring, assignment, and remediated corrective actions as necessary.

In Policy, an *initiative* is a container object associated with one or more individual policy definitions. The initiative's use case is businesses that want to manage multiple related policy assignments as a single entity. This chapter, however, focuses on individual policies.

Creating a policy

You can define a policy linked to the subscription scope that limits the regions to which administrators can deploy resources. Follow these steps in the Azure portal:

1. **Browse to the Policy blade, and choose Settings ⇨ Definitions.**

2. **On the Policy - Definitions blade, type** location **in the Search box.**

You see a list of results for the search term as you type. Spend a moment browsing the results list. I show you this interface in Figure 12-4.

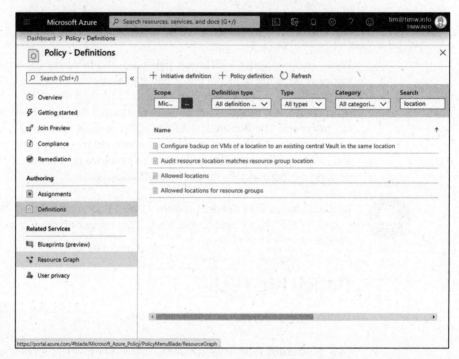

FIGURE 12-4:
Browsing built-in
Azure Policy
definitions.

3. **Select the Allowed Locations built-in policy definition, and click Duplicate Definition from the toolbar.**

The policy definition appears. The built-in templates are read-only, so you need to duplicate it to make it your own.

4. **Complete the new policy definition.**

Here is some guidance on the properties:

- *Definition Location:* Options are management group and subscription. I recommend you choose your subscription.

- *Name:* Make the policy name meaningful in accordance with your corporate Azure naming convention.

- *Category:* Store the policy in a built-in category or create your own.

5. **Edit the policy rule to remove the following lines:**

```
{
  "field": "location",
  "notEquals": "global"
},
{
  "field": "type",
  "notEquals": "Microsoft.AzureActiveDirectory/b2cDirectories"
}
```

The only policy condition you need, strictly speaking, is the one that references the listOfAllowedLocations parameter value(s).

6. **Click Save to commit your changes.**

TIP Microsoft's Policy engineering team hosts an Azure Policy Samples GitHub repository that contains hundreds of policies across most Azure services. These policy definitions should give you a head start on governing your own environments. You can find them at https://github.com/Azure/azure-policy.

Assigning the policy

After you've created a custom policy definition, assign it to your subscription and test it. Follow these steps:

1. **On the Policy - Definitions blade, choose Custom from the Type drop-down list.**

   It's helpful to filter your view so that you see only your custom policies.

2. **Select your policy, and click Assign on the toolbar.**

   You can also edit or delete your policy definition from this configuration blade.

3. **Complete the form.**

   Here are my recommendations for filling out the form:

   - *Scope:* Because you linked the definition to the subscription level, select that subscription as your assignment scope. You can further limit policy scope to a particular resource group within the subscription.

- *Exclusions:* You can exempt resource groups and individual resources from the policy. In this case, you may have resources already present in the subscription that have authorized to exist in disallowed regions.

- *Assignment Name:* The assignment name can have a different display name from its underlying policy definition.

- *Parameters:* In this case, you should see an Allowed Locations drop-down list populated with Azure regions. Choose whichever regions you want to allow.

- *Create a Managed Identity:* This option is necessary only when your policy will perform deployment. A Managed Identity in Azure Active Directory (AD) is analogous to a service account in local AD; see Chapter 11.

4. **Click Assign to submit your policy.**

WARNING

Open the notification menu; you may see an information message informing you that Policy assignments take around 30 minutes to go into effect.

If you browse to the Assignments blade, you should see your newly assigned policy, as shown in Figure 12-5. To get a clearer view, open the Definition type drop-down list and filter for Policy.

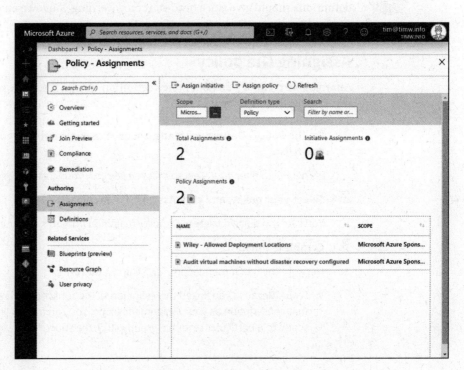

FIGURE 12-5:
List of Policy assignments.

Testing the policy

To test the policy, attempt to deploy an Azure resource to a disallowed location. For example, try to deploy a new storage account; Chapter 3 describes how to do this.

The deployment should fail, as shown in Figure 12-6.

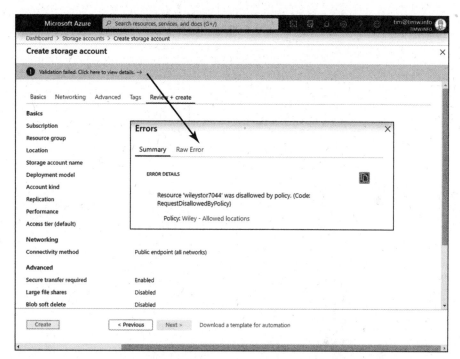

FIGURE 12-6: Azure Policy blocked this deployment.

Notice that the Azure failure text explains that the desired storage account resource is disallowed by policy, and it even helpfully reminds you which policy was the protector.

TECHNICAL STUFF

AZURE BLUEPRINTS

Azure Blueprints is a service in which you can package related Azure artifacts (including ARM templates, RBAC role assignments, and Policy definitions) into deployable units that you manage centrally. I suggest that you look into Blueprints as a way to apply your new skills in using these artifacts individually. See the Azure Blueprints documentation at https://docs.microsoft.com/en-us/azure/governance/blueprints/.

5

Migrating to Microsoft Azure and Monitoring Your Infrastructure

IN THIS PART . . .

Extending your on-premises environment to Azure

Mastering how to migrate massive amounts of data from your on-premises network to Azure

Grasping the difference between Azure VPN and ExpressRoute

Monitoring your Azure resource health

IN THIS CHAPTER

» Migrating on-premises data and databases into Azure

» Migrating on-premises physical and virtual servers into Azure

» Establishing a VPN to connect your on-premises network to Azure

Chapter **13**

Extending Your On-Premises Environment to Azure

I n this chapter, I cover the task of migrating on-premises data and applications into Azure. The good news is that Microsoft provides many tools to make the process easier. I also discuss how to create a hybrid cloud in which you extend your on-premises network infrastructure into an Azure virtual network.

Data Migration Options

Managing data on-premises can be both expensive and stressful. There's data resiliency to consider, as well as disaster recovery. You have security issues such as data encryption, and you have to be concerned about running out of space and having to make additional capital expenditures to expand your local storage fabric.

For these reasons and more, you may want or need to move local data into Azure. You have three options for doing that:

» Blob copy

» Azure Data Box

» Azure Migrate

Blob copy

The most straightforward way to get local blob data into a storage account is to do file copies. You could use Azure Storage Explorer, but a better option is the AzCopy command-line tool, available free at `https://docs.microsoft.com/en-us/` `azure/storage/common/storage-use-azcopy-v10?WT.mc_id=thomasmaurer-` `blog-thmaure`.

Suppose that you have 2 TB of data in a server directory called D:\backup-archive, and you want to copy these files to a container on Azure named backup-archive in your wileystorage704 storage account.

After you open an elevated command prompt on the file server, you'd authenticate to Azure with AzCopy this way:

```
azcopy login
```

Next, you perform the copy (note that the following code should be on one line; I had to break the line so it would fit on the printed page):

```
azcopy copy "D:\backup-archive" https://wileystorage704.
          blob.core.windows.net/
          backup-archive
          --recursive --put-md5
```

The `--recursive` flag ensures that you copy all subfolders inside the parent folder. The `--put-md5` flag instructs AzCopy to verify that the copied files match their local versions through MD5 checksum verification.

The upside to this data migration method is that it's very inexpensive, barring network bandwidth. The downside is that the process could take hours or days to complete. Also, although AzCopy includes retry logic in the event of a copy interruption, the program will abort after a 15-minute timeout, which can make your data migration process take longer yet.

Azure Data Box

Azure Data Box is a collection of physical storage appliances (and one virtual option) that you rent from Microsoft. The high-level Data Box workflow is

1. Order your Data Box from the Azure portal.

2. Connect Data Box to your local computer or network.

3. Use Data Box's local web portal to structure how you want the Azure-side data to look (storage accounts, containers, and so on).

4. Copy data from your local environment to Data Box.

5. Ship the Data Box to your primary Azure region.

   Microsoft unpacks your data into your Azure subscription.

Here's a rundown of the Data Box family members:

>> **Data Box Disk:** 8 TB SSD drive, available in packs of five (40 TB). Plug the disks into your local workstation by using a USB/SATA interface.

>> **Data Box:** Ruggedized appliance with 100 TB capacity; connects to your LAN with high-speed Ethernet ports.

>> **Data Box Heavy:** Wheeled drive cart with 1 PB capacity.

>> **Azure Stack Edge:** On-premises physical appliance; includes logic for transforming data before uploading it to Azure.

>> **Data Box Gateway:** A virtual appliance version of Data Box Edge.

TIP

Azure has a legacy offline data migration product called Import/Export Service whereby you prepare your own hard drives and ship them to Microsoft. I chose to ignore this option for this book because Data Box is much more flexible and cost-effective. Check the docs for more info: https://docs.microsoft.com/en-us/azure/storage/common/storage-import-export-service.

Figure 13-1 shows the various physical Data Box form factors. The Data Box Gateway is a software appliance; therefore, it's not shown.

The advantage of Data Box is that it's a convenient way to get large data volumes into Azure. The disadvantage (with the exception of Data Box Edge and Data Box Gateway) is the latency between ordering, filling, shipping, and unpacking the appliance. You may not be able to afford that kind of data latency.

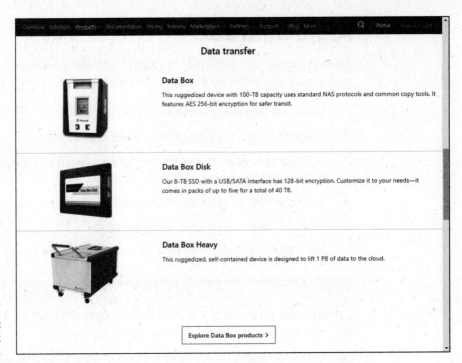

Data transfer

Data Box

This ruggedized device with 100-TB capacity uses standard NAS protocols and common copy tools. It features AES 256-bit encryption for safer transit.

Data Box Disk

Our 8-TB SSD with a USB/SATA interface has 128-bit encryption. Customize it to your needs—it comes in packs of up to five for a total of 40 TB.

Data Box Heavy

This ruggedized, self-contained device is designed to lift 1 PB of data to the cloud.

Explore Data Box products >

FIGURE 13-1:
The Data Box
product family.

What is your alternative, then? In the "Hybrid Cloud Options" section, I describe the virtual private network (VPN) and ExpressRoute options for establishing secure, high-speed, always-on connectivity to Azure.

Azure Migrate: Database Assessment

Instead of or in addition to blob (file) data, you likely have on-premises SQL Server databases that you want to migrate to Azure in an offline or online manner. The Microsoft-supported database migration workflow involves two phases:

>> **Assessment:** Evaluate your current workload parameters, and determine which Azure product is the best fit and at which pricing tier/scale.

>> **Migration:** Determine your tolerance for network latency, and then decide on an offline or online migration method.

Performing the database assessment

Practically all data migration options nowadays happen under the Azure Migrate product umbrella. Follow these steps to create a new database migration project and kick off an assessment:

1. **In the Azure portal, browse to the Azure Migrate blade.**

2. **In the Migration Goals section, click Databases.**

   The Getting Started blade appears.

3. **On the Details pane, in the Getting Started section, click Add Tool(s).**

4. **On the Add a Tool tab, complete the Migrate Project blade.**

   Specify subscription, resource group, migration project name, and geography.

5. **Click Next to continue.**

6. **On the Select Assessment tool blade, choose Azure Migrate: Database Assessment.**

   I show you this interface in Figure 13-2.

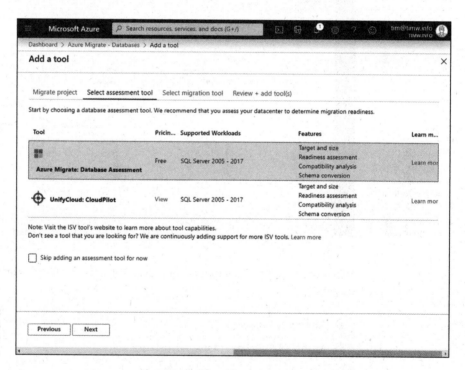

FIGURE 13-2:
Adding tools
to an Azure
Migrate project.

7. **On the Select Migration tool blade, choose Azure Migrate: Database Migration.**

8. **Deselect Skip Adding a Migration Tool.**

9. **Go back to the Azure Migrate - Databases blade, and click the link to download Data Migration Assistant (DMA).**

DMA is a free desktop app that you'll download and run on your administrative workstation.

Figure 13-3 shows the DMA interface.

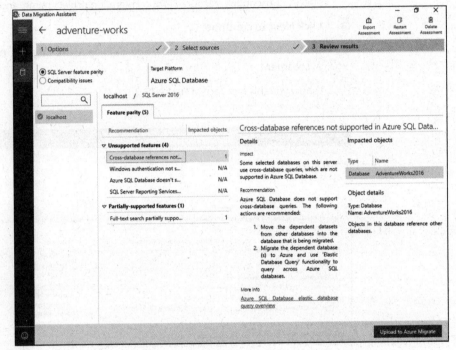

FIGURE 13-3: Use DMA to assess your local SQL Server databases for Azure readiness.

When you run DMA, you model your local SQL Server database against one of four targets:

» Azure SQL Database

» Azure SQL Database Managed Instance

» SQL Server on Azure Virtual Machines

» SQL Server

DMA checks your database compatibility against your defined Azure database option, and it checks feature parity to ensure that you're not using features on-premises that aren't available in Azure. It also allows you to upload your assessment results to your Azure Migrate project, which feeds into the next phase: migration.

TECHNICAL STUFF

Microsoft designed Azure Migrate to work without need for a secure virtual private network (VPN) connection. Instead, your connection to Azure is encrypted using the TLS/SSL protocol. Therefore, you can be assured of data privacy before, during, and after the migration process.

Performing the database migration with DMS

In Azure, you use Database Migration Service (DMS) to migrate your assessed on-premises SQL Server databases to Azure. DMS supports several other database platforms, including

>> MongoDB

>> MySQL

>> AWS RDS for MySQL

>> PostgreSQL

>> AWS RDS for PostgreSQL

>> Oracle

Follow these steps to get started with DMS in the Azure portal:

1. **In your Azure Migrate - Databases project, below the heading Get Started with DMS, click the link to create a DMS service instance.**

The Create Migration Service blade appears.

2. **Complete the Create Migration Service deployment blade.**

You're required to place the database migration project on a virtual network in your home region. You also choose a pricing tier. Besides speed and capacity, the biggest difference between the Standard and Premium pricing tiers is that only Premium supports online migration. In my consulting work, I've found that most customers go with Premium because online migration is a business requirement for them.

3. **Open your Azure Database Migration Services service instance, and click New Migration Project.**

4. **Give the project a meaningful name, and complete the New Migration Project form, as follows:**

- *Source Server Type:* Select the source server type, such as SQL Server.

- *Target Server Type:* Select the type of server you're migrating to, such as SQL Database.

- *Type of Activity:* If you chose the Premium pricing tier, your options are Offline Data Migration, Schema-Only Migration, Online Data Migration, and Create the Project Shell Only.

The Migration Wizard takes over with various phases and options, depending on your source database platform.

One important note: Whereas database assessment required no VPN, you need to have an existing, secure connection path between your on-premises database server and Azure to complete the database migration with Azure Database Migration Services. This could be a point-to-site VPN, site-to-site VPN, or an ExpressRoute circuit.

Performing database migration with DMA

If establishing a VPN isn't workable, you can perform the database migration with the DMA tool, which uses standard secure web protocols and requires no VPN. Figure 13-4 shows the interface.

You're likely asking, "Tim, why would I use DMS when DMA can not only assess my local databases, but migrate them too?"

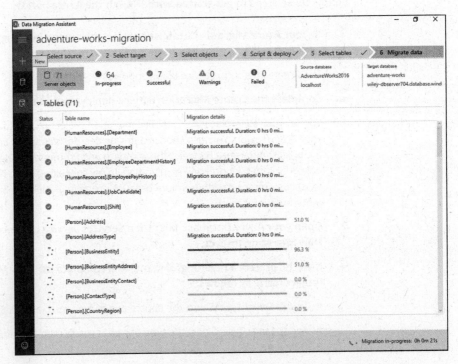

FIGURE 13-4:
The DMA tool can perform database migration as well as assessment.

The answer to that question is twofold:

>> Only DMS supports migration of non-SQL Server databases.

>> DMS was built to perform at great scale.

In conclusion, if you need to migrate only a small number of SQL Server databases, you likely don't need DMS. But if you're operating on a large number of potentially gigantic databases across vendors, DMS is a great fit.

Server Migration Options

The last category of migration is server migration. The most convenient way to migrate servers is with Azure Site Recovery (ASR), which supports physical and virtual servers, and also fully supports VMware and Hyper-V virtualization environments.

However, you also can migrate on-premises VHDs to an Azure storage account by using AzCopy; then you convert the uploaded VHDs to managed disks.

VHD upload

A common, still-valid use for a tool such as AzCopy is migrating generalized VHDs from on-premises into Azure to Azure virtual machine (VM) deployments. To do that, you first upload your generalized Generation 1 VHD.

WARNING

Although Azure is gradually rolling out support for Hyper-V Generation 2 VHDX files, I suggest that you take the safe route and upload only Generation 1 VHDs. You may need to do some format conversion on your VM disks before transferring them to Azure, especially if you use VMware or another non-Microsoft hypervisor.

When you have your generalized VHD tucked into a storage account, you can use Azure PowerShell to create a managed disk. Follow these steps:

1. Create some variables, as follows:

```
$vmName = "vm-template"
$rgName = "myResourceGroup"
$location = "EastUS2"
$imageName = "myImage"
```

2. Create a reference to your generalized VHD in Azure, as follows:

```
$osVhdUri = https://mystorageaccount.blob.core.windows.net/vhdcontainer/
    vhdfilename.vhd
```

3. Run a series of AzImage cmdlets to create the image:

```
$imageConfig = New-AzImageConfig -Location $location
$imageConfig = Set-AzImageOsDisk -Image $imageConfig
        -OsType Windows -OsState Generalized
        -BlobUri $osVhdUri
$image = New-AzImage -ImageName $imageName
        -ResourceGroupName $rgName -Image $imageConfig
```

When you have your managed image in place, you can deploy new VMs based on that image. On the Basics tab of the Create a Virtual Machine blade, click Browse All Public and Private Images, and switch to the My Items tab, shown in the composite image in Figure 13-5. Chapter 5 covers creating an Azure VM.

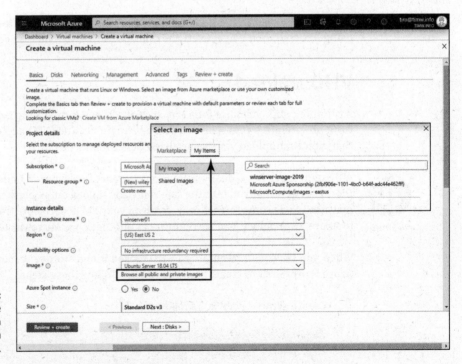

FIGURE 13-5: Deploy Azure VMs based on your own custom VHD images.

Azure Migrate: Server Assessment

The other alternative is to use Azure Migrate as your on-premises server migration base of operations. Follow these steps to get things rolling:

1. **In the Azure portal, browse to the Azure Migrate blade, select Servers, and then click Add Tool(s).**

2. **Complete the Migrate Project tab.**

   You need to fill in metadata: subscription, resource group, migrate project name, and geography.

3. **On the Select Assessment Tool tab, select Azure Migrate: Server Assessment.**

   Microsoft allows certain independent software vendor partners to include their tools in this list. Figure 13-6 shows this interface.

4. **On the Select Migration Tool tab, click Azure Migrate: Server Migration.**

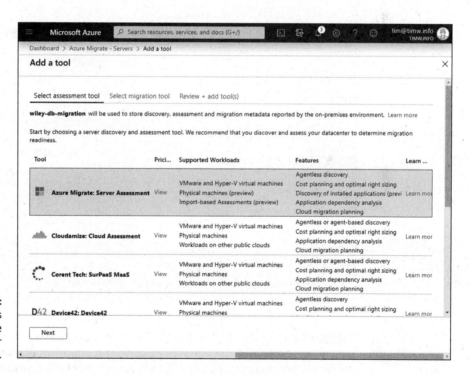

FIGURE 13-6: Adding tools to an Azure Migrate server migration project.

Then you can kick off a discovery and assessment process that takes different forms, depending on whether you have a Hyper-V or a VMware environment on-premises.

The discovery and assessment workflow

You download a Migrate VM appliance, stand it up in your local network, and let it do its work. The appliance does a good job of enumerating all your local servers and reporting on how they might translate into Azure VMs.

The collector appliance also sends its discovery and assessment data to your Migrate project for centralized tracking. The deliverables are a series of Microsoft Excel spreadsheets and Migrate data sent to your project.

Figure 13-7 shows an example server assessment report. Besides giving you VM size recommendations, the server assessment engine gives you cost estimates. In my work as an Azure solutions architect, I've never yet met a customer for whom minimizing cost wasn't a principal concern.

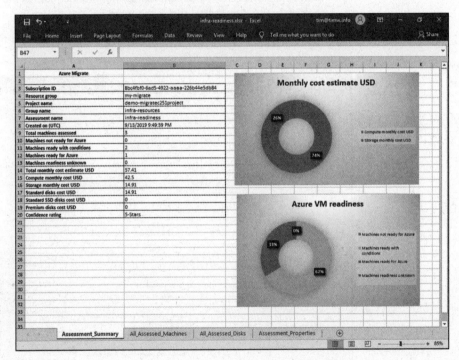

FIGURE 13-7:
Azure server assessment reports include graphs and table data.

TIP

In its documentation, Microsoft advises you to run your assessment for as long as possible to gather all peaks and valleys of your on-premises servers' performance. It isn't uncommon to run an assessment for two weeks to a month or more.

Azure Migrate: Server Migration

Before Migrate came along, the option for migrating on-premises servers via replication was using the Recovery Services vault and ASR. You still use ASR, but work is under way to incorporate the technology into Migrate.

Here a high-level overview of what happens:

1. Create a virtual network environment in Azure for your on-premises VMs and physical servers.

2. Replicate your on-premises servers' disks to Azure until their data is synchronized.

3. Perform a failover from your local environment to your Azure virtual network.

4. Stop replication.

5. Decommission your on-premises servers because you no longer need them.

6. Continue to use your services in Azure.

You don't need a VPN or ExpressRoute connection to perform this Azure Migrate/ASR replication. Eventually, the replication process will be agentless for VMware environments (Hyper-V is already agentless), but agentless VMware replication is in preview status at this writing.

The upside of Migrate server migration is that replication means nearly zero downtime. The downside is the initial replication hit can be substantial and costly if you have a metered Internet connection.

TECHNICAL STUFF

In Migrate terminology, *server migration* translates to "Replicate, failover, and don't fail back to the on-premises environment."

Hybrid Cloud Options

I'm closing this chapter with a survey of the two primary ways you can extend your on-premises environment into Azure:

>> Site-to-site (S2S) VPN

>> ExpressRoute circuit

Deploying a hybrid cloud is cost-, labor-, and time-intensive, so I can't get into the minute details of the process in this book, but I want to give you global understanding of these technologies.

S2S VPN

A VPN is a secure connection across an unsecure medium: the Internet. Azure S2S VPNs are always-on secure connections that tunnel your Internet traffic by using the Internet Protocol Security (IPSec) and Internet Key Exchange (IKE) security protocols.

The value propositions of establishing a VPN tunnel between your local network and an Azure virtual network are manifold. The VPN allows you to do the following:

>> Join Azure VMs to your on-premises Active Directory domain.

>> Manage Azure VMs with System Center or other configuration management and monitoring platforms.

>> Administer on-premises VMs by using Azure management solutions.

>> Ensure data confidentiality between the local environment and Azure.

Extend is an appropriate word for an Azure hybrid cloud because the hybrid cloud enables you to make your on-premises network available to your Azure subscription, and vice versa.

Let me walk you through the parts and pieces of the S2S VPN. Figure 13-8 shows a high-level view of an Azure hybrid cloud:

>> The on-premises gateway

>> The virtual network gateway

>> The local network gateway

>> The connection

On-premises VPN gateway

Azure needs to know your local VPN gateway's public IP address as well as the network addresses of all your local virtual local area networks (VLANs). Azure stores this information in a resource called the local network gateway; you're responsible for configuring your on-premises VPN gateway with the Azure gateway's public IP address and preshared key.

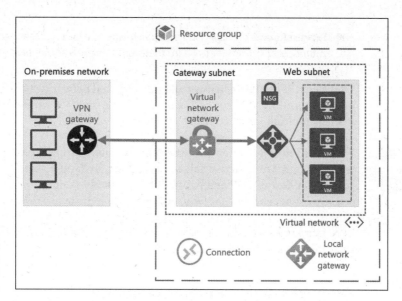

FIGURE 13-8:
Representative
Azure S2S VPN
topology.

TIP

I recommend that you read "About VPN devices and IPsec/IKE parameters for Site-to-Site VPN Gateway connections" (heck of an article title, isn't it?) at `https://docs.microsoft.com/en-us/azure/vpn-gateway/vpn-gateway-about-vpn-devices`. That article lists all the validated VPN devices that Microsoft guarantees will work with Azure. You'll likely find a link to a detailed configuration guide provided by your device manufacturer or Microsoft.

Azure VPNs use garden-variety VPN and routing protocols such as IPSec, IKE, and Border Gateway Protocol (BGP), so you shouldn't have difficulty configuring your local side of the VPN tunnel even if your hardware isn't on Microsoft's list of validated devices.

Virtual network gateway

This Azure resource is called a virtual network gateway rather than a VPN gateway because it's multifunctional. With this single resource, you can create any combination of the following connections:

» **S2S VPN:** You configure this secure IPSec tunnel between an on-premises network or another cloud-hosted network and your Azure VNet.

» **VNet-to-VNet VPN:** You configure this secure IPSec tunnel between two Azure virtual networks. Strictly speaking, this gateway is no longer necessary thanks to VNet peering.

» **Point-to-Site VPN:** You can configure specific client computers to create their own private VPN tunnels into your virtual network. See the sidebar "Azure P2S VPN" later in this chapter for details.

» **ExpressRoute:** You can configure a high-speed, always-on connection from your local environment to Azure that bypasses the Internet entirely.

That said, I'll use *VPN gateway* to signify a virtual network gateway configured for one or more S2S VPN connections. Yes, that's right: A single VPN gateway can manage multiple connections at the same time.

TIP

When used in conjunction with the BGP dynamic routing protocol, the VPN gateway supports active-active failover scenarios for fault tolerance. For more info, read "Overview of BGP and Azure VPN Gateways" at `https://docs.microsoft.com/en-us/azure/vpn-gateway/vpn-gateway-bgp-overview`.

VPN gateway is available in four stock-keeping units (SKUs); Table 13-1 summarizes their major distinctions.

TABLE 13-1

Azure VPN Gateway SKU Comparison

Gateway Type	Max Bandwidth	Maximum S2S Tunnels
Basic	100 Mbps	10
VpnGw1	650 Mbps	30
VpnGw2	1 Gbps	30
VpnGw3	1.25 Gbps	30

Another VPN gateway configuration choice is how the device handles IPSec traffic routing. Route-based gateways use static routing tables, whereas policy-based gateways take advantage of dynamic routing protocols such as BGP. Your choice largely depends on how old your on-premises VPN hardware is. The general guidance is that older VPN hardware normally requires you select the route-based gateway for the Azure side of the tunnel.

Finally, know that your VPN gateway needs to be placed on its own subnet in your hub virtual network. You may have noticed the Gateway Subnet button in your virtual network's Subnets blade (see Figure 13-9). You don't have to use this button to create your gateway subnet, but the subnet does need the name GatewaySubnet (with no spaces).

Microsoft recommends using the smallest possible IP address space for the gateway subnet so that you conserve your private IP addresses. A /29 network address is a common choice.

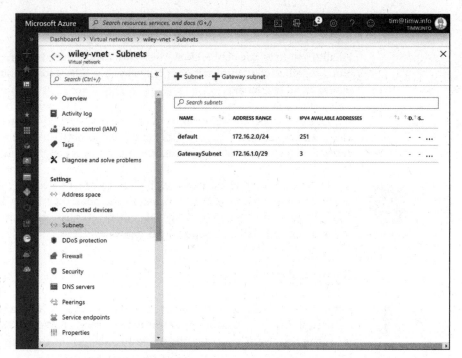

FIGURE 13-9:
Your Azure VPN gateway needs to be on its own subnet in your virtual network.

Local network gateway

In Azure, the local network gateway is a resource that represents your local network. The local network gateway contains two or three important configuration values:

>> Public IP address of your on-premises VPN endpoint

>> The IP address ranges of your local network(s)

>> (Optionally) BGP settings such as autonomous system number and peer IP address

When you think about this, it makes sense inasmuch as Azure needs to be able to identify not only the VPN concentrator at the other end of the tunnel, but also the remote network segments that facilitate hybrid cloud traffic routing.

WARNING

Be careful of the private IP address ranges you use in Azure. The last thing you want to do is troubleshoot/unwind IP address conflicts between your on-premises networks and Azure VNets. Always use nonoverlapping IP address ranges.

Connection

Finally, you have the connection. The Azure connection resource is the glue that binds together your local network gateway and VPN gateway, and defines your hybrid cloud handshake.

Within the Connection definition, you define the connection type (S2S, VNet-to-VNet, or ExpressRoute) and the preshared key that both the local gateway and VPN gateway will store for mutual authentication and data encryption.

REMEMBER

All the Azure hybrid cloud parts and pieces I've discussed are part of the Azure product family, so all the stuff covered in the book thus far — including RBAC, Policy, taxonomic tags, and so on — applies here just as much as to any other resource. Don't be afraid to apply your new knowledge.

ExpressRoute

ExpressRoute is similar to the Azure S2S VPN in that it is an always-on private connection between your on-premises network and an Azure VNet. ExpressRoute is unique because it's a truly private Azure connection that bypasses the public Internet. ExpressRoute links require no tunneling protocols.

The ExpressRoute circuit bandwidth options go from 50 Mbps to 10 Gbps. This means you can have a connection to Azure that's as fast as your local network's speed. Data ingress into ExpressRoute is free, but you're charged for data download unless you purchase ExpressRoute's unlimited data plan.

ExpressRoute has two peering options that you can use separately or in combination:

>> **Azure private peering:** ExpressRoute link from on-premises into an Azure VNet

TECHNICAL STUFF

AZURE P2S VPN

You may want to give some of your IT staff remote access to your Azure environment but you need all their data encrypted within a VPN tunnel. One option is the point-to-site (P2S) VPN, configured in your Azure VPN Gateway settings. The P2S VPN uses firewall-friendly security protocols and digital certificates to give users a VPN link to Azure no matter where they are in the world. Specifically, Azure creates a client installation package based on your VPN settings. You deploy this package to your remote users, and they can start and end P2S sessions at their convenience.

>> **Microsoft peering:** ExpressRoute link from on-premises into Office 365 or Dynamics 365

Figure 13-10 depicts a typical ExpressRoute implementation.

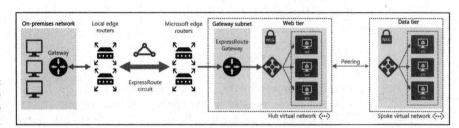

FIGURE 13-10:
ExpressRoute
representative
topology.

You need two edge routers to build an ExpressRoute connection. You also need to work with a local third-party ExpressRoute connectivity provider to help you peer into the Microsoft cloud platform.

Most customers locate a local ExpressRoute service provider by asking their Internet Service Provider, consulting with a Microsoft Partner, or performing a good old-fashioned online search.

TECHNICAL
STUFF

Microsoft requires you to provide two edge routers on your side of the ExpressRoute circuit for three reasons:

>> To allow Microsoft to offer its ExpressRoute service-level agreements (SLAs)

>> To provide failover redundancy

>> To enable you to combine the two links to maximize bandwidth

At this writing, ExpressRoute offers three connectivity models:

>> **Cloud exchange co-location:** You co-locate your edge equipment at an ExpressRoute service provider's data center.

>> **Point-to-point Ethernet connection:** You establish your ExpressRoute circuit from your campus by using point-to-point Ethernet (also called Metro Ethernet) connectivity.

>> **Any-to-any (IPVPN) connection:** You add Microsoft Cloud as a node in your existing Multiprotocol Label Switching wide-area network cloud.

Introducing Azure Arc

For Azure professionals, the most significant new product announcement to arise from Microsoft's Ignite 2019 conference was Azure Arc. Arc is a solution for deploying Azure services anywhere and extending Azure-based management to a hybrid, multicloud infrastructure.

The Arc use case

TECHNICAL STUFF

In information technology, *governance* refers to the policies and procedures your business has in place to ensure compliance with organizational and legal requirements. In Azure, governance is also used to limit cost, maximize security, and understand which groups own which Azure-based resources.

The Azure VPN and ExpressRoute options extend your on-premises network into Azure so that you can integrate Azure-based VMs and other resources more directly into your local IT governance strategy.

By contrast, Arc brings core elements of Azure Resource Manager (ARM) into your local networks as well as those you maintain in other clouds. Figure 13-11 shows an overview of the Azure topology.

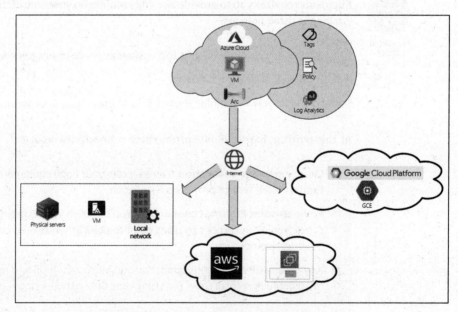

FIGURE 13-11: Arc topology overview.

In Figure 13-11, notice how the flow works. Without any VPN or ExpressRoute requirement, you can extend core Azure features such as tags, policy, and log analytics not only to your local network, but also to other clouds, such as Amazon Web Services and Google Cloud Platform.

The second value proposition that Arc brings to the table is the notion of deploying Azure resources directly in your local environment. You can use ARM templates, for example, to deploy VMs, databases, and Kubernetes clusters into your own data centers and then manage these resources right alongside your cloud-native resources using Azure tools.

Arc family members

As of this writing, the Arc product family includes three members that enable you to complete certain tasks:

» **Azure Arc for Servers:** Manage virtual and physical machines that are outside Azure by using native Azure tools.

» **Azure Arc for Data Services:** Run Azure data services such as Azure SQL Database and Azure Database for PostgreSQL on-premises or in another cloud environment.

» **Azure Arc for Kubernetes:** Deploy and manage Kubernetes applications across environments.

WARNING

Arc for Servers is in public preview, and Arc for Kubernetes and data platform are in private preview status. You normally have to apply to be a part of a private preview, whereas public preview features are available to some or all Azure customers. Be aware that Microsoft normally doesn't support or supply an SLA on Azure preview features. The general guidance is you should run Azure preview features only in your testing/development environments.

Arc for Servers is the only feature that's publicly available at this writing, so that product is the focus of the following sections.

Preparing your environment

In my local lab environment, I have two VMs: one running Windows Server 2019 and one running Ubuntu Linux 16.04. To keep my Arc environment tidy, I create a resource group to hold my two on-premises machines. In this section, I show you how to use Arc for Servers to onboard these machines into an Azure subscription.

Follow these steps to create a new resource group in the Azure portal:

1. **Search for** resource groups, **and browse to the Resource Groups blade.**

   The Resource groups blade appears.

2. **On the Resource Groups blade, click Add.**

   The Create a Resource Group blade appears.

3. **On the Create a Resource Group blade, fill out the Basics form and then click Review + Create.**

   All you provide here is the appropriate Azure subscription, resource group name, and region. As of this writing, Azure Arc is available only in selected regions. Don't be surprised by this; Microsoft rolls out preview features gradually with the goal of the product being available in all regions by its general availability date.

4. **Click Create to submit the deployment.**

   This operation should take only a few seconds to complete.

Adding a Windows Server system to Arc

You can add a Windows-based server to your Arc environment. According to the Arc documentation, the service supports systems running Windows Server 2012 R2 and newer.

You don't need a VPN or ExpressRoute connection to Azure to add a server. All you need to do to make a local system manageable by Azure is install a single agent.

Follow these steps to onboard a Windows Server system to Arc. Of course, you can perform these steps only if you have local servers available:

1. **In the Azure portal, search for** azure arc.

   The search results include entries for Azure Arc and Machines - Azure Arc.

2. **Click the first icon to see the full product.**

3. **On the Arc welcome page, click Manage Servers.**

   The Machines - Azure Arc blade appears.

REMEMBER

   At this writing, the Kubernetes and data platform products aren't yet available.

4. **On the Machines - Azure Arc blade, click Add.**

   The Select a Method blade appears.

5. **On the Select a Method blade, click the Generate Script button in the Add Machines Using Interactive Script section (see Figure 13-12).**

   The interface may have *changed*, and what you see may look different from Figure 13-12; such is the nature of Azure's evolving ecosystem.

   When you click this button, the Generate Script blade appears.

   Read the nearby sidebar "Adding servers at scale" for more information on the other Arc server onboarding method.

TIP

6. **On the Generate Script blade, complete the Basics tab.**

   Choose your subscription, resource group, and region; then select your local computer's operating system (Windows or Linux).

FIGURE 13-12: Choosing a server onboarding method for Arc.

7. **Click Review + Generate.**

   The Review + Generate tab appears.

   For Windows machines, you see the following script (or something like it if Microsoft updates the code after this book is published):

```
# Download the package
Invoke-WebRequest -Uri https://aka.ms/AzureConnectedMachineAgent
    -OutFile AzureConnectedMachineAgent.msi
```

```
# Install the package
msiexec /i AzureConnectedMachineAgent.msi /l*v
          installationlog.txt /qn | Out-String

# Run connect command
& "$env:ProgramFiles\AzureConnectedMachineAgent\azcmagent.exe"
          connect --resource-group "AzureArc" --tenant-id
          "133f6972-44a7-4037-8eea-1d9afd1ebfc8"
          --location "westus2" --subscription-id
          "2fbf906e-1101-4bc0-b64f-adc44e462fff"
```

The Azure portal dynamically populated this PowerShell code with the
environment details you specified earlier in the deployment process.

PowerShell accomplishes the following three tasks: downloads the Azure
Connected Machine Agent in Microsoft Installer (.msi) format, installs the
agent on your system by using the msiexec command-line utility that's
built into Windows, and links the local system to your Azure subscription
in general and to Arc in particular.

8. **Click Download.**

9. **Copy the onboarding script to your target system.**

   You run the script directly on the system.

10. **On the target system, start an elevated PowerShell console by opening
    Start, typing** powershell, **right-clicking the PowerShell icon, and choosing
    Run as Administrator from the shortcut menu.**

    An administrative PowerShell console appears.

11. **Temporarily set the script execution policy to Bypass.**

    For security reasons, Windows doesn't run all PowerShell scripts by default. To
    ensure that you can run the Arc onboarding script, type and run the following
    command:

    ```
    Set-ExecutionPolicy -ExecutionPolicy Bypass -Scope Process -Force
    ```

    This code relaxes the system's script execution policy for the duration of this
    PowerShell session.

12. **Run the script.**

    All you have to do is type the full or qualified path to the script file. If you used
    the cd command to set your command prompt location to the same directory
    as the script file, for example, you could type the following to run the script:

    ```
    .\OnboardingScript.ps1
    ```

TECHNICAL STUFF

On Windows and Linux systems, specifying the *dot slash* syntax instructs your computer to run the script from the present working directory.

The Arc for Servers onboarding script pauses to ask you to authenticate to Azure. Figure 13-13 shows the device login process.

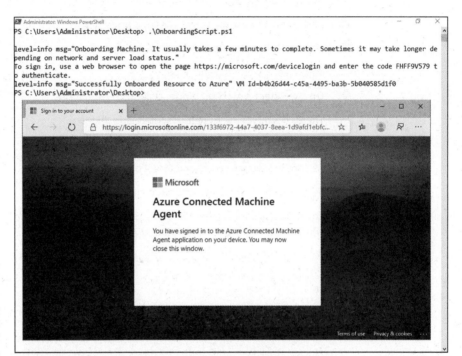

FIGURE 13-13: Onboarding a Windows Server system to Arc.

TECHNICAL STUFF

ADDING SERVERS AT SCALE

Microsoft understands that some Azure administrators need to add dozens, hundreds, or thousands of their local machines to Arc. If you need to add many machines, you can use PowerShell to script the deployment and target as many local systems as you need to onboard. You can automate the script by using a *service principal* — a special Azure AD identity that uses a digital certificate for authentication.

For more information on onboarding systems to Arc at scale, see "Quickstart: Connect machines to Azure using Azure Arc for servers - PowerShell" at https://docs. microsoft.com/en-us/azure/azure-arc/servers/quickstart-onboard-powershell.

Adding a Linux system to Arc

At this writing, Arc for Servers supports only Ubuntu 16.04 and 18.04. Follow these steps to onboard a Linux system to Arc:

1. **In the Azure portal, search for** azure arc.

2. **In the search results, select the Machines - Azure Arc icon.**

3. **On the Machines - Azure Arc blade, click Add.**

   The Select a Method blade appears.

4. **On the Select a Method blade, click Generate Script.**

   The Basics tab of the Generate Script blade appears.

5. **Fill in the Basics tab.**

   Be sure to select Linux as your target operating system.

6. **Click Review + Generate and then click Download.**

   The following code is the OnboardingScript.sh Linux onboarding script, which uses Bash shell syntax rather than PowerShell syntax:

   ```
   # Download the installation package
   wget https://aka.ms/azcmagent -O ~/install_linux_azcmagent.sh

   # Install the hybrid agent
   bash ~/install_linux_azcmagent.sh

   # Run connect command
   azcmagent connect --resource-group "AzureArc" --tenant-id
   "133f6972-44a7-4037-8eea-1d9afd1ebfc8" --location "westus2"
   --subscription-id "2fbf906e-1101-4bc0-b64f-adc44e462fff"
   ```

   The Linux code performs the following three actions: downloads the Connected Machine Agent, installs it, and then links the local system to your Arc environment.

7. **Transfer the** OnboardingScript.sh **script to your target system, and run it to complete the onboarding process.**

   Open a Terminal on the Linux system, browse to the directory where you copied the OnboardingScript.sh script, and execute it. If your Terminal command prompt is in the same directory as the script, for example, type and run the following Bash command:

   ```
   sudo sh ./OnboardingScript.sh
   ```

You're required to enter a one-time code in a separate browser window to authenticate to Azure.

8. **When the agent installation completes, go back to the Azure portal, and refresh the Machines - Azure Arc blade.**

As you see in Figure 13-14, your Arc environment now has two managed, on-premises VMs.

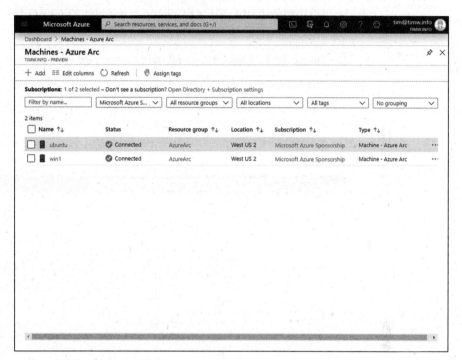

FIGURE 13-14:
Viewing
onboarded
local VMs in the
Azure portal.

Managing local systems with Arc

Now it's time to answer the question "What can I do with onboarded machines with Arc for Servers?" At this writing, Arc for Servers supports the following management actions on onboarded systems:

>> Role-Based Access Control (RBAC)

>> Azure Monitor

>> Taxonomic tags

>> Azure Policy

Implementing Azure Policy

Policy is a powerful platform for Azure resource governance. Suppose that your business is located in the western United States. You need to ensure that all systems are assigned the Pacific time zone by using Policy.

Follow these steps to configure a Windows Server–based Arc machine for policy assignment:

1. **On the Machines - Azure Arc blade, select your Windows server.**

The server's Overview blade appears.

2. **Select the Policies setting and then click Assign Policy on the toolbar.**

The Assign Policy blade appears.

Figure 13-15 shows the VM's settings interface. If you're thinking that managing an on-premises system works exactly as it does for managing an Azure native VM, you understand the Arc for Servers use case.

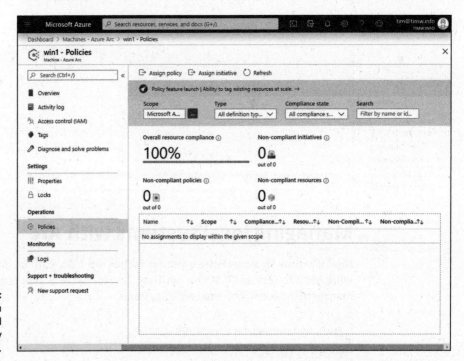

FIGURE 13-15: Viewing an Arc-managed system's policy settings.

3. **On the Basics tab of the Assign Policy blade, complete the form, and click Next to continue.**

   Complete the following information:

   - *Scope:* Make sure that this setting is set to your Azure subscription and your Azure Arc resource group.

   - *Exclusions:* Use this control to exclude the Ubuntu system from this policy. The time-zone policy you're about to assign is for Windows systems only.

   - *Policy Definition:* Search the built-in policy definitions for the one named Configure Time Zone on Windows Machines.

   - *Assignment Name* (optional): You can give the policy a custom name, if you want. By default, the name is set to the policy definition name.

   - *Policy Enforcement:* The options are Enabled and Disabled. You want to use this policy, so ensure that it's set to Enabled.

4. **On the Parameters tab of the Assign Policy blade, choose your desired time zone from the Time Zone drop-down list and then click Next to continue.**

   In this scenario, you're assigning all systems to Pacific time: UTC – 8 hours in the United States and Canada.

5. **On the Remediation tab of the Assign Policy blade, create a remediation task and then click Review + Create to continue.**

   Policy can do much more than simply audit compliance. Here, select the Create a Remediation Task check box to instruct Azure to set the Windows server's time zone to match your policy definition.

REMEMBER

   Make sure that the Policy to Remediate drop-down list is set to your policy. Azure creates a managed identity to provide a security context for the remediation task. By default, Azure grants the managed identity temporarily.

TECHNICAL STUFF

   A *managed identity* is a special-purpose Azure AD identity that acts very much like a service account in a local network environment. For more information about managed identities in Azure, read "What is managed identities for Azure resources?" at https://docs.microsoft.com/en-us/azure/active-directory/managed-identities-azure-resources/overview.

6. **Click Create to submit the deployment.**

You can follow up on policy remediation status by navigating to the Windows server's Policies blade, selecting your policy, and switching to the Remediation Tasks tab (see Figure 13-16).

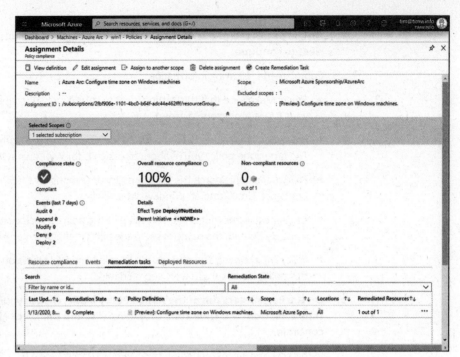

FIGURE 13-16:
Verifying policy
compliance and
remediation
status.

I checked the time zone on my Windows Server VM, and sure enough, it was set from the Central time zone (my original time zone) to Pacific.

Implementing taxonomic tags

You can create a taxonomic tag set for your Arc servers. Specifically, you define a tag called env:arc on your Ubuntu VM.

Follow these steps to assign a taxonomic tag to an Arc (or native Azure) resource:

1. **On the Machines - Azure Arc blade, select your Linux VM.**

The VM's Overview Settings blade appears.

2. **Select the Tags setting in the Settings list.**

3. **Define the** env:arc **tag and then click Save to save your changes.**

Note that taxonomic tags are name:value pairs. You simply type the tag name and tag value; alternatively, you can reuse previously defined tag names and/or values.

Figure 13-17 shows the finished configuration.

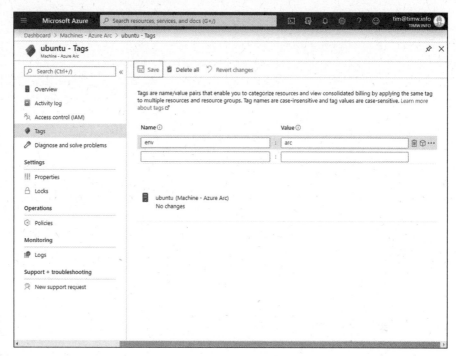

FIGURE 13-17:
Applying
taxonomic tags to
an Arc resource.

For more information on taxonomic tags, see the nearby sidebar "What can you do with tags in Azure?"

WHAT CAN YOU DO WITH TAGS IN AZURE?

TECHNICAL STUFF

Most businesses need to manage multiple Azure deployments and to track cost and utilization separately for each environment. At first blush, the resource group seems to be the most appropriate container for these tracked deployments. The reality, however, is that most cost centers also span entire Azure subscriptions.

Thus, by applying taxonomic tags to your resource groups and resources, you can aggregate Azure resources throughout your environment and then report on them, using tools such as Azure Monitor, Azure Cost Management, and Azure Log Analytics. For best practices on tag use in Azure, see "Resource naming and tagging decision guide" at `https://docs.microsoft.com/en-us/azure/cloud-adoption-framework/decision-guides/resource-tagging/`.

Chapter **14**

Monitoring Your Azure Environment

T his chapter explains how to check the pulse of all your Azure resources. Monitoring is an important skill for many reasons:

» Track the who, what, when, and where of deployments

» Generate performance baselines

» Manage resource usage costs

» Troubleshoot issues

» Identify and resolve security red flags

» Optimize your environment for cost, speed, security, and availability

By the end of this chapter, you'll be up to speed with Azure Monitor and Azure Log Analytics.

Azure Monitor

Azure Monitor is your baseline monitoring platform. I say *baseline* because Azure itself collects essential metric data and allows you to access it at no additional cost. By contrast, Application Insights and Log Analytics are premium monitoring services with their own pricing plans.

Azure Monitor collects two fundamental data types from your resources:

>> **Metrics:** Numerical time-series data that describes some aspect of your Azure resource

>> **Logs:** Text files or tables that describe various system events and metric data

The term *telemetry* gets a lot of press with regard to Azure; this term simply refers to a resource's ability to transmit its metric and log data to a collector resource.

TECHNICAL
STUFF

The word *telemetry* derives from two Greek words: *tele,* meaning *at a distance,* and *métron,* meaning *measure.* In contemporary English, you can say that telemetry signifies remote measurement.

Enabling diagnostic logging

For non-VM Azure resources, you can enable diagnostic logging and metrics individually by visiting each resource's configuration blade in the Azure portal or by visiting Azure Monitor. You always enable diagnostics for your Windows Server and Linux virtual machines (VMs) at the VM resource level.

Azure Monitor Activity Log

The Azure Monitor Activity Log tracks what Microsoft calls "control plane events," which are administrative events issued by Azure itself or by you and your fellow Azure administrators. Some examples of control plane events include restarting a virtual machine, deploying an Azure Key Vault, or fetching storage account access keys.

I like to describe Activity Log as being essentially an operational/auditing log. With it, you can determine who executed which action in your subscriptions, at what time, and whether the action succeeded or failed.

WARNING

The Activity Log collects only subscription-level events. If you want to aggregate Activity Log data from multiple subscriptions, you need to take a look at Azure Activity Log Analytics, which is covered later in this chapter.

Follow these steps to tour your Activity Log environment:

1. **In the Azure portal, browse to the Monitor blade, and click Activity Log.**

2. **Click each filter button to gain insight into how to adjust Activity Log view.**

I show you this interface in Figure 14-1.

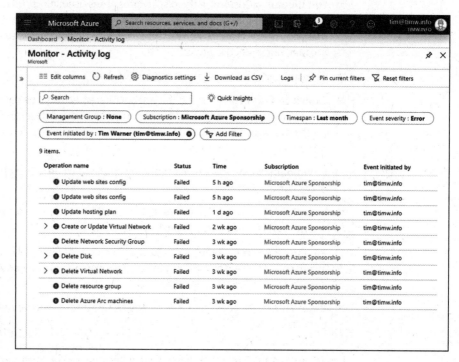

FIGURE 14-1: Azure Activity Log records administrative events initiated by you or by Azure itself.

You can type your Azure AD user name in the Search box to see only control plane events initiated by your user account, for example.

You can filter based on several criteria:

- *Resource Type:* Display VMs, web apps, databases, and so forth.
- *Operation:* Display create, delete, write, or perform any other action that affects Azure resources.
- *Event Initiated By:* Search for an Azure AD username.
- *Event Category:* Show administrative, security, alert, and so on.
- *Event Severity:* Show critical, error, warning, and informational.
- *Timespan:* List events that occurred within the last hour or month, or a custom interval.

3. **Select an Activity Log event to view its details.**

In Figure 14-1 you can see exactly who successfully started a virtual machine (me) and when. The JavaScript Object Notation (JSON) source data shown in Figure 14-2 reveals the VM name and additional details.

The toolbar at the top of Figure 14-2 contains some useful buttons:

>> **Edit Columns:** Customize the display properties used in resource list views. You should get into the habit of using this control in all resource lists. Note that your customizations here affect only your Azure Active Directory (AD) account, not your colleagues'.

>> **Refresh:** Click to ensure you see the latest data.

>> **Export to Event Hub:** Stream the current filtered Activity Log data into an Event Hub namespace. Then you can subscribe to this Activity Log stream by using other Azure resources and process the data according to your business requirements.

>> **Download As CSV:** Pull down a comma-separated value (CSV) representation of the current Activity Log view.

>> **Logs:** Takes you to Activity Log Analytics. You'll be prompted to create a Log Analytics workspace if you haven't already done so.

>> **Pin Current Filters:** Enables you to place the current filtered result set in a dashboard tile. This option can be convenient when you need to keep a steady eye on Activity Log data.

>> **Reset Filters:** Removes any user-defined filters and resets the view to the default.

Clicking an Activity Log event shows you a summary. The Summary tab, shown in Figure 14-2, shows general information. Click the JSON tab to reveal details in JSON format. This JSON provides deep details concerning the event, and is useful when you perform forensic troubleshooting to figure out exactly who did what, when, in your subscription.

TECHNICAL
STUFF

Activity Log Analytics is a premium (paid) service that allows you to consolidate Activity Log data from multiple subscriptions; configure longer data archival policies; run interactive queries; and build dynamic reports on query data. You can find out more about Activity Log Analytics at https://docs.microsoft.com/en-us/azure/azure-monitor/platform/activity-log-collect.

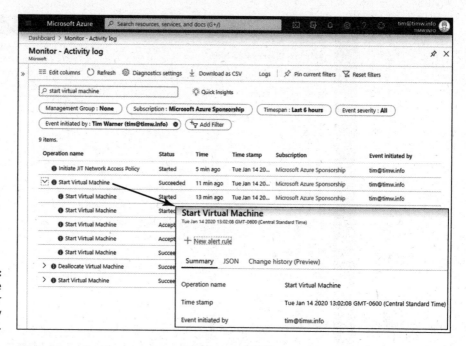

FIGURE 14-2:
Viewing the
JSON source for
an Azure Activity
Log event.

Azure Monitor Diagnostics Settings

Azure Monitor Diagnostics Settings is a central control station for enabling non-VM resource diagnostics. Follow these steps to enable resource diagnostics in Azure Monitor:

1. **In Azure Monitor, select the Diagnostics Settings blade.**

2. **Use the filter controls to narrow your view, and select a resource from the list.**

In Figure 14-3, you see four resources from two subscriptions. This example selects the vm1-nsg network security group.

3. **On the Diagnostics Settings blade, click Add Diagnostic Setting.**

The two types of Azure Monitor diagnostics data are logs and metrics. Some Azure resources have both; others have one or the other.

REMEMBER

4. **Complete the Diagnostics Settings blade.**

Compare what you see with Figure 14-4. Give the diagnostics stream a name; I always append -diag to the resource name.

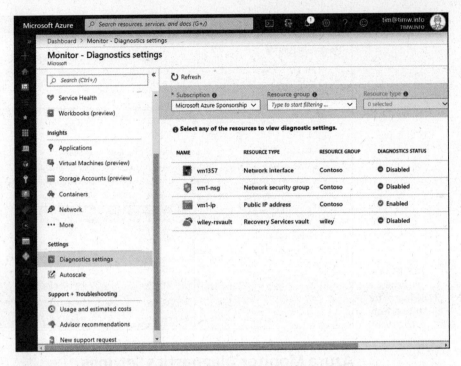

FIGURE 14-3:
Azure Monitor
Diagnostics
settings allow
you to enable
diagnostics
centrally for
several resources.

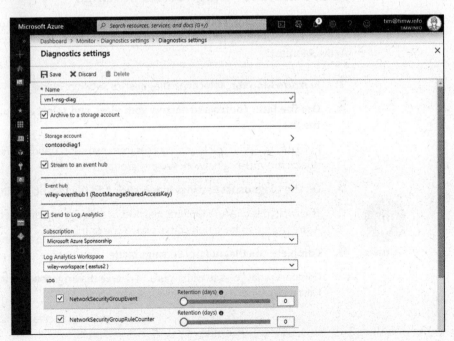

FIGURE 14-4:
Configuring
Azure resource
diagnostics.

You can send diagnostics data to one or more of the following targets:

- *Storage Account:* The benefit is long-term archival storage.

- *Event Hub:* The benefit is subscribing to the diagnostics streams in real time.

- *Log Analytics:* The benefit is the powerful querying/reporting functionality inherent in Log Analytics.

You can revisit these settings later if you need to change them.

Besides the diagnostics settings targets, you need to specify which log(s) and metrics categories you want to collect. Different resources collect different types of metrics and logs. For example, network security group diagnostics logs any time an NSG rule is fired.

5. **Click Save to commit your changes.**

WARNING

You'll be charged for using any other Azure resource, even as part of a separate configuration. In configuring diagnostics to store resource diagnostics data in a storage account, for example, you're accepting those additional storage account-related charges.

VM diagnostic settings

VM resource diagnostics are handled separately from other Azure resources. Enabling VM diagnostics involves installing the Azure Diagnostics extension. As you might expect, the specific metrics and logs collected by this extension depend on the operating system (Windows or Linux).

To enable VM diagnostics, follow these steps:

1. **Navigate to the VM for which you want to enable diagnostics, and select the Diagnostics Settings menu item.**

2. **On the Diagnostic Settings Overview page, click Enable Guest-Level Monitoring.**

It's important to note that Azure collects very basic VM data with no agent required. By enabling guest diagnostics, you instruct Azure to collect more detailed, granular diagnostics data for the virtual machine.

3. **In the VM's settings list, click Extensions, and verify that the Azure Diagnostics extension has been installed.**

In Figure 14-5, you can see my VM1 virtual machine has the VM diagnostics and other extensions installed.

At the time I'm writing, the extension's formal name is Microsoft.Insights. VMDiagnosticsSettings (Windows).

VIEWING YOUR DIAGNOSTICS DATA

How you analyze your resource diagnostics data depends on which target(s) you chose for those data streams. If you choose Log Analytics, for example, you'd run KQL queries in Azure's Log Search interface.

You can also use Monitor's metrics and alerting systems, which I cover later in this chapter.

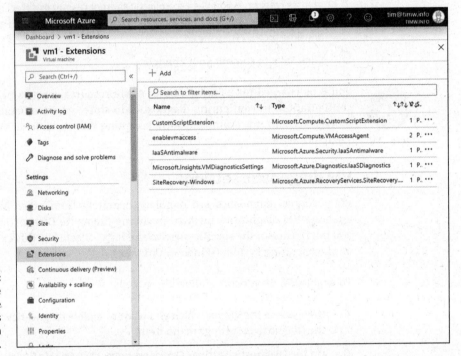

FIGURE 14-5:
Verifying the presence of the VM diagnostics extension for an Azure VM.

4. **Return to the VM's Diagnostics Settings blade, and review the configuration options.**

   You can collect the following data on Windows VMs:

   - Performance counters
   - Event logs
   - Memory crash dumps

You can collect the following data on Linux VMs:

- System hardware metrics (processor, memory, network, file system, and disk)

- Syslog events from any enabled daemons running on the VM

I show you this interface in Figure 14-6.

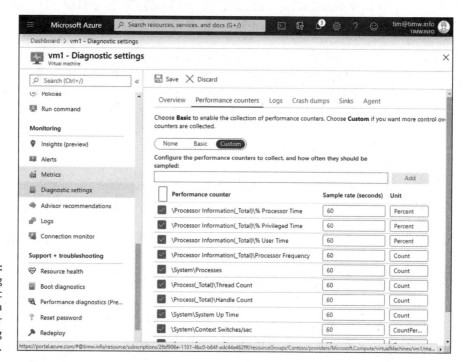

FIGURE 14-6: Customizing the diagnostic logging in a Windows Server VM running in Azure.

TECHNICAL STUFF

You must have an existing storage account in a Linux VM's region to enable guest diagnostics on that VM.

VM boot diagnostics

I nearly always recommend that my customers enable boot diagnostics on Windows Server and Linux VMs. Boot diagnostics data is stored in a designated storage account's blob service. This feature provides two benefits to administrators:

» Boot diagnostics periodically take a screenshot of your VM's screen — a convenient sanity check to ensure that your VM isn't in a stopped state.

>> Boot diagnostics enables the serial console — a diagnostic back door into your system whereby you obtain a command-line connection directly through the Azure portal. Serial console can be life-saving when your VM's networking stack is offline and you can't reach the VM via the Internet or your VPN connection.

Plotting resource metrics and raising alerts

In this section, I return to Azure Monitor to examine Azure resource and VM diagnostic data. As mentioned earlier, the Azure platform gathers basic resource metrics that viewable in Azure Monitor. You gain much deeper insight, however, when you formally enable diagnostics on your resources.

Charting metrics

Metrics are time-series values sampled from your resource periodically. Follow these steps to use Azure Monitor's Metrics Explorer to plot CPU consumption on multiple VMs:

1. **Browse to the Azure Monitor settings list, and select Metrics.**

Metrics explorer appears on the Details blade.

2. **Click the pencil icon next to Chart Title, and give your chart a meaningful name.**

I called mine Multi-VM CPU Utilization.

3. **Complete the first resource row, as follows:**

- *Resource:* You can select multiple subscriptions and/or resource groups to get a wide span of resources to choose among. Make sure you select the Virtual Machines resource type. Sadly, you can choose only one VM here; you'll need to create additional resource rows to plot metrics from other VMs on the same chart.

- *Metric Namespace:* Select Virtual Machine Host. This value depends on the resource you've loaded into the Resource property.

- *Metric:* Select Percentage CPU. The metrics are specific both to the resource and may be a longer or shorter list depending on whether you've enabled resource diagnostics.

- *Aggregation:* Select Average.

4. **Add at least one more resource row to plot metrics from additional VMs.**

To do so, click Add Metric on the toolbar\ and then choose the same properties you selected when you defined the first resource row. Figure 14-7 shows a resulting chart.

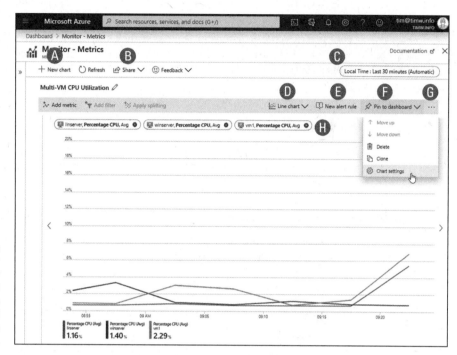

FIGURE 14-7: Metrics Explorer in Azure Monitor gives you at-a-glance diagnostics and performance data.

Here's a bit more detail about the interface in Figure 14-7:

>> Use New Chart (A) to create more than one chart in Metrics Explorer.

>> Click Share (B) to download your chart definition as a Microsoft Excel work-book. Be aware that if you don't pin the chart to your dashboard or save its definition, it's lost when you leave Metrics Explorer! Be sure to save a link, download the definition, or save your metric chart to your dashboard if you'll need it in the future.

>> Click the Time range/Time granularity drop-down list (C) to set the time range.

>> Use the Line Chart drop-down list (D) to display your data in one of five chart formats: line, area, bar, scatter, and grid.

>> Click New Alert Rule (E) to configure an alert rule based on the currently loaded metrics.

» Click Pin to Dashboard (F) to display the chart persistently on your Azure portal dashboard.

» Click the More button (G) and choose Chart Settings to modify the chart properties.

» Click the metric row (H) to adjust the metric count displayed on your chart.

TIP

Your metrics charts disappear when you click away from Metrics Explorer in Azure Monitor. Click Share and then select Copy Link, and save that link in your web browser's Favorites list. That way, you can get your chart back when Azure vaporizes it.

Configuring alerts

Alerts in Azure are super-powerful because you can configure Azure to take automated corrective actions whenever an alert is triggered. An action group can contain one or more of the following action types:

» **Automation Runbook:** Runs your Azure PowerShell or Python script

» **Azure Function:** Runs your Function App function

» **Logic App:** Runs a designated Logic App workflow

» **Email/SMS/Push/Voice:** Notifies one or more accounts in various ways

» **ITSM:** Creates a ticket in your IT service management platform

» **Webhook:** Sends a particularly formatted HTTP(S) response to a receiving service (Azure Event Grid, Function App, Logic App, and so forth)

Suppose that you need to configure an alert such that you receive an email notification whenever your winserver VM is restarted. You define your action group, create the alert rule, and restart the VM to test the alert.

Creating an action group

Follow these steps to create an action group that sends you an email notification:

1. In Azure Monitor, select the Alerts blade and then click Manage Actions.

2. On the Manage Actions blade, click Add Action group.

You can consider an action group to be a container that holds one or more individual action rules.

3. Complete the Add Action Group form.

After you supply an action group name, short name, subscription, and resource group, the real work begins: defining your action. Here's how I set my email-alert Action group action rule:

- *Action Name:* Send-email.

- *Action Type:* Email/SMS/Push/Voice. You're prompted to specify the destination email address.

    As you'd expect, each action type has its own subconfiguration.

4. **Click OK to confirm your configuration.**

Now it's time to create the rule, which you bind to the action group.

TIP

Microsoft intentionally separated the action groups and action rules from your alerts. This way you can easily reuse the same action groups and rules with different alerts. Pretty convenient, eh?

Defining an alert rule

Azure alerts supports two signal types:

>> **Metrics:** These are the same metrics you've been working with throughout the chapter.

>> **Activity Log:** These are events tracked in Activity Log. For a VM restart condition, you need this signal type.

WARNING

Due to Azure platform limitations, you're limited to two metrics signals or one Activity Log signal per alert rule.

Follow these steps to create an alert rule that triggers whenever a given VM is restarted:

1. **On the Azure Monitor Alerts blade, click New Alert Rule.**

The Create Rule blade appears.

2. **In the Resource section of the Create Rule blade, click Select.**

3. **Choose the VM you want to monitor.**

Use the filter controls to drill through your subscriptions, locations, and resource types.

4. **In the Condition section, click Add, choose the Restart Virtual Machine Activity Log signal, and then click Done.**

The specific configuration options depend on which metric or Activity Log signal you selected. I show you this interface in Figure 14-8.

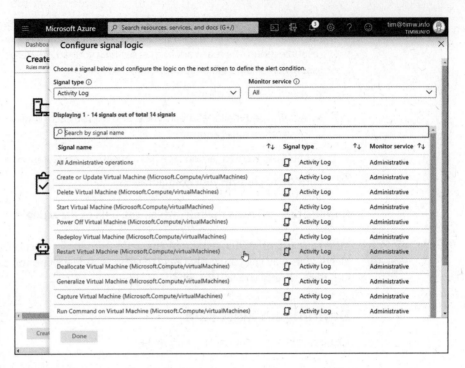

FIGURE 14-8:
Configuring signal logic for an Azure Monitor alert rule.

5. **In the Actions section, click Select Action Group, and choose your action group.**

6. **In the Alert Details section, complete the alert metadata.**

   This metadata consists of the alert rule name, optional description, target resource group, and whether you want to enable the rule. Figure 14-9 shows my completed rule definition.

   Be sure to select Yes for Enable Rule upon Creation so you can test it out.

7. **Click Create Alert Rule to complete the configuration.**

Testing the alert

You can view your alert rule definitions by revisiting the Azure Monitor Alerts blade and clicking Manage Alert Rules.

In my environment, I restarted my winserver VM and waited. Within a few minutes, I received my alert notifications. The composite screenshot in Figure 14-10 shows the Azure portal, the notification email, and the SMS text message alert.

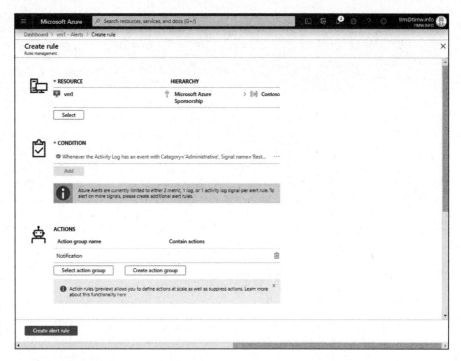

FIGURE 14-9:
Completing the alert rule definition.

FIGURE 14-10:
Different ways Azure informs you that an alert rule was triggered.

APPLICATION INSIGHTS

TECHNICAL STUFF

Sadly, an in-depth discussion of Application Insights falls outside the scope of this book. To give you the briefest possible introduction, however, let me tell you that Application Insights is an Azure application performance management product that works with all Azure App Service applications. Application Insights enables you to collect detailed telemetry from your applications and display the data meaningfully in numeric and/or chart views. It shows developers where users go in their App Service apps and what sorts of performance-related troubles happen so the developers can identify and resolve these bugs. For more information about Application Insights, visit `https://docs.microsoft.com/en-us/azure/azure-monitor/app/app-insights-overview`.

Azure Log Analytics

Having spent some time in Azure Monitor, you've seen some of the myriad log files that your Azure resources create. Think of all the ways that data is represented, and imagine a way to put all your logs in a single data lake and run queries against it seamlessly. "Are you leading me again, Tim?" you ask.

Yes, I am. Log Analytics is a platform in which you do just that: aggregate VM and Azure resource log files into a single data lake (called a *Log Analytics workspace*) and then run queries against the data, using a Microsoft-created data access language called Kusto (pronounced KOO-stoh) Query Language (KQL).

You'll find that Log Analytics somehow normalizes all these different log streams into a tabular structure. You'll also discover that KQL is similar to Structured Query Language (SQL), the data access language that is standard for relational databases.

Creating a Log Analytics workspace

The first order of business is to deploy a Log Analytics workspace. Then you can on-board as few or as many Azure resources to the workspace as you need. You can also deploy more than one Log Analytics workspace to keep your log data separate.

To create a new Azure Log Analytics workspace, follow these steps:

1. **In the Azure portal, browse to the Log Analytics Workspaces blade, and click Add.**

   The Log Analytics workspace blade appears.

2. **Complete the Log Analytics workspace blade.**

   You'll need to provide the following details:

   - Workspace name
   - Subscription name
   - Resource group name
   - Location
   - Pricing tier

3. **Click OK to create the workspace.**

4. **Click OK to submit your deployment.**

Pricing is beyond the scope of this book, but Log Analytics has a free tier as well as several paid tiers. The biggest free tier limitations are

>> Data ingestion limit of 5 GB per month

>> 30-day data retention limit

Connecting data sources to the workspace

With your workspace online, you're ready to on-board Azure resources into said workspace. To connect Azure resources to the workspace, go back to Monitor Diagnostic Settings, enable diagnostics, and point the log streams to your workspace. (Refer to Figure 14-4 to see what the interface looks like.)

You can connect VMs to the workspace directly from the workspace's Settings menu. Follow these steps:

1. **In your Log Analytics workspace settings menu, click Virtual Machines.**

   You see a list of all VMs in the workspace's region. You can see which VMs are connected to the workspace and which are not.

2. **If necessary, use the filter controls until you see the VM you want to connect.**

   You can link a VM to only one workspace at a time. In Figure 14-11, for example, my vm1 virtual machine is linked to another workspace.

3. **Select the desired VM, and click Connect.**

   Behind the scenes, Azure deploys the Log Analytics agent (formerly called Microsoft Monitoring Agent) to the VM.

4. **Verify that the VM is connected to the workspace.**

   You can see this information in your workspace settings. Or you can revisit your VM's Extensions blade (see Chapter 5 for more information about how to do this) and verify that the MicrosoftMonitoringAgent extension is installed.

Chapter 13 discusses hybrid cloud possibilities. You should know that Log Analytics can on-board on-premises VMs, particularly those managed by Systems Center Operations Manager, just as it can native cloud Linux and Windows Server VMs.

TIP

You can disconnect a VM from its current workspace and connect it to another one. This operation is trivial, taking only 2 minutes or so to complete. To do this, simply select the VM from within the workspace and click Disconnect from the toolbar.

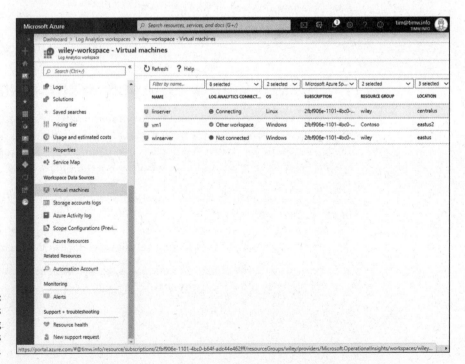

FIGURE 14-11:
Connecting VMs
to an Azure Log
Analytics
workspace.

USING BOTH DIAGNOSTICS AND LOG ANALYTICS

You may be thinking, "Tim, you said that the Azure platform collects basic VM diagnostics with no agent required. Then you deployed the Azure Diagnostics agent to collect deeper metrics and logs. Now the VM is connected to a Log Analytics workspace. What now?"

Specifically, the question is whether you need both the Diagnostics and Log Analytics extensions installed simultaneously and what effect they have on performance.

There's no noticeable performance penalty for having both agents installed on your VMs simultaneously. Diagnostics tracks metrics and log data, whereas Log Analytics stores only log/table data.

Writing KQL queries

You need to know a bit about how to access your Log Analytics workspace data with KQL. KQL is fast and easy to learn, and it should seem familiar to you if you've used Splunk Search Processing Language, SQL, PowerShell, or Bash shell.

Touring the Log Search interface

You can get to the Log Search interface by opening Monitor and selecting the Logs blade. Another way to get there (and the way I prefer) is to go to your Log Analytics workspace and click the Log setting.

A third method is to use the Log Analytics Query Playground, where you can work with an enormous data set, getting to know Log Analytics before generating a meaningful data set.

Follow these steps to run some sample KQL queries:

1. **Open a new browser tab, and navigate to** `https://portal.loganalytics.io/demo`.

This site is authenticated, but don't worry: You're using Microsoft's subscription, not your own.

2. **Expand some of the tables in the Schema list (shown in Figure 14-12).**

There's a lot in this list. Log Analytics normalizes all incoming data streams and projects them into a table-based structure.

Expand the LogManagement category; then expand the Alert table, where you can use KQL to query Azure Monitor alerts. The t entries (shown under the expanded SecurityEvent item in Figure 14-12) are properties that behave like columns in a relational database table.

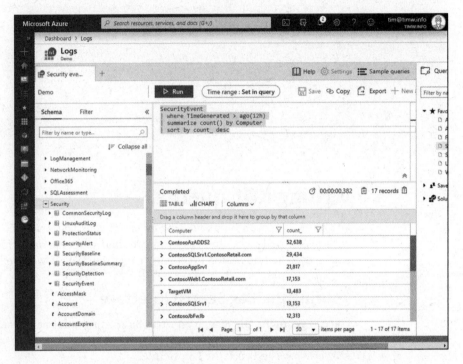

FIGURE 14-12:
Azure Log
Analytics Log
Search interface.

3. **On the Log Search toolbar, click Query Explorer, expand the Favorites list, and run the query Security Events Count by Computer During the Last 12 Hours.**

   This environment is a sandbox. Microsoft has not only on-boarded untold resources into this workspace but also written sample queries to let you kick the tires.

4. **In the results list, click Chart to switch from Table to Chart view.**

   You can visualize your query results automatically with a single button click. Not every results set lends itself to graphical representation, but the capability is tremendous.

5. **Click Export, and save your query results (displayed columns only) to a CSV file.**

   Note the link to Power BI, Microsoft's cloud-based business intelligence/ dashboard generation tool.

**TECHNICAL
STUFF**

AZURE SOLUTIONS

You may have noticed in the Log Search query interface tables that reference Azure products beyond VMs and individual resources. I'm talking about categories such as DNS Analytics, Office 365, Security Center, SQL Assessment, and Network Monitoring.

These Log Analytics tables appear when you enable Azure Solutions. In the Azure Marketplace, for example, you can load the Azure SQL Analytics solution, which gives Log Analytics insight into your SQL Servers (virtual, physical, on-premises or cloud) along with their databases.

The idea is that eventually, all monitoring roads in Azure will lead to Log Analytics. This platform is extremely wide-reaching and powerful; dive into it with gusto.

Writing basic KQL queries

For fun, I'd like to put you through an obstacle course of common KQL queries. Click the plus sign in the Log Search query interface (visible in Figure 14-12) to open a new tab — a multitab interface like those in Visual Studio and Visual Studio Code.

To get a feel for a table, you can instruct Azure to display any number of rows in no particular order. To display 10 records from the SecurityEvent table, for example, use the following command:

```
SecurityEvent
| take 10
```

Did you notice that the query editor attempted to autocomplete your query as you typed? Take advantage of that convenience by pressing Tab when you see the appropriate autocomplete choice appear.

Use the search keyword to perform a free-text query. The following query looks in the SecurityEvent table for any records that include the string "Cryptographic":

```
search in (SecurityEvent) "Cryptographic"
| take 20
```

When you press Enter, you'll doubtless notice the pipe character (|). This character functions the same way here as it does in PowerShell or the Bash shell. Output from one query segment is passed to the next segment via pipe — a powerful construct for sure.

You can ramp up the complexity by finishing with filtering and sorting. The following code both filters on a condition and sorts the results in a descending manner based on time:

```
SecurityEvent
| where Level == 8 and EventID == 4672
| sort by TimeGenerated desc
```

If you're thinking, "Wow, these KQL queries act an awful lot like SQL!" you're right on the money. Welcome to Log Analytics!

TIP

I adapted the KQL examples in this chapter from the Microsoft docs. For more information, see the "Getting Started with Log Queries in Azure Monitor" tutorial at https://docs.microsoft.com/en-us/azure/azure-monitor/log-query/get-started-queries.

6

The Part of Tens

IN THIS PART . . .

Getting to know the top 10 Azure news resources

Finding out how to remain current with the ever-expanding Azure ecosystem

Chapter **15**

Top Ten Azure News Resources

've found that Microsoft Azure is the technology stack that's kept me most on my toes, forcing me to adopt both a growth mindset and an always-learning perspective. Given how rapidly Azure evolves, how can you keep up with the changes? Well, here are ten handpicked websites that I use and strongly believe will benefit you.

I suggest that you create a bookmarks folder in your favorite browser, create bookmarks for each of these sites, and get into the habit of reviewing them regularly. Stay current, and have fun!

TIP

Most websites listed in this chapter have a Really Simple Syndication (RSS) feed. Consider subscribing to these feeds and viewing updates by using your favorite RSS feed reader. (I like Feedly.)

Azure Status

```
https://status.azure.com/status
```

The Azure Status dashboard is a real-time index of global service availability. Here, you can check the status of every Azure service in every public and government region. The status categories are

>> Good

>> Information

>> Warning

>> Critical

Microsoft is quite good about providing details, including postmortem root-cause analysis when there's been an outage. The dashboard also provides announcements regarding planned maintenance events that might affect your services.

Azure Blog

https://azure.microsoft.com/blog

Not every Azure product/engineering team contributes to the official Azure blog, but enough do to make subscribing worthwhile. You'll find product announcements that chart an Azure product's path through private preview and public preview into genera-availability status. You'll also find white papers and case studies written by Microsoft program managers, product marketing managers, and sometimes C-suite executives such as Mark Russinovich.

Azure Updates

https://azure.microsoft.com/updates

The Azure Updates page provides detailed product tracking and road-map information. The three tabs correspond to product development phases:

>> In development

>> In preview

>> Now available

Each quarter, Microsoft publishes a free updates retrospective that you can download at no cost from this site.

This site is the one to watch when you're excited about a new Azure feature under development and ask "When will this product finally be released to production?"

Azure.Source

https://azure.microsoft.com/blog/topics/last-week-in-azure

Technically, Azure.Source (also called Last Week in Azure) is part of the official Azure blog, but this weekly newsletter is important enough to warrant its own entry in this chapter.

Azure.Source is essentially a roll-up of product announcements and road-map updates. You may prefer reading this weekly summary to getting updates via RSS as they happen.

Build5Nines Weekly

https://build5nines.com/category/weekly

Microsoft MVP (and my friend) Chris Pietschmann runs a blog, Build5Nines.com (formerly BuildAzure.com), that's one of the world's best Azure educational resources. The blog rounds up not only the most important Azure product announcements from the previous week, but also the best Azure-related community blog posts that Pietschmann has read. You'll pick up a lot of information by reading this electronic newsletter each week.

Azure Weekly (Endjin)

https://azureweekly.info

Endjin is a London-based cloud consultancy that puts a lot of effort into community outreach. Its weekly email digest is super-comprehensive; I suspect that staff members pack every Azure product update that they found during the previous week into the newsletters.

What's especially cool about Azure Weekly is that the entire back-issue archive (since 2014) is accessible and searchable on the website — absolutely for free.

Azure Official YouTube Channel

https://www.youtube.com/user/windowsazure

This media channel, which has existed since November 2008, hosts hundreds of videos. (Microsoft appears to have culled any videos posted before 2017, however.)

Here, you'll find a plethora of content, including product feature overviews, Azure-related Microsoft conference sessions, and tutorials.

The Azure Friday episodes (see the next section) are also available on this channel.

Channel 9: Azure Friday

https://channel9.msdn.com/Shows/Azure-Friday

Azure Friday is a weekly video series hosted by Scott Hanselman (a Microsoft product evangelist famous for his ability to provide simple explanations for complicated technical subjects) or one of his colleagues. Hanselman is popular because he's both a knowledgeable developer and a fine teacher. The series features interviews with Azure product team members and often offers demonstrations.

Azure Feedback

https://feedback.azure.com

You can go to the Azure Feedback portal to submit new-product and/or product improvement suggestions, vote on existing issues, and interact directly with Microsoft product team members. As you see in Figure 15-1, some customer feedback results in feature enhancements and even new-product development.

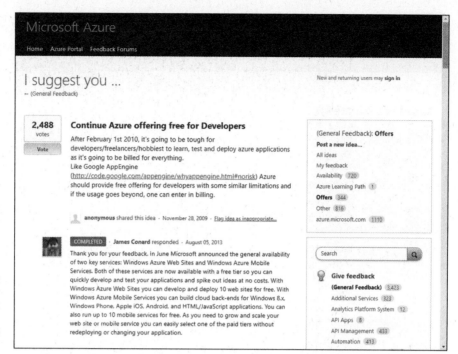

FIGURE 15-1:
Sometimes, your Azure feedback results in new-product development.

Tim's Twitter Feed

`https://twitter.com/techtrainertim`

If you want to be meta about keeping current with Azure stuff, you could simply follow my Twitter feed and be done with it. After all, I read the previous nine websites on a daily basis and post related tweets three to five times per day.

Chapter **16**

Top Ten Azure Educational Resources

I f I've tried to make one thing clear in this book, it's that to be successful with Microsoft Azure, you've got to keep up to date with it.

To that end, I'm closing this book by offering you ten hand-selected Azure educational resources. Happy reading!

Azure Documentation

```
https://docs.microsoft.com/azure
```

The Azure documentation library is your ultimate source of truth on how Azure products work. Microsoft has open-sourced the documents to GitHub, so community members (like you!) can edit them and submit your review.

The living nature of the library means that the documentation evolves with Azure products. You'll also find plenty of multimedia resources to address educational styles that cater more to a hands-on or visual approach.

TIP

If you have yet to skill up on Git source-code control and the GitHub collaboration workflow, consider checking out Sarah Guthals's and Phil Haack's splendid *GitHub For Dummies* (John Wiley & Sons, Inc.).

Azure Architecture Center

https://docs.microsoft.com/azure/architecture

Microsoft has long since eaten its own dog food, so to speak, which means two things:

>> It uses the products, technologies, and frameworks that it develops.

>> It shares its best practices with customers.

The Azure Architecture Center includes two super-valuable online guides:

>> *Azure Application Architecture Guide:* How Microsoft approaches designing scalable, resilient, performant, and secure application architectures in Azure

>> *Microsoft Cloud Adoption Framework for Azure:* How Microsoft helps customers transition from fully on-premises to hybrid cloud to cloud-native architectures

The center also includes a reference architecture library as well as a varied collection of topology diagrams and explanations. Many of the diagrams are available for free as Microsoft Visio drawing files. In my work as an Azure solutions architect, I often use a published reference architecture as a starting point for the topologies that I recommend to customers.

TECHNICAL STUFF

If you haven't invested in Visio or an equally good technical diagramming tool, consider doing so. Practically every Azure architect in my life uses either Visio or Microsoft PowerPoint to create Azure architectural diagrams.

Azure REST API Browser

https://docs.microsoft.com/rest/api/?view=Azure

Every action you take in your Azure subscription translates into Representational State Transfer (REST) API calls to the Azure public cloud. The Azure REST API Browser enables you to deep-dive into resource providers, view available operations, and even test them (see Figure 16-1).

After the API Browser shows you how the Azure Resource Manager API request/response life cycle works, you can productively build custom applications that interact directly with the ARM REST API.

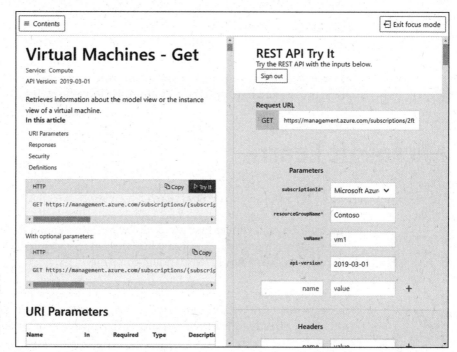

FIGURE 16-1: Work from the bare metal by using the Azure REST API Browser.

Microsoft @ edX

https://www.edx.org/learn/azure

edX is a not-for-profit company that hosts massive open online courses (MOOCs, pronounced *mooks*). Microsoft bought into the edX ecosystem heavily. You'll find a large collection of Azure-related courses that cover most disciplines, including

>> Architecture

>> Administration

>> Development

>> Security

>> Internet of Things

>> Data engineering

>> Data science

>> Machine learning

These courses are free and require only that you log in with your Microsoft account to track your progress. The company's multimedia approach is an excellent way to reach people who have different (or multiple) learning styles.

Microsoft Learn

https://docs.microsoft.com/learn

Microsoft Learn is similar in ways to edX, with the exception that Learn is entirely homegrown at Microsoft. You'll find hundreds of free, curated labs on most Azure job roles; the labs are well-written and complete.

Microsoft includes a sandbox environment in many hands-on labs that gives you access to Microsoft's Azure subscription. This means you learn Azure by working with Azure directly rather than working with a mock-up or simulation.

Azure Certification

https://www.microsoft.com/learning/azure-exams.aspx

I've found that if you ask five IT professionals their views on professional certification, you'll get five different responses. Some folks require Azure certification to keep up their Microsoft Partner status; other people want certification to differentiate themselves in a crowded job market.

Regardless, this site is the one you want to delve into for Azure role-based certification. In 2018, Microsoft moved from a monolithic Azure certification title to role-based badges. This way, you can demonstrate your Azure expertise in a way that's closely aligned with your present or desired job role, be it administrator, developer, architect, DevOps specialist, and so forth.

TIP

I highly recommend that you bookmark the Microsoft Worldwide Learning Certification and Exam Offers page (https://www.microsoft.com/en-us/learning/offers.aspx). Most of the time, you can find the Exam Replay offer, as well as discounts on MeasureUp practice tests (see the next section). Exam Replay gives you a voucher for a second exam if you don't pass on your first attempt.

MeasureUp

https://www.measureup.com/azure-products

MeasureUp is Microsoft's only authorized practice exam provider. I can't overstate how crucial practice exams are to success on the Azure certification exam. I've observed seasoned experts walk into an exam session smiling and exit crying because they didn't pass because they weren't expecting the myriad ways that Microsoft Worldwide Learning tests the candidate's skills.

Oh, by the way: Microsoft Learn, discussed earlier in this chapter, refers to Microsoft Worldwide Learning's online technical education hub. Yes, they are different things.

MeasureUp gives you an accurate exam experience. Just as important as understanding the theory is understanding and being comfortable with how Microsoft assesses your knowledge.

On the Azure exams, you can expect to see performance-based labs in which you're given an Active Directory (AD) login to the real Azure portal and required to complete a series of deployment and/or configuration tasks.

The exams also feature case studies that present a fictional company's current situations, Azure-related goals, and technical limitations; then you're asked to answer several questions by analyzing each the case. These exams are no joke and deserve dedicated preparation time.

Meetup

`https://www.meetup.com/topics/azure`

I must confess to you candidly that practically every professional engagement I've had in my 20-plus year career came about through professional networking. When you make professional connections, it's a natural outcome that your name will arise when opportunities make themselves manifest.

To that point, I suggest that you visit Meetup.com and search for Azure user groups in your area. At this writing, there are 716 groups worldwide with more than 300,000 members (see Figure 16-2).

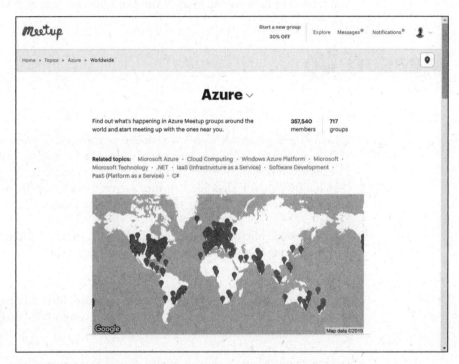

FIGURE 16-2: Find an Azure user group near you.

Azure meetups are great opportunities to find out new stuff, and you'll meet neighbors who do the kind of work you're doing or want to do in the future. IT recruiters make a habit of sponsoring user groups, so you can get plugged into job-search networks at meetups as well.

While I'm on this subject, I'd also like to recommend Microsoft Reactor (`https://developer.microsoft.com/en-us/reactor/`), which is a Microsoft-run community hub listing free meetups for learners and community organizers. The subject matter covers Azure and most other Microsoft technologies and job roles.

CloudSkills

```
https://cloudskills.io
```

CloudSkills is a boutique cloud consultancy that has Microsoft Azure education as its principal aim. My friend Mike Pfeiffer is a Microsoft Most Valuable Professional (MVP) who has worked as a cloud architect for both Amazon Web Services and Microsoft. He created CloudSkills as a training company that offers free and paid training, professional consulting, and general cloud and career guidance. You can find training sessions at CloudSkills.io, free podcasts interviews at Cloud-Skills.fm, and free tutorials at CloudSkills.tv.

Pluralsight

```
https://www.pluralsight.com/partners/microsoft/azure
```

Full disclosure: I'm a full-time trainer with Pluralsight. Then again, so are (seemingly) most of the world's Azure experts. Pluralsight and the Azure teams partnered to create an industry-leading online learning library.

Many of these video training courses, covering all the major Azure job roles, are available for free. Pluralsight also offers pre- and post-skills assessments as well as mentoring services.

Index

Symbols

` (backtick), 71–72

. . . (ellipsis) icon, 216

A

"About VPN devices and IPsec/IKE parameters for Site-to-Site VPN Gateway connections" article, 283

abstract, 41

access rules, 74

Accounting tags, 253

accounts

  adding to Azure AD roles, 245–247

  Cosmos DB, 202–203

  for storage, 49–61

ACI (Azure Container Instances), 121

ACR (Azure Container Registry), 121

action groups, 312–313

Action Pack, 22

Action property, 74

actions

  about, 170

  testing, 183

Active Directory (AD)

  about, 229–230

  AD *vs.* AD DS, 231

  Azure Advisor, 247–249

  Azure roles, 243–245

  compared with Active Directory Domain Services (AD DS), 231

  configuring Role-Based Access Control (RBAC), 242–247

  creating users and groups, 234–241

  pricing, 239

  subscriptions *vs.* AD tenants, 231–234

Active Directory Domain Services (AD DS), 231, 236

AD (Active Directory)

  about, 229–230

  AD *vs.* AD DS, 231

  Azure Advisor, 247–249

  Azure roles, 243–245

  compared with Active Directory Domain Services (AD DS), 231

  configuring Role-Based Access Control (RBAC), 242–247

  creating users and groups, 234–241

  pricing, 239

  subscriptions *vs.* AD tenants, 231–234

adding

  accounts to Azure AD roles, 245–247

  Application Insights resource, 164

  application security groups (ASGs), 77–78

  custom domains, 158–160

  domains to Active Directory, 234–235

  Linux systems to Arc, 294–295

  servers at scale, 293

  service tags, 77–78

  tags in Azure portal, 253–254

  tags programmatically, 254–255

  Windows Server systems to Arc, 290–293

address space, 66

administration notes (AKS), 132–133

ADO.NET, 195

AdventureWorks sample database, 192

AKS. *See* Azure Kubernetes Service (AKS)

alerts

  configuring, 312

  defining rules for, 313–314

  testing, 314–315

`AllowAzureLoadBalancerInBound`, 74

`AllowInternetBound`, 75

`AllowVnetInBound`, 74

`AllowVnetOutBound`, 75

Amazon Web Services (AWS), 11, 12, 88

analytics, 8

Any-to-any (IPVPN) connection, 287

API. *See* application programming interface (API)

App Service Certificates, 162

App Service plan, for Azure Functions, 168

Application Administrator role, 243

Application Insights resource, 164, 316

Application Insights telemetry data, 165–166

application programming interface (API)

  about, 13

  access to tags and billing, 258–259

  apps, 141

application security groups (ASGs), 77–78

Application settings, 158

application-consistent consistency level, 221

applying tags to resource groups and resources, 252–256

architectural considerations, 94–96

archive tier, 58

ARM. *See* Azure Resource Manager (ARM)

ASGs (application security groups), 77–78

ASM (Azure Service Management), 18

ASR (Azure Site Recovery), 277

Assessment phase, in Azure Migrate Database Assessment, 272–275

Assigned membership group (AD), 236

assigning

  licenses to users, 238–240

  policies, 263–264

Assignment phase, of policies, 261

associating NSGs with subnets, 78

Authoring phase, of policies, 261

autoscaling, configuring, 161–163

availability set, 94–95

availability zones, 33–34

AWS (Amazon Web Services), 11, 12, 88

az aks browse command, 133

AzCopy, 216–217, 270

Azure. *See* Microsoft Azure

Azure Active Directory. *See* Active Directory (AD)

Azure AD Business-to-Business (B2B), 233

Azure AD Business-to-Consumer (B2C), 234

Azure AD Connect/Connect Health, 234

Azure AD Domain Services, 234

Azure Advisor, 247–249

Azure App Service

  about, 139–141

  API apps, 141

  configuring Web Apps, 157–163

  deploying Web Apps, 144–157

  development frameworks and compute environments, 140

  domains, 162

  function apps, 141–142

  logic apps, 141

  logical components, 142–144

  mobile apps, 141

  monitoring Web Apps, 163–166

  as a PaaS product, 19

  protecting, 223–225

  publishing to, 154–155

  using containers with, 133–136

  Web App for Containers, 122

  Web Apps, 141, 144–166

Azure Application Architecture Guide, 332

Azure Arc

  about, 288

  adding Linux systems, 294–295

  adding servers at scale, 293

  adding Windows Server systems, 290–293

  family members, 289

  managing local systems with, 295–299

  preparing environment, 289–290

  tags, 299

  use case, 288–289

Azure Architecture Center, 332

Azure Blob Storage, 171

Azure Blog, 326

Azure Blueprints, 265

Azure certification, 334–335

Azure CLI/Azure Cloud Shell, 39–41

Azure Compute Unit, 143

Azure connection resource, 286

"Azure consumption API overview" article, 259

Azure Container Instances (ACI)
  about, 121
  deploying, 123–124
  disposing of, 124–125
  implementing, 122–126
  verifying, 124–125

Azure Container Registry (ACR)
  about, 121
  deploying, 126–127
  storing images in, 126–130

Azure Cosmos DB
  about, 200–201
  backing up and restoring, 227–228
  creating an account, 202–203
  debugging sample apps, 203–204
  implementing, 200–208
  interacting with, 204–207
  as a multimodel, 201
  multiple consistency levels, 202
  running sample apps, 203–204
  turnkey global distribution, 201

Azure Cosmos DB for MongoDB API, 201

Azure Cosmos DB table API, 61

Azure Data Box, 271–272

Azure Database for MariaDB Servers, 189

Azure Database for MySQL, 16

Azure Database for PostgreSQL Servers, 189

Azure Downloads page (website), 41

Azure Feedback, 328–329

Azure for Students, 22

Azure Free Account FAQ, 21

Azure Functions. See also Function Apps
  creating, 171–177
  defining, 173–174
  testing, 176–177

Azure Government Cloud, 12

Azure Kubernetes Service (AKS)
  about, 121–122, 131
  architecture of, 131–132

Azure Log Analytics
  about, 316

Applications Insights telemetry streams and, 165
  connecting data sources to workspaces, 317–318
  creating workspaces, 316–317

Azure Marketplace
  deploying VMS from, 96–106
  preinstalled virtual machines (VMs) from, 186–187
  starting deployment from, 89
  website, 85

Azure Migrate Database Assessment, 272–277

Azure Migrate Server Assessment, 279–280

Azure Migrate Server Migration, 281

Azure Monitor
  about, 302
  Activity Log, 302–305
  enabling diagnostic logging, 302–310
  viewing diagnostics data in, 112–113

Azure Monitor Log Analytics, 111

Azure Official YouTube Channel, 328

Azure P2S VPN, 286

Azure Pass, 22

Azure Policy
  assigning policies, 263–264
  creating policies, 262–263
  implementing, 296–298
  testing policies, 265

"Azure Policy definition structure" article, 260

Azure Policy Samples GitHub repository (website), 263

Azure portal
  about, 24, 36–37
  adding tags in, 253–254
  Applications Insights telemetry streams and, 165, 166
  creating storage accounts in, 50–53
  deploying from, 96–99, 144–145
  deploying resources in, 180
  deploying with, 68–71

Azure PowerShell, 38–39, 71–72

Azure private peering, 286

Azure Queue Storage, 48, 171

Azure Resource Explorer, 42

Azure Resource Manager (ARM)
  about, 13, 27
  JSON, 30–31
  management scopes, 31–33
  resource providers, 28–30
  REST APIs, 28, 42–43
Azure REST API Browser, 333
Azure SDKs, 41–42
Azure Service Bus Queue, 171
Azure Service Bus Topic, 171
Azure Service Management (ASM), 18
Azure Site Recovery (ASR), 277
Azure Solutions, 321
Azure Speed Test 2.0, 36
Azure Stack, 12
Azure Status, 325–326
Azure Storage Explorer, 54–56, 174
"Azure subscription and service limits, quotas, and constraints" article, 67
Azure Table, 201
Azure Updates, 326–327
Azure Visio stencils, 71
Azure Weekly (Endjin), 327–328
AzureCloud service tag, 77
AzureLoadBalance service tag, 77
Azure.Source, 327

B

backtick (`), 71–72
backups and restoring
  about, 211–212
  Azure Cosmos DB, 227–228
  backing up storage blobs in bulk, 216–217
  protecting App Services, 223–225
  protecting databases, 225–228
  protecting storage account's blob data, 212–217
  protecting virtual machines, 217–223
  SQL database, 225–227
  virtual machines, 219–221
Billing Administrator role, 243
binary large objects. *See* blobs (binary large objects)

binding TLS/SSL certificates, 160–161
blade, 21, 24
blob service, 54
Blob storage option, 49
blobs (binary large objects)
  about, 48
  copying, 270
  rehydrating archived, 58
  uploading, 56–57
boot diagnostics, 309–310
Build5Nines Weekly, 327

C

CaaS (Code as a Service), 141
capital expenditure (CapEx), 9, 10
Cassandra, 201
changing
  blob access tiers, 57–59
  user passwords, 241
Channel 9: Azure Friday, 328
charting metrics, 310–312
Cheat Sheet (website), 4
Classification tags, 253
CLI (command-line interface), 39
cloud apps, 230
cloud computing
  about, 7–9
  benefits of, 10
  economies of scale, 11
  models, 11–17
  NIST definition of, 9
  providers of, 11
Cloud Cost Management API, 259
Cloud exchange co-location, 287
Cloud Shell (C), 36, 136
CloudSkills, 337
cmdlets, 90
Code as a Service (CaaS), 141
code version-control systems, 150
Code View button (Logic App designer toolbar), 182

command-line interface (CLI), 39

Compliance phase, of policies, 261

compute environments, 92, 140

computer, 8

Configuration blade (I), 37

Configure blade, 197–198

configuring

  alerts, 312

  autoscaling, 161–163

  Function App settings, 177–178

  Git, 145–147

  network security groups (NSGs), 74–78

  peering, 84

  Role-Based Access Control (RBAC), 242–247

  SQL database, 194–198

  SQL database backup retention, 226–227

  virtual machines (VMs), 106–108

  virtual networks, 73–80

  VNet peering, 81–82

  Web apps, 157–163

connecting

  data sources to workspaces, 317–318

  to SQL database, 199–200

  virtual networks, 81–86

  to VMs, 99, 105–106

  to Web apps from Visual Studio, 147–152

connection strings, 195

Connectors button (Logic App designer toolbar), 182

consistency levels

  of Azure Cosmos DB, 202

  of VM backup, 221

consumption plan, for Azure Functions, 168

containers, as a PaaS product, 19. *See also* Docker containers

content delivery network, Azure App Service and, 143

Contributor role, 245

cool tier, 58

copying blobs, 270

Core (SQL), 201

cost

  Active Directory (AD), 239

Developer plan, 25

Premier plan, 26

Professional Direct plan, 26

Standard plan, 25

Cost Management + Billing blade, 257–258

crash-consistent consistency level, 221

"Create an Azure Service Principal with Azure PowerShell" article, 39

creating

  action groups, 312–313

  AD groups, 237

  Azure accounts, 22–24

  Azure AD users, 238

  Azure Functions, 171–177, 174–176

  backup policies, 218–219

  blob containers, 174

  Cosmos DB account, 202–203

  Function App, 172–173

  Git repositories for Web apps, 148–150

  groups, 234–241

  Log Analytics workspaces, 316–317

  Logic Apps, 179

  policies, 262–263

  snapshot backups, 213–214

  storage accounts, 49–54

  users, 234–241

  virtual networks, 68–72

  Web app projects in Visual Studio, 153

  workflows with Logic Apps, 179–183

Crockford, Douglas (JSON inventor), 31

custom connectors, 170

custom domains, adding, 158–160

"Custom roles for Azure resources" article, 246

customizing app settings, 158

D

data

  consistency of, 202

  options for migrating, 269–277

  semistructured, 48

  structured, 48

  types of, 47–48

  unstructured, 48

data egress network traffic, 58

data sources, connecting to workspaces, 317–318

Database Migration Service (DMS), performing database migration with, 275–276

Database Transaction Unit (DTU), 190

databases

  about, 185

  Azure App Service and, 142

  comparing relational and nonrelational, 187–189

  implementing Azure Cosmos DB, 200–208

  implementing SQL, 190–200

  as a PaaS product, 19

  PaaS vs IaaS, 185–187

  protecting, 225–228

  SQL, 188–189

debugging sample Cosmos DB apps, 203–204

declarative code, 105

Default Documents, 158

defining workflows, 180–182

DELETE method, 28

deleting snapshots, 214–216

DenyAllInBound, 74, 75

deploying

  Azure Container instances, 123–124

  Azure Container Registry (ACR), 126–127

  from Azure portal, 68–71, 96–99, 144–145

  Linux VMs, 96–99

  models for, 12–14

  with PowerShell, 71–72

  Recovery Services vault, 218

  resources in Azure portal, 180

  SQL database, 192–194

  SQL database virtual servers, 191–192

  virtual machines (VMs), 88–91, 96–106

  virtual machines (VMs) from Marketplace, 96–106

  from Visual Studio, 153–155

  Web Apps, 144–157

  Windows Server VMs, 99–106

Deployment Slots, 155–157

Designer button (Logic App designer toolbar), 182

Destination property, 74

Developer plan, 25

development environment, 100–101

development frameworks, 140

DevOps, as a PaaS product, 19

Dev/Test tier, 143

diagnostic logging, enabling, 111–112, 302–310

disaster recovery (DR), 13

disk storage, 61–63

distributing licenses, 240

Docker containers

  about, 115–117

  Azure Kubernetes Service (AKS), 131–133

  documentation website, 116

  implementing instances, 122–126

  running in Azure, 120–122

  setting on workstations, 117–120

  storing images in Azure Container Registry (ACR), 126–130

  using, 117

  using with Azure App Service, 133–136

Docker Desktop, installing, 118

domains

  adding to Active Directory, 234–235

  Azure App Service, 162

Download As CSV button (Azure Monitor), 304

DR (disaster recovery), 13

DTU (Database Transaction Unit), 190

DTU-based service tier, 190

Durable Functions HTTP Starter, as an Azure Function trigger, 171

Dynamic group (AD), 236

E

EA (Enterprise Agreement), 21

economies of scale, 11

Edit Columns button (Azure Monitor), 304

elastic pool model, 190

elasticity, rapid, as a characteristic of cloud computing, 9

ellipsis (. . .) icon, 216

enabling

  diagnostic logging, 111–112, 302–310

  instrumentation in Web apps, 165

Enterprise Agreement (EA), 21

environments
  about, 301
  Application Insights, 316
  Azure Log Analytics, 316–322
  Azure Monitor, 302–315
  controlling, 186
  preparing, 289–290
events, 170
Export to Event Hub button (Azure Monitor), 304
ExpressRoute, 284, 286–287
extending capabilities of VMs, 111–113
External Azure AD, 236

F

Favorites (G), 37
features, availability of, 36
File, as a storage account service, 48
File Recovery feature, 222
File service, 59–60
file-system-consistent consistency level, 221
firewall, 195
force-deleting resource groups, 208
Fowler, Adam (author)
  NoSQL For Dummies, 188
Function Apps
  about, 141–142, 168, 171
  compared with Logic Apps, 170
  configuring settings, 177–178
  creating, 172–173
Functional tags, 253
functions, 168

G

GCP (Google Cloud Platform), 11, 12
General settings, 158
General-purpose v1 option, 49
General-purpose v2 option, 49
geographies, 34
geo-redundant storage (GRS), 50
georeplication, 196–197
GET method, 28

"Getting Started with Log Queries in Azure Monitor" tutorial, 322
Git
  configuring, 145–147
  creating repositories for Web apps, 148–150
GitHub For Dummies (Guthals and Haack), 145
Global Administrator role, 243
global navigation, 36
Global Search (B), 36
Global Subscription filter (D), 36
Google Cloud Platform (GCP), 11, 12
governance
  implementing Azure policy, 259–265
  implementing taxonomic tags, 251–259
Gremlin, 201
groups
  action, 312–313
  creating, 234–241
GRS (geo-redundant storage), 50
Guest Inviter role, 243
Guest user (AD), 236
guest-level metrics, 111–112
Guthals, Sarah (author)
  GitHub For Dummies, 145

H

Haack, Phil (author)
  GitHub For Dummies, 145
hello-world container, 118–120
host-level metrics, 111
hot tier, 58
HTTP (Hypertext Transfer Protocol), 28, 171
hybrid cloud, 13–14, 281–287
Hypertext Transfer Protocol (HTTP), 28, 171

I

IaaS (Infrastructure as a Service), 16–17
IBM Cloud, 11, 12
icons, explained, 3
IDaaS (Identity as a Service), 16
idempotent, 105

identity, as a PaaS product, 20

Identity as a Service (IDaaS), 16

images, storing in Azure Container Registry, 126–130

implementing

  Azure Container instances, 122–126

  Azure Cosmos DB, 200–208

  Azure policy, 259–265

  Azure Policy, 296–298

  built-in RBAC roles, 243–245

  SQL database, 190–200

  taxonomic tags, 251–259, 298–299

incremental mode, 105

Infrastructure as a Service (IaaS), 16–17, 185–187

inspecting virtual servers, 198

installing

  Azure Storage Explorer, 54–56

  Docker Desktop, 118

instrumentation, enabling in Web apps, 165

interacting, with Cosmos DB, 204–207

Internet of Things (IoT), as a PaaS product, 19

Internet resources

  "About VPN devices and IPsec/IKE parameters for Site-to-Site VPN Gateway connections" article, 283

  Active Directory (AD) pricing, 239

  Activity Log Analytics, 304

  AdventureWorks sample database, 192

  Application Insights resource, 316

  AzCopy, 217

  Azure AD Connect, 231

  Azure Architecture Center, 332

  Azure Blog, 326

  Azure Blueprints, 265

  Azure certification, 334

  "Azure consumption API overview" article, 259

  Azure Cosmos DB table API, 61

  Azure Data Box, 271

  Azure documentation, 331–332

  Azure Downloads page (website), 41

  Azure Feedback, 328

  Azure Free Account FAQ, 21

  Azure Marketplace, 85

  Azure Official YouTube Channel, 328

  "Azure Policy definition structure" article, 260

  Azure Policy Samples GitHub repository, 263

  Azure portal, 24, 36, 50

  Azure pricing, 168

  Azure Resource Explorer, 42

  Azure REST API Browser, 333

  Azure Speed Test 2.0, 36

  Azure Status, 325

  Azure Storage Explorer, 174

  "Azure subscription and service limits, quotas, and constraints" article, 67

  Azure Updates, 326

  Azure Visio stencils, 71

  Azure Weekly (Endjin), 327

  Azure.Source, 327

  Build5Nines Weekly, 327

  Channel 9: Azure Friday, 328

  Cheat Sheet, 4

  CloudSkills, 337

  "Create an Azure Service Principal with Azure PowerShell" article, 39

  "Custom roles for Azure resources" article, 246

  Docker container documentation, 116

  File Recovery feature, 222

  "Getting Started with Log Queries in Azure Monitor" tutorial, 322

  keyboard shortcuts, 57

  MeasureUp, 335

  Meetup, 336

  Microsoft @ edx, 333

  Microsoft Learn, 334

  Microsoft Reactor, 336

  Microsoft Worldwide Learning Certification and Exam Offers page, 335

  "Modify Visual Studio" article, 41

  NIST Special Publication 800-145, *The NIST Definition of Cloud Computing*, 9

  "Overview of BGP and Azure VPN Gateways" article, 284

  Pluralsight, 337

  Postman, 29

price information, 50

Products Available by Region page, 36

"Quickstart: Connect machines to Azure using Azure Arc for servers - PowerShell" article, 293

"Resource naming and tagging decision guide" article, 299

RFC 1918 source document, 66

"Security Groups" article, 78

services directory, 17

SQL Server Management Studio, 199

Tim's Twitter Feed, 329

"Understand Azure Policy Effects" article, 261

Visual Studio 2019 Community Edition, 100, 144

"What are Azure Reservations?" article, 194

"What is managed identities for Azure resources" article, 297

Internet service tag, 77

IPv6, 67

IPVPN (Any-to-any) connection, 287

Isolated tier, 143

J

JDBC, 195

JSON, 30–31, 170, 259

K

keyboard shortcuts, 57

KQL queries, writing, 319–322

kubectl command-line tool, 132

Kubernetes Web UI, 133

L

licenses

  assigning to users, 238–240

  distributing, 240

life cycle, of Azure policies, 261–265

Linux VMs

  adding to Arc, 294–295

  deploying, 96–99

local network gateway, 285

local systems, managing with Arc, 295–299

locally redundant storage (LRS), 49

Log Search interface, 319–320

logging in, as Azure AD users, 240–241

Logic Apps

  about, 141, 168–169, 179

  building workflows with, 179–183

  compared with Function Apps, 170

  creating, 179

  designer toolbar, 182

logical components, Azure App Service, 142–144

logs, 302

Logs button (Azure Monitor), 304

low-obligation, 20

LRS (locally redundant storage), 49

M

machine learning, as a PaaS product, 20

Managed Disks, 61–63

managed identity, 297

management group scope, 242

management scopes, 31–33

management tools

  about, 36

  ARM REST API, 42–43

  Azure CLI/Azure Cloud Shell, 39–41

  Azure portal, 36–37

  Azure PowerShell, 38–39

  Azure SDKs, 41–42

managing

  environments, 186

  local systems with Arc, 295–299

Marketplace. *See* Azure Marketplace

Master node, 131

measured service, as a characteristic of cloud computing, 9

MeasureUp, 335

Meetup, 336

Member user (AD), 236

methods, of HTTP, 28

metrics, 302, 310–312

microservices, 61

Microsoft Account, 237

Microsoft Azure. *See also specific topics*

  creating an account, 22–24

  disk storage, 61–63

  documentation, 331–332

  history of, 17–19

  implementing policy, 259–265

  management tools, 36–43

  regions, 33–36

  running Docker containers in, 120–122

  services, 17–20

  starting subscription to, 20–26

Microsoft BizTalk Server, 169

Microsoft Cloud Adoption Framework for Azure, 332

Microsoft @ edx, 333–334

Microsoft Flow, 170

Microsoft Learn, 334

Microsoft Office 365, 14–15

Microsoft peering, 287

Microsoft Reactor, 336

Microsoft Visio license, 70

Microsoft Worldwide Learning Certification and Exam Offers page (website), 335

`Microsoft.Storage`, 29

migrating data. *See* data

Migration phase, in Azure Migrate Database Assessment, 272, 275–277

mobile apps, 141

models

  of cloud computing, 11–17

  deployment, 12–14

  RM deployment, 18

  service delivery, 14–17

  shared responsibility, 17

"Modify Visual Studio" article, 41

monitoring

  environments. *See* Azure Monitor

  as a PaaS product, 20

  Web apps, 163–166

multitenant, 230

multitenant Azure AD, 232–233

N

Nadella, Satya (COO), 17

Name property, 74

name resolution strategy, 73

National Institute of Standards and Technology (NIST), 9

Network File System (NFS), 48

network security groups (NSGs), 74–78

network virtual appliance (NVA), 85

networks

  about, 8, 65, 93

  broad access, as a characteristic of cloud computing, 9

  components of, 66–67

  configuring virtual networks, 73–80

  connecting virtual networks, 81–86

  creating virtual networks, 68–72

NFS (Network File System), 48

NIST (National Institute of Standards and Technology), 9

NIST Special Publication 800-145, *The NIST Definition of Cloud Computing,* 9

nonrelational databases, compared with relational databases, 187–189

NoSQL databases, 48

NoSQL For Dummies (Fowler), 188

Notifications (E), 37

NSGs (network security groups), 74–78

NVA (network virtual appliance), 85

O

ODBC, 195

on-premises environments

  about, 14, 269

  Azure Arc, 288–299

  data migration options, 269–277

  hybrid cloud options, 281–287

  server migration options, 277–281

  starting deployment from, 89–91

operational expenditure (OpEx), 10

operational security, 35

operations, of HTTP, 28

OpEx (operational expenditure), 10
Oracle Cloud, 11, 12
"Overview of BGP and Azure VPN Gateways" article, 284
Owner role, 245

P

PaaS. *See* Platform as a Service (PaaS)
Page header (A), 36
paired regions, 35–36
Partnership tags, 253
Password Administrator role, 243
PATCH method, 28
Path Mappings, 158
Pay-As-You-Go (PAYG), 20
peering, 84, 286–287
PHP, 195
Pin Current Filters button (Azure Monitor), 304
pipelining, 110
Platform as a Service (PaaS)
  about, 15–16
  compared to Infrastructure as a Service (IaaS), 185–187
  products, 19–20
plotting resource metrics, 310–312
Pluralsight, 337
pod, 131
Point-to-point Ethernet connection, 287
Point-to-Site VPN, 283, 286
Port property, 74
POST method, 28
Postman, 29
power, 8
preinstalled virtual machines, 186–187
Premier plan, 26
preparing environments, 289–290
Priority property, 74
private cloud, 12–13
Production tier, 143
Products Available by Region page (website), 36
Professional Direct plan, 26
properties, 74

protecting
  App Services, 223–225
  databases, 225–228
  storage account's blob data, 212–217
  virtual machines, 217–223
Protocol property, 74
providers, 29
public cloud, 12
publishing, to App Service, 154–155
Purpose tags, 253
pushing code changes to Azure, 151–152
PUT method, 28

Q

Queue service, 61
Quick Start blade, 194
"Quickstart: Connect machines to Azure using Azure Arc for servers - PowerShell" article, 293

R

RA-GRS (read-access georedundant storage), 50
RateCard API, 259
RBAC (Role-Based Access Control), 242–247
read-access georedundant storage (RA-GRS), 50
Reader role, 245
Recovery Services vault, 217–219
Refresh button (Azure Monitor), 304
regions, 33–36
rehydrating archived blobs, 58
relational databases, compared with nonrelational databases, 187–189
Remember icon, 3
removing tags, 256
replication, 50
reporting, via tags, 257–259
Reports Reader role, 243
repository images, pulling via ACI, 128–130
representational state transfer (REST), 28, 170
Request for Comments (RFC), 66
Reservations button, 194

Reset Filters button (Azure Monitor), 304
resizing virtual machines (VMs), 108–109, 110–111
resource group scope, 242
resource groups
  applying tags to, 252–256
  force-deleting, 208
resource metrics, plotting, 310–312
"Resource naming and tagging decision guide" article, 299
resource pooling, as a characteristic of cloud computing, 9
resource providers, 28–30
resource roles, 245
resource scope, 242
Resource Usage API, 259
resourceGroups, 29
resources
  applying tags to, 252–256
  recommended, 325–329, 331–337
Resources pane (H), 37
REST (representational state transfer), 28, 170
REST APIs, 28, 58
restoring
  data. See backups and restoring
  snapshots, 214–216
  virtual machines, 221–223
RFC (Request for Comments), 66
RFC 1918 source document, 66
RM deployment model, 18
Role-Based Access Control (RBAC), 242–247
Run button (Logic App designer toolbar), 182
running
  Docker containers in Azure, 120–122
  hello-world container, 118–120
  sample Cosmos DB apps, 203–204
  serverless apps, 167–183
  versions of databases, 186
Russinovich, Mark (CTO), 35

S
SaaS (Software as a Service), 14–15
Salesforce, 11

scalability, 95–96
SDKs (software development kits), 41
security and configuration overhead, 9
"Security Groups" article, 78
self-service, on-demand, as a characteristic of cloud computing, 9
semistructured data, 48
Server Message Block (SMB), 48
server sizes, 92
serverless apps
  about, 167
  actions, 170
  events, 170
  Function Apps, 168, 171–178
  Logic Apps, 168–170, 179–183
  triggers, 170
servers
  adding at scale, 293
  options for migrating, 277–281
service chaining, 82–86
service delivery models, 14–17
service endpoints, 78–80
service tags, adding, 77–78
service tiers, 190
services, 17–20
settings
  Azure Monitor Diagnostics, 305–307
  virtual machines, 307–309
setup
  development environment, 100–101
  Docker containers on workstations, 117–120
shared responsibility model, 17
Site-to-Site (S2S) VPN, 282–286
SMB (Server Message Block), 48
snapshot backups, 213–214
snapshots, 214–216
Software as a Service (SaaS), 14–15
software development kits (SDKs), 41
Source property, 74
special regions, 34–35
SQL Azure Relational Database, 17
SQL database

about, 188–189
backing up and restoring, 225–227
Configure blade, 197–198
configuring, 194–198
connecting to, 199–200
connection strings, 195
deploying, 192–194
deploying virtual servers, 191–192
firewall, 195
georeplication, 196–197
implementing, 190–200
SQL Database for MySQL Servers, 189
SQL For Dummies, 8th Edition (Taylor), 188
SQL Server Management Studio (website), 199
STaaS (Storage as a Service), 16
Standard plan, 25
starting
   Azure subscription, 20–26
   virtual machines (VMs), 108–110
stopping virtual machines (VMs), 108–110
storage
   about, 8, 93
   accounts for, 49–61
   Azure App Service and, 142
   data types, 47–48
   images in Azure Container Registry, 126–130
   protecting blob data, 212–217
Storage as a Service (STaaS), 16
storage blobs, backing up in bulk, 216–217
Storage service tag, 77
storage volume, 57
storageAccounts, 29
structured data, 48
subnets, 66–67, 78
subscription scope, 242
subscriptions
   compared with AD tenants, 231–234
   types of, 20–22
   viewing details of, 24–26
subscriptions, 29

T

Table service, 60–61
tags
   adding in Azure portal, 253–254
   adding programatically, 254–255
   applying to resource groups and resources, 252–256
   removing, 256
   reporting via, 257–259
   taxonomic tags, implementing, 251–259, 298–299
Taylor, Allen G. (author)
   SQL For Dummies, 8th Edition, 188
Technical Stuff icon, 3
telemetry, 302
Templates button (Logic App designer toolbar), 182
tenant root scope, 242
tenants
   compared with subscriptions, 231–234
   defined, 230
testing
   actions, 183
   alerts, 314–315
   Azure Functions, 176–177
   policies, 265
   triggers, 183
Timer, as an Azure Function trigger, 171
Tim's Twitter Feed, 329
Tip icon, 3
TLS/SSL certificates, binding, 160–161
tlwstor270, 29
triggers
   about, 170
   for Function Apps, 171
   testing, 183
turnkey global distribution, 201
2fb..., 29
twtech, 29

U

"Understand Azure Policy Effects" article, 261
Uniform Resource Identifier (URI), 29
unstructured data, 48
uploading blobs, 56–57
URI (Uniform Resource Identifier), 29
User Administrator role, 243
users
  assigning licenses to, 238–240
  changing passwords, 241
  creating, 234–241
  logging in, 240–241

V

vCore service tier, 190
verbs, of HTTP, 28
verifying Azure Container instances, 124–125
versions, of databases, 186
VHD Upload, 277–278
VHDs (virtual hard disks), 61–63
viewing
  Application Insights telemetry data, 165–166
  diagnostics data in Azure Monitor, 112–113
  snapshot backups, 213–214
  subscription details, 24–26
virtual hard disks (VHDs), 61–63
Virtual Machine Administrator Login role, 245
Virtual Machine Contributor role, 245
Virtual Machine Scale Sets (VMSS), 95
virtual machines (VMs)
  about, 13, 87
  architectural considerations, 94–96
  backing up, 219–221
  boot diagnostics, 309–310
  components of, 91–93
  configuring, 106–108
  connecting to, 99, 105–106
  deploying from Marketplace, 96–106
  diagnostic settings, 307–309
  extending capabilities of, 111–113
  planning deployment of, 88–91

  preinstalled, 186–187
  protecting, 217–223
  resizing, 108–109, 110–111
  restoring, 221–223
  starting, 108–110
  stopping, 108–110
virtual network gateway, 283–285
virtual networks
  Azure App Service and, 142
  configuring, 73–80
  connecting, 81–86
  creating, 68–72
virtual private network (VPN) gateway, 14
virtual servers, inspecting, 198
VirtualNetwork service tag, 77
Visual Studio
  about, 22
  Applications Insights telemetry streams and, 165, 166
  connecting to Web apps from, 147–152
  creating Web app projects in, 153
  deploying from, 153–155
Visual Studio 2019 Community Edition, 100, 144
VM-based container hosts, 121
VMs (virtual machines)
  about, 13, 87
  architectural considerations, 94–96
  backing up, 219–221
  boot diagnostics, 309–310
  components of, 91–93
  configuring, 106–108
  connecting to, 99, 105–106
  deploying from Marketplace, 96–106
  diagnostic settings, 307–309
  extending capabilities of, 111–113
  planning deployment of, 88–91
  preinstalled, 186–187
  protecting, 217–223
  resizing, 108–109, 110–111
  restoring, 221–223
  starting, 108–110
  stopping, 108–110

VMSS (Virtual Machine Scale Sets), 95

VNet peering, configuring, 81–82

VNet-to-VNet VPN, 283

VPN (virtual private network) gateway, 14

W

Warning icon, 3

Web App for Containers, 122

Web Apps

  about, 141

  configuring, 157–163

  connecting to from Visual Studio, 147–152

  creating projects in Visual Studio, 153

  customizing settings, 158

  deploying, 144–157

  enabling instrumentation in, 165

  monitoring, 163–166

websites

  "About VPN devices and IPsec/IKE parameters for Site-to-Site VPN Gateway connections" article, 283

  Active Directory (AD) pricing, 239

  Activity Log Analytics, 304

  AdventureWorks sample database, 192

  Application Insights resource, 316

  AzCopy, 217

  Azure AD Connect, 231

  Azure Architecture Center, 332

  Azure Blog, 326

  Azure Blueprints, 265

  Azure certification, 334

  "Azure consumption API overview" article, 259

  Azure Cosmos DB table API, 61

  Azure Data Box, 271

  Azure documentation, 331–332

  Azure Downloads page (website), 41

  Azure Feedback, 328

  Azure Free Account FAQ, 21

  Azure Marketplace, 85

  Azure Official YouTube Channel, 328

  "Azure Policy definition structure" article, 260

  Azure Policy Samples GitHub repository, 263

  Azure portal, 24, 36, 50

  Azure pricing, 168

  Azure Resource Explorer, 42

  Azure REST API Browser, 333

  Azure Speed Test 2.0, 36

  Azure Status, 325

  Azure Storage Explorer, 174

  "Azure subscription and service limits, quotas, and constraints" article, 67

  Azure Updates, 326

  Azure Visio stencils, 71

  Azure Weekly (Endjin), 327

  Azure.Source, 327

  Build5Nines Weekly, 327

  Channel 9: Azure Friday, 328

  Cheat Sheet, 4

  CloudSkills, 337

  "Create an Azure Service Principal with Azure PowerShell" article, 39

  "Custom roles for Azure resources" article, 246

  Docker container documentation, 116

  File Recovery feature, 222

  "Getting Started with Log Queries in Azure Monitor" tutorial, 322

  keyboard shortcuts, 57

  MeasureUp, 335

  Meetup, 336

  Microsoft @ edx, 333

  Microsoft Learn, 334

  Microsoft Reactor, 336

  Microsoft Worldwide Learning Certification and Exam Offers page, 335

  "Modify Visual Studio" article, 41

  NIST Special Publication 800-145, *The NIST Definition of Cloud Computing,* 9

  "Overview of BGP and Azure VPN Gateways" article, 284

  Pluralsight, 337

  Postman, 29

  price information, 50

  Products Available by Region page, 36

  "Quickstart: Connect machines to Azure using Azure Arc for servers - PowerShell" article, 293 websites *(continued)*

  "Resource naming and tagging decision guide"
     article, 299

  RFC 1918 source document, 66

  "Security Groups" article, 78

  services directory, 17

  SQL Server Management Studio, 199

  Tim's Twitter Feed, 329

  "Understand Azure Policy Effects" article, 261

  Visual Studio 2019 Community Edition, 100, 144

  "What are Azure Reservations?" article, 194

  "What is managed identities for Azure resources"
     article, 297

  "What are Azure Reservations?" article, 194

  "What is managed identities for Azure resources"
     article, 297

  Windows Server AD, 237

Windows Server VMs

  adding to Arc, 290–293

  deploying, 99–106

Worker node, 131

workflows

  building with Logic Apps, 179–183

  defining, 180–182

workstations, setting up Docker containers on,
     117–120

writing KQL queries, 319–322

Y

Your account (F), 37

Z

zone-redundant storage (ZRS), 49

About the Author

Tim Warner had his first exposure to computers in 1981 when his father bought him the much-vaunted "$99 computer," the Timex-Sinclair 1000. From there, Tim graduated to the Commodore 64, Tandy TRS-80, and then the x86 machines, which introduced him to Microsoft Windows. The rest, as they say, is history!

Tim's been an IT professional since 1997. He has written close to 20 technical books, has authored more than 200 computer-based training (CBT) courses, and speaks internationally on Microsoft Azure. Tim holds Microsoft certifications in Azure architecture, administration, and development.

You can reach Tim via Twitter (@TechTrainerTim) or his website, `https://techtrainertim.com/`.

Author's Acknowledgments

Thanks to my Wiley editor, Steve Hayes, for giving me this opportunity to become a *For Dummies* author. It was actually Peter Weverka's *Word for Windows 95 For Dummies* that helped me get into the IT industry in 1997, so let me thank Peter as well. I hope this book represents one small way to "pay it forward."

Thanks to my project editor, Charlotte Kughen, for your fine skills, availability, and guidance throughout the manuscript production process. You and your husband, Rick, have been part of my writer's journey for quite a few years now!

Thanks to everyone in the Microsoft Azure community — Microsoft product team members, community MVPs, my colleagues, and my students. It's a cliché, but I indeed couldn't have done this without you!

Finally, thanks to my wife, Susan, and daughter, Zoey. I love yaaa!

Publisher's Acknowledgments

Executive Editor: Steve Hayes

Project Editor: Charlotte Kughen

Copy Editor: Kathy Simpson

Technical Editor: Sarah Guthals

Proofreader: Debbye Butler

Sr. Editorial Assistant: Cherie Case

Production Editor: Magesh Elangovan

Cover Image: © gremlin/Getty Images